"I SUGGEST THAT YOU KEEP IT TO YOURSELF."

A man arrived at the hotel and asked to see Billy Doyle. He flashed a card at the reception to indicate he was with the police, at which, of course, he was directed to see the witness straight away. Billy says that he claimed to be some sort of ''special officer'' with the ''CID'' but would not be drawn to say more. He was there to investigate Billy's UFO sighting.

The two men relocated to an empty room and the stranger asked Billy to tell his story. After he had finished the stranger said, ''What would you say if I asked you not to report this? That it was a government matter?'' Billy replied that he would agree, naturally. He was not interested in breaking secrets. The man nodded in return, as if satisfied with the answer, but did not insist on silence. Instead he simply reasoned with Billy saying, ''You do realise that nobody will ever believe your story. I suggest that you keep it to yourself.''

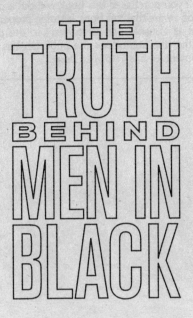

THE TRUTH BEHIND MEN IN BLACK

GOVERNMENT AGENTS— OR VISITORS FROM BEYOND

JENNY RANDLES

St. Martin's Paperbacks

The moral right of the author has been asserted.

Published in Great Britain by Judy Piatkus (Publishers) Ltd.

THE TRUTH BEHIND MEN IN BLACK

ISBN: 0-312-96521-4

Printed in the United States of America

St. Martin's Paperbacks edition/August 1997

10 9 8 7 6 5 4 3 2 1

CONTENTS

1　MIB: Strangers in the Night　　　　　1
2　Maury Island: Birth of a Mystery　　　23
3　The Three Men　　　　　　　　　　42
4　The 1950s: Missing in Action　　　　52
5　1957: Men from Gharnasvarn　　　　60
6　1963: Fields of Folly　　　　　　　69
7　1964: Intruder on the Shore　　　　77
8　1965–1967: Imposters　　　　　　　92
9　1972–1977: Hidden Depths　　　　　105
10　1980–1988: Men of Mystery　　　　125
11　Foreign Affairs　　　　　　　　　148
12　Grand Deceptions　　　　　　　　157
13　Evidence of Aliens　　　　　　　　170
14　A History in Black　　　　　　　　179
15　Enforcers of the Cover-Up　　　　197
16　Conclusion: Dark Thoughts　　　　233

References　　　　　　　　　　　241
Index　　　　　　　　　　　　　245

THE TRUTH BEHIND MEN IN BLACK

mysteries everywhere I go but identify a simple cause nine times out of ten.

Most UFO cases crumble upon investigation and turn out to be the result of the natural wonders that surround us in this world, often going unrecognized to our unobservant eyes. The vagaries of human perception can also make even the humblest of things at the fringes of our vision seem like something that would be more at home in a scene out of *Star Wars*.

With experience, you learn to recognize when a witness is being sincere and is describing something that is unlikely to be identified in mundane terms. Not that this obviates the need to seek for explanations. I find it part of the challenge to hunt for answers and resolve cases. Indeed, if it were proven beyond question that there were no aliens coming here in flying saucers, it would not perturb me one bit. People will go on seeing UFOs and the task of a UFOlogist, such as myself, is not to prove vast government conspiracies that hide pickled bodies of captured aliens or the wreckage of a starship from another galaxy. It is to probe the evidence that we have and try to understand what is happening.

Unfortunately, the media all too rarely appreciate this distinction. They seem amazed—or do not even realize—that it is perfectly possible to believe in UFOs without therefore meaning that there are visitors from another planet coming to earth. There may, or there may not, be any such aliens. The evidence is conflicting. But one thing is certain—Unidentified Flying Objects (UFOs) exist.

This conviction comes not merely from the hundreds of responsible witnesses that I have interviewed. There is evidence of a more scientific nature as well. Film and photographs that have been analyzed by top researchers and organisations such as Kodak establish to the satisfaction of most who study the data that something is really flying around. Ground traces have been left which are amenable to laboratory investigation. These have on numerous occasions been shown by science to involve radiation fields and other forms of energy that appear to be directly connected with a hovering or landed UFO. There are even reliable and remarkably consistent cases involving interference to the engine and lighting systems of motor vehicles. Data that any physicist could use to good effect in theorising what is taking place during a close encounter.

Many people only see the lurid tabloid headlines about UFOs. They are probably unaware of the more sober and widespread reality that underpins the few highly touted cases. In fact countless scientists—from geologists to psychologists and atmospheric physicists to folklore PhDs—have spent many hours studying the gathered evidence, and there is an impressive body of research, scientific experimentation and—in my view—*absolute proof* regarding UFO reality. This is waiting to be examined by anyone who resists the urge to scoff and chooses to look for themselves. This is why the governments of the world have pursued the UFO question for 50 years.

What is the purpose behind these government investigations? I will assess that more thoroughly later in this book, for it is an area that I have spent a good deal of time pursuing as I researched and wrote a BBC TV documentary called *Britain's Secret UFO Files*. In my work I have been invited to the Houses of Parliament to brief politicians on the UFO situation in Britain. I have had the cooperation of many MPs (of all parties) and top defense officials in trying to seek out a rational answer. I have even had covert files leaked to me and spent many days at the Public Record Office learning what is publicly available on governmental UFO study—if you know *where* and *how* to look.

I do not believe from all of this that there is a major cover-up of guilty secrets. But I *do* think that there is much circumspection about the UFO mystery—and with very good cause. We, as a society, trivialise and sensationalise what are in fact often very intriguing questions about these strange phenomena. The sightings and data may provide insights into new propulsion systems or energy resources that could benefit us all. A government may well properly believe that it is best to conduct such studies in private rather than to face the combined wrath of the media and the UFO community.

During the years that I have investigated cases—from the

simplest light in the sky to the most amazing claims of alien abduction—I have increasingly confronted witnesses who have told me about the more disturbing aftermath. The visits or the phone calls from what appear to be ''Men in Black'' who enforce their demands for silence—although, of course, most often these people have never heard the term MIB.

I had long assumed that the legend of Men in Black was just part of American UFO mythology. Once you have been told worryingly similar stories from a growing band of seemingly reliable witnesses, however, you do have to reassess the situation. These people were not in contact with one another. Most had no knowledge of the American legends. The cases were scattered across the UK and over 30 or 40 years. I soon came to realize that something was going on here and I had a responsibility to take note of what these people said.

There has never been a mainstream book on the MIB mystery in Britain and only one—to my knowledge—published in the USA. This came from a magazine publisher and did not attempt to investigate the issues raised but merely told a few stories gathered from American UFOlogists with various degrees of credulity. I discovered that most people had taken the view that there was no serious evidence to be investigated and so chose to pretend that the problem did not exist.

I cannot have that luxury. The problem *does* exist, and I was finding more and more examples as my work continued. The patterns that link the cases together were becoming obvious. I had to delve into this difficult area and set out for the first time the full story of the Men in Black.

As a result, this book is unique and full of shocking new evidence. It goes beyond reports of UFOs and aliens and looks at the aftermath told by a large number of people. For the first time anywhere it sets out the history of the MIB phenomenon from its American roots to its global spread. It presents firsthand investigations conducted by myself which I believe clearly establish that this matter is more than just a myth. There is a *real* Men in Black mystery to be unravelled, and this leads me onto review the theories proposed to explain these intimidating visitors.

That they are part of the phenomenon itself—some sort of shape-changing alien manifestation—may well seem rather absurd to you. Frankly, it sits uncomfortably with me although the UFO world is full of surprises and I rule nothing out. This is an idea proposed by some researchers and has at least traces of tantalising evidence in support. Honesty dictates that I must take an impartial look.

The other option—and the one that I suspect most readers will find easier to accept—is that the MIB are the product of a covert operation on the fringes of government study into UFOs. Even if this turns out to be the truth it still poses huge questions.

Why would any government act in this way, particularly given the bizarre nature of many of the MIB stories? Where do these visitors come from, given that the official line of all major powers is that they categorically do not send investigators to frighten witnesses? What is the purpose of the MIB activities—from simple threats to impersonation and even theft of evidence such as films and tapes?

Such issues go right to the heart of the need for a free society in which open government is practiced and not just preached. They are also bound to throw light on the hardly irrelevant but—in this book—somewhat peripheral question of what causes the UFO mystery in the first place.

Today's culture has dictated the remarkable success of TV shows such as *The X Files*, followed more recently by *Dark Skies*, a 1996 drama series that re-writes political history of the past 40 years on the premise that we are involved in a secret war with aliens. Men in Black are key players in the deadly games of agents Mulder and Scully and serve as puppets of the covert agency "Majestic" featured in *Dark Skies*. But Hollywood caught the mood even more openly during 1997 by producing the movie *Men in Black* with Will Smith and Tommy Lee Jones.

These somewhat comic movie characters ensure that witnesses remain ignorant of alien activity on earth in ways rather less sinister (and more amusing) than reported in real life. But that film provides the spur for this book. Millions will see it all over the world and need to know that the Men in Black are not just figures on a cinema screen. To many, they are an undoubted reality.

This book is full of the real life stories that have inspired TV series and movies like *The X Files* and *Men in Black*. Such fiction requires no explanation in order to maintain its suspense. It can afford to take the legend simply on trust. We are forced to look much deeper than that.

The cases in this book are told first hand, often by very frightened people. Fear alone should not prevent us from debating the issues that are at stake although, until now, many of these witnesses were bullied into silence and the shocking truth behind their claims has never been revealed. That is about to change, for Men in Black exist in the real world and seemingly refuse to go away. How could they disappear? It seems that the MIB have a job to do, and we are in their way.

SEEKING MIB

Just how do we find cases of Men in Black? Unfortunately, it is not as easy as going up to someone and asking. If they *have* been frightened by a mysterious visitor who demanded their silence then they could well choose to obey him for fear of the consequence of speaking out.

A witness has to *want* to talk. Often they will have broached the subject carefully over the years, gradually sharing the story with family and friends. Perhaps after a suitable passage of time they may feel the need to talk to an investigator. Or, indeed, they may have been so angered from the start that anyone should order them about that they quickly opt to tell all—although usually with some discretion. Sadly, the latter possibility is less likely. Cases usually emerge *years* after they happen.

As a result, many MIB will *never* be reported. To those wrestling with the decision as to whether to relate their own account I can add that I know of no cases where any serious repercussions have followed the decision to speak out. MIB threats may *seem* scary, but they appear rather hollow.

In truth, when hunting MIB reports we can only keep alert for the possibility. It would be poor investigation to lead witnesses from their story of a strange encounter into urgings that they tell you about weird visitors who came to call. If they do not do so *voluntarily* we cannot force the issue.

This means that we have to look at the evidence that is already available to see whether there are types of cases, categories of witnesses or geographical areas where MIB tend to call more often. We know that the evidence will almost invariably follow a witness encounter with a UFO or alleged alien contact. This is is a place to start. There may be something special that alerts the MIB—whoever they are—to pay a call on witness A, whilst ignoring witnesses B,C and D. As this book develops I believe that you will find that there are indeed clues of this nature about all of these things.

We also need to look at where cases of Men in Black first appeared in history. Are they only contemporary to the UFO mystery, which itself is a largely post-World War II phenomenon? UFOs predating modern times do exist—far back into history, in fact. There are also tales of dark strangers frightening people that might well be early examples of MIB. We will look at those in a later chapter.

For now, let us start with a case that came my way just as many MIB stories do. It arrived bit by bit and very slowly with the witness gradually finding that time had turned fear into anger and frustration, then inspired the very understandable desire to know what on earth was going on.

THE LONG WALK HOME

For Shirley Greenfield* the nightmare began one winter's evening as she walked home from work. It would only come to an end 12 years later when she purged herself of the horrors that now plagued her life. She was about to come face to face

*Shirley Greenfield is a pseudonym

with the Men in Black, and they would stun her into silence for a long time. Talking in public led her inexorably down a path that she could not have predicted—a path that took her from an innocent teenage witness to a young woman who was frightened out of her wits.

On 23 January 1976, Shirley Greenfield was aged 17 and was working in an office in the town of Bolton, Lancashire. As usual, she took the bus out of the center to her new home amidst the Pennine ridges. This is a part of Britain that has been fraught with high levels of UFO activity for many years.

Shirley got off the bus at around 5:20 pm. It was almost dark and the streets were quiet. Her walk from the bus took less than ten minutes and she was nearly home when she saw two lights over a reservoir about half a mile away. Mildy curious, she looked closer to see that one was amber and the other red. They moved through the air as if bumping into one another in some kind of aerial dance.

Moments later these lights had inexplicably swooped toward Shirley. It was as if they had somehow picked her out amidst the gloom of the streets. Now it was evident that these eerie glows were on an object—akin to an upturned pudding basin. The base was curved and the top flattened. There were what seemed to be windows in the side from which the orange light was coming.

Desperately Shirley looked about the road, seeking help, but the pavements were deserted. Fear was clogging her throat as the craft floated above her at a height no greater than a rooftop. It was 20 or 30 feet across and rotating like a spinning top.

The whole thing was quite oppressive in the way that it loomed above her. The sense of isolation increased the tension, as did a physical pressure that appeared to emerge from the object. It was a cold night and snowstorms were heading toward Lancashire that weekend. As a precaution, Shirley had carried her umbrella. A mysterious force invisibly emanated from this object and pressed the witness strongly into the ground, but she rebelled by pushing her umbrella back and resisting the downward thrust. It felt as if she might be crushed by this thing that was now directly on top of her head.

Now there was a further problem to add to the pain that was beginning to throb in her shoulders. The girl's teeth were vibrating—not chattering in fear but resonating like a piece of metal does when a sound of the right frequency is emitted. Shirley had some metal fillings. This force was definitely affecting them, causing these to tingle. A tangy taste was also filling her mouth.

From this point onward memories become confused. Shirley recalls that the object appeared to rotate and flip as if moving away. She took the opportunity to push herself upward from the decreasing pressure and flee in a kind of stumbling run. It was difficult. Everything seemed to enter slow motion. It took her ages to make her legs move and a cocoon of silence swallowed her up. She opened her mouth and attempted to scream in a pure reaction to the terror, but no sounds emerged.

Shirley's next memory is of bursting into her home. She was still unable to speak, presumably as a result of the severe shock. Grabbing hold of her perplexed mother she physically dragged her outside and pointed vaguely at the sky. Nothing was visible, and the last thing that Mrs. Greenfield expected was that her daughter had just seen a UFO.

SOMETHING DREADFUL MUST HAVE HAPPENED

Unsurprisingly, Mrs. Greenfield concluded that her daughter must have been attacked, perhaps even raped, and that the only solution was to contact the police.

At that point neither woman realized there was an anomaly with the time. The UFO must have been seen at about 5:30 pm. It ought now to have been about 5:40. In fact it was 6:10 pm.

One female police officer arrived at the Greenfields' semi at about 7 pm. Shirley was still visibly upset and claiming to feel unwell, no doubt as a direct result of this terrible ordeal. But she spoke fairly coherently to the young woman officer, talking about UFOs and denying that she had met an attacker. A statement was taken from her, but it was obvious that this was done with an air of disinterest and that the incident was not going to be considered a matter for police investigation.

Mrs. Greenfield later told me, "I think they thought Shirley was a hysterical teenager who had seen an aircraft or helicopter and gone crazy. They did not know her like I did. There was not the slightest doubt in my mind that something dreadful must have happened."

Given the lack of interest shown by the police, it is a surprise that they appear to have passed Shirley's story on to the local paper. At least the newspaper says that the police alerted them to this encounter—not the witness. Unfortunately, but not untypically, the police refused to cooperate with UFOlogists and would neither confirm nor deny this allegation.

Three other Bolton girls had seen lights in the sky that week. Their sighting was two days after Shirley's encounter and was a low grade report, featuring a fuzzy white light in the sky. It is probable that this was just a bright star or planet affected by ice crystals then in the atmosphere. However, the report had attracted the local press and the police offered confirmatory evidence.

To her credit, Shirley was not interested in the glut of publicity on offer. She refused to cooperate with the local paper, and when the story about the other girls was picked up by local television she resisted their more lucrative suggestion of money in return for a filmed interview.

Shirley told me, "The money was very tempting to a 17-year-old who liked the odd night out. But these people from TV were clowns. They were not taking the story seriously at all. In any case all I wanted to do by then was forget about it. I told the paper and TV to go away."

A more reluctant self-publicist one could not imagine.

AFTERMATH

There was another reason for Shirley's desire not to talk. Her health had markedly deteriorated in the days since the sighting. After the policewoman left that Friday evening Shirley's mouth had become sore and this problem grew worse over the next day or two. Eventually, she made an appointment to see a dentist.

Shirley was also not very well in other ways. She felt a little light-headed and next morning found a small burn mark on her arm and side as she took a bath. This did not hurt but she pointed it out to her parents. More disconcerting was the pain in her eyes, which by now were watering and looked quite red. She also began to feel nauseous and vomited. Her muscles ached. Then a purple rash formed on her neck and shoulders over the weekend—in fact covering the areas that had been most directly exposed to the UFO. Understandably, Shirley took to her bed at this point.

When she did not improve by the next Sunday the doctor was called out. The rash intrigued him, but he was not convinced that a UFO was responsible. The family GP told the Greenfields that the teenager probably just had flu and prescribed medication. Shirley gradually improved and was back at work by the Tuesday, although it was to be two weeks before she was fully on her feet.

On his way out of the house, her doctor had taken Mr. and Mrs. Greenfield aside and said that Shirley was probably seeking attention—a phase all teenagers go through. They were tempted to believe him, if only to ease their fears, but when they saw her turn down the opportunity of press and TV appearances they knew that this idea was nonsense.

By now Shirley's mouth was causing real problems and her dentist was baffled. Her top fillings had crumbled into a powder and had fallen out. Some in her lower mouth had become embedded in the gums and extensive dental work was needed to sort her out. After the attitude of both the police and her doctor Shirley was reluctant to refer to the cause of this injury for fear the dentist might not treat her if UFOs were cited. He told her that in all his years of work he had never come across a case like this one, especially as the fillings were not very recent.

Another problem was that Shirley did not describe these medical troubles to the UFO community until some time after the encounter. By then the trail was cold and the investigating UFO group, involving myself and colleague Peter Hough, were not able to make the progress we might have made to verify this medical evidence.

Her doctor was another obstacle. The elderly GP died soon after the encounter. A woman GP took over Shirley's notes but absolutely refused to discuss the case with us. In Britain there is no Freedom of Information Act. Patients do not even have the right to access their own files, and despite Shirley's personal request no records were made available. We persuaded an independent doctor to appeal for the woman's records from her GP, using a cover letter from Shirley giving permission. He tried to get her doctor to talk to him as a medical confidence. This man was a hospital specialist but hit the same brick wall that we did.

I have no idea why Shirley's doctor refused to cooperate. The GP may simply have been a stickler for the rules, but perhaps there were things that she preferred not to discuss with UFOlogists—although Shirley's total cooperation and desire to see the records openly released seems to argue strongly against the possibility that she has anything to hide.

In the immediate wake of her encounter, on the following Thursday, Shirley had spoken with a local man called Arthur Tomlinson. Arthur is a long-term UFO investigator with a group called DIGAP (Direct Action Group into Aerial Phenomena). Formed in 1955, this is one of the oldest UFO associations in the world. Shirley reluctantly agreed to tell him about the sighting, just as she had done with the police, but refrained from talking about the medical aftermath.

Shirley only chose to break her silence on these matters in 1984 when she chanced upon my book, *The Pennine UFO Mystery*. The book does not mention her sighting, nor does it refer to Men in Black. As of this time, Shirley had never come across that term at all.

Now aged 26 and far more self-assured, Shirley had tracked down my phone number and given me a call. As she said then, "There are things I have not talked about to anyone but which I really need to describe. I just have to get them off my chest.

For years I have been living with them gnawing at me inside."
She was about to uncork the bottle and let the genie pop out.

REGRESSION

During the next two years I had several meetings with Shirley.
She also had sessions with doctors and psychiatrists which
were coordinated by the local UFO group MUFORA (Manchester UFO Research Association,—today known as NARO—
the Northern Anomalies Research Organisation). These sessions included both assessment and subsequent regression hypnosis.

The first appointment was set up by UFOlogist Harry Harris
with Dr. Albert Kellar, a Manchester specialist. The other
work came under the auspices of Dr. John Dale, a clinical
psychologist in Stockport. I was present on all of these occasions.

There is considerable debate about the use of hypnosis as a
successful means to retrieve bona fide memories. Experiments
have shown that just as often as it brings out memory the
process also stimulates the person into fantasy. If you check
back and see what parts of any hypnotic testimony fit in well
with the facts, then you can decide what might be considered
as valid evidence. But how does anyone decide what is memory and what is fantasy about an experience with strange alien
creatures that may not even exist?

The "missing memory" that did emerge through hypnosis
tells how Shirley was somehow taken into a large room where
she was made to get onto a table or bed. She was being studied
by a being whom she could only just see as her head was
paralyzed in a grip. The entity was very much like a human,
although over six feet tall. It appeared to be female with a
long gown and hair that was so blond it was almost white.

This being was not unkind to her captive. A voice was constantly impressing the line "Do not be afraid." As it did so,
the tall entity was examining Shirley, notably her feet. Shirley
repeated the word "Babinski" under hypnosis. The Babinski

reflex is a test doctors use into muscle function and which involves stroking the underside of the feet.

The entity was also putting images into Shirley's head—"like hundreds and thousands," as she described it. These told of things that would stimulate a response at some unspecified time. Shirley was not to know what these were, but the truth would later be revealed "during and after the sequence of events." This phrase meant nothing to the witness, but the aliens had assured her that they would pay her a return visit, and some sort of subconscious trigger would then be released.

THE COMMANDER CALLS

On Monday, 2 February 1976, nine days after Shirley's encounter, Mrs. Greenfield took a call just before her daughter came home from work. A man who would only identify himself as "someone who investigates these things" posed questions about the girl's state of health. Specifically, he wanted to know if any marks had been left on her body. Mrs. Greenfield fobbed him off.

She initially (and reasonably) assumed that this was someone from Arthur Tomlinson's UFO group, because Arthur had visited only a few days before. It was not. Indeed, the man enigmatically refused to say how he had got hold of the family address and phone number. In any case, why ask about the medical problems that Shirley did not want to discuss? How could he know of these?

At 7 pm the following night the weather was atrocious with a major downpour. Shirley was upstairs unwinding after work. Her medical condition was improving and she was putting the whole episode behind her at last. Then there was a knock at the door.

Two men stood there. They said that they had come to "interrogate" Shirley. Mr. Greenfield, who answered the door, suffered no fools gladly. When they denied being from a UFO group he assumed they must be journalists, but they refuted that possibility as well, without adding where they were actually from. By now Mr. Greenfield was determined not to let them in and told them firmly that his daughter had no interest in discussing the matter further.

Only one of the two men was doing all the talking, and he responded quite sternly to this rebuff: "If you do not let us in now we will come back later and make Shirley speak to us." The threat was not uttered lightly. It seemed very believable.

Shirley had overheard the conversation from the top of the stairs and shouted down that she would speak to them. She told me later that this was definitely against her better judgment and she is unsure why she did it. Her father was even more baffled. He said to me that he could not understand why he let these men into his house given their attitude of intimidation toward his daughter. But things were to get a lot stranger very quickly after they stepped through the door.

Both men were aged about 40 and wore smart black suits. They had a definite air of power and authority about them, clearly convinced that they had a right to do and say whatever they chose. But they were also rather eccentric in behavior and appearance.

The one who did all the talking was tall and fair, almost blond. He never refered to either himself or his colleague by name. Instead he simply used the term "Commander" to introduce himself and created the impression that he was with the RAF. If so, Commander is an inappropriate title. Wing Commander would be correct, but Commander is a naval rank.

There is a curious disagreement between Shirley and her parents with regard to the physical appearance of the "Commander." She says that he had only one arm, a feature that one would assume was noteworthy. Indeed she says that he described losing the appendage during an aircraft accident. But Shirley's parents were less certain. It was the only serious discrepancy in the account of this visit, and they did not try to hide it. Indeed their bafflement was quite evident during our initial discussions.

All three witnesses recall how the "Commander" admired an image of Sir Winston Churchill that the Greenfields had in their living room. He made a point of explaining that he had attended the former Prime Minister's funeral ten years earlier.

Whilst this was occurring the other man sat on a chair holding a square-shaped black box. It was said to be a sophisticated tape recorder but had no visible moving parts. Although he sat on the opposite side of the room from Shirley, no microphone was used to record her voice. Also, the interrogation lasted until after 10 pm, but at no point was the box opened to change a tape.

There was little time for the Greenfields to think about the absurdity of such matters, for during the whole evening the "Commander" was fiercely grilling the teenager in a style that would have done the SS proud. He had her go through every tiny detail of her story repeatedly in precise fashion and was unwilling to accept any hint of uncertainty or vagueness in reply. Indeed, several times he jumped on minor changes in words used by the witness as if it were evidence of a hoax— accusing her of fraud. He was rude to the point of aggression.

Several times during this gruelling session the family had attempted to find out who these men were, but they refused to budge. They admitted that they knew Arthur's group, DIGAP, and called them "meddlers." In fact they seemed disrespectful of UFO investigators in general.

Mr. Greenfield said to me, with a glazed expression conveying much even though it was now eight years since the visit, "You know, I have never been able to understand why I did not throw them out. Why I let them hound Shirley for hour after hour. I would normally not tolerate something like this. Why did I let them do this thing?"

THIS IS WHAT YOU SAW!

After Shirley had related her story, without reference to either the time lapse or the physical after-effects, the "Commander" suddenly announced, "This is what you saw!" It had been a weather balloon launched by an RAF station. Shirley told him that the idea was ridiculous, so he changed the explanation to "an experimental military aircraft," a theory to which she gave only slightly more credence. He practically beat her into an acceptance of this explanation, but she would not agree to it.

At this point the conversation took off in new directions. The "Commander" began to ask things that seemed baffling to Shirley. He was very insistent that she must have had physical illness and marks on her body following the encounter. He seemed unable to accept the girl's insistence that she had not and then demanded to see her arms. Understandably, she declined. Shirley told me that she deliberately lied to him about this point of her story. "It was the only untruthful thing I said to these men all night. But I was not going to talk about those marks."

Other questions that were posed included whether she had seen anyone inside the object. When Shirley truthfully said no, the question was extended to "any moving objects or parts inside it?" More perplexing was a series of questions about psychic phenomena. Could Shirley read minds? Did she have dreams about something before it happened? Could she move objects through mental effort alone? To all of these things Shirley said no.

In fact, during childhood she had indeed experienced many vivid dreams, including what we might well term "out of body" experiences. In other instances she believed that she had consciously levitated—literally floated down the stairs. Shirley had not only one witness but two. Her sister and her mother had allegedly seen her levitate down the stairs and confirmed this story from memory later. Whilst it proves nothing, of course, it raises the matter beyond the level of a single person's account.

When Shirley told me this I was stunned but let the fantastic claim wash over me. I was aware that close encounter witnesses and abductees often did profess a strong track record of other paranormal happenings within their lives—particularly in early childhood. It was to me a vital clue to what was going on. The UFO or alien contact was not an isolated experience. Most of the time it was part of a lifelong continuum of incredible incidents, from poltergeist outbreaks to apparitions.

The sophisticated nature of the questions asked during the visit by these two men was what was really perturbing me. Why had they asked about so many obscure things? Even in 1997 most researchers into alien abductions would think you were wasting your time if you grilled the witness about whether they had floated into the air as a child.

Whoever these visitors were at the Greenfield house that February night, they were doing their job in a way that was unlike how a UFO group would have handled matters back then. Who were they?

YOU MUST NOT TALK

At the end of a long night the "Commander" conveyed a stern warning to Shirley: "You must not talk about this matter. It is in your interests not to do so. Nobody will believe you, in any case. In particular you must not talk to UFO investigators."

Shirley took the warning seriously. It fitted in with her own desire to forget the entire experience. In fact, it would be several years before she came round to thinking that nobody had the right to order her about like this and her natural assertiveness won the day.

When the two men left they got into a large black car that was parked outside. The make was not noticed in the rainy night, but it could have been a Mercedes or a Jaguar.

Mrs. Greenfield could not get over how the man who had not spoken all night had stared intently at her daughter throughout the evening. "He gave me the creeps," she told me. "He was just watching Shirley all of the time." Only when the family talked about the events of that evening in the cold light of day did they begin to realize the peculiarity and the stunning way in which they had accepted it all so meekly.

The next day the "Commander" phoned again and Mrs. Greenfield answered. He asked her to relay a question to Shirley, which she did. "Was Shirley certain that she had no marks on her body?" The teenager denied it yet again.

About a week later he called one more time and asked exactly the same thing. This time Shirley took the phone and determined to end things once and for all. Her marks were now practically gone, so she told him that, yes, she did have a rash and other problems, but these had cleared up now.

The "Commander" seemed relieved by this news and thanked her for the information. Then he hung up. The Greenfields never heard from him again.

However, during the first regression experiment in Dr. Kellar's surgery in St. John Street, Manchester, it was decided to try a unique experiment. Shirley would be asked to relive the visit by the two men in addition to her UFO encounter. This proved a horrific ordeal. Whilst her "abduction" was stressful to describe, she reacted in absolute terror to the recounting of the visit by the two Men in Black. Indeed, Dr. Kellar quickly stopped the experiment because he was monitoring her vital signs, such as pulse rate and heartbeat, and these began to climb to dangerous levels.

Even so, Shirley surprised us by stating of the "Commander": "I don't understand—he's talking to me twice." It seems that during the visit a message was acting on her subconscious mind like a subliminal communication. The man was somehow interrogating her on two different levels. Was this a kind of hypnotic suggestion, and is this why the family submitted themselves to hour after hour of interrogation without batting an eyelid?

FINAL WARNING

After the hypnosis sessions had concluded in 1984, Shirley got a telephone call at home. It was not the "Commander." She did not recognize the male voice. Although very few people were yet aware of the experiment this caller told Shirley that he knew all about its outcome. He warned that she should cease cooperation with the MUFORA team and agree to meet with him if she wanted to learn the truth. He would not name himself and never called back. She refused to cooperate with this threat.

A week later Shirley received another mystifying call. This was to invite her to a Manchester city center hotel so that she could be vetted for a plush job. The job paid well but would involve her moving immediately to Zimbabwe. According to the caller she had applied for the post. Shirley had done no such thing and so did not attend the interview. She has no idea how the offer came about.

In view of all these things, it is little wonder that when a wave of unsought media pressure came through an unannounced radio ad not long afterwards this served as the final straw, and Shirley decided to give up talking about her experience altogether. She headed off for a quiet life away from her former home and the intimidating tactics of these mystery men.

ASSESSMENT

Assessing a case of this nature is very difficult, for there are two types of evidence: the verifiable data from fully conscious recall, and the material that emerges under regression hypnosis—which is almost impossible to validate. The two cannot be considered of equal validity.

That Shirley Greenfield saw something strange in the sky and that it left serious physical after-effects on her body seems to me completely inescapable. The physical symptoms are not unlike mild radiation exposure and have been recounted by witnesses in many other close encounter cases from around the world. I am reasonably certain that Shirley was not familiar with these facts in 1976. The dental problems are also significant. Something caused those fillings to fall out. Was it an ultrasonic sound emerging from the UFO? Does this also explain her nausea?

The image of a tall, blond-haired being performing medical tests is extraordinarily consistent within European UFO events. In 1984, what publicity there had been surrounded American cases in which the entities are quite different (short and squat with big black eyes). Shirley cannot have known that European witnesses tend to describe tall blond beings, just as she had.

Other consistent features occur in Shirley's account, such as the use of telepathy to communicate and the implantation of tasks to be unleashed at some future point as part of a grand plan. It is hard to know why people fantasising under regression would plump for this same storyline.

However, the question of alien abduction is a very complex one beyond the scope of this book. Many psychologists, psychiatrists and sociologists have studied it since 1984 and their arguments are voluminously documented elsewhere. They involve the study of various possible theories, ranging from stimulation of the brain's temporal lobe by an atmospheric energy to individuals with unusually vivid imaging capabilities. We should explore all options, but research has proved one thing very clearly—that the vast majority of abductees are not pathologically ill or making up stories. Whatever these encounters may be, the witnesses believe implicitly in what they say.

As for the visit by the two mysterious Men in Black, this does not rely on hypnosis. Nor is it down to Shirley's memory alone. We have no reason to conclude other than that it really did take place.

2

MAURY ISLAND:
BIRTH OF A MYSTERY

When did Men in Black first enter our awareness? There is one encounter through which we can definitely pinpoint the start of the MIB phenomenon in its modern guise. It comes from the very starting point of the flying saucer enigma.

Whilst there have probably always been UFO reports, in the sense of strange lights seen in skies, one man is widely considered to be the father of the mystery. He was a 32-year-old Boise, Idaho, businessman and light aircraft pilot named Kenneth Arnold who saw something odd around 3 pm on the afternoon of 24 June 1947 amidst a wave of reports that swept the western USA. Earlier sightings went virtually unreported, but Arnold's story caught the public imagination.

The witness was flying his small, single-engined Callair across Washington state from Chehalis, where he had just installed some fire fighting equipment for an air company. His destination was the small airport at Yakima. A C-46 transport had vanished in the mountains around Mount Rainier, and the search had so far revealed nothing. There was a $5000 reward on offer (a considerable sum in those days), and Arnold decided to route his journey in such a way that he could circle the peaks and look for the wreckage.

He never found the crashed C-46, but he did open a huge can of worms. Scanning the ground above the town of Mineral, he was startled by a very bright flash that he took to be the approach of an aircraft on a collision course. A few moments later another flash appeared, and this time he spotted the source—a formation of nine curious objects above Mount Baker. They were many miles away but moving at great speed across his path. He could not make out their shape as they strongly reflected the sunlight, but they flew in formation. Arnold had no doubt that they were military jets of a type he had never encountered before.

Most intriguing to the witness was their motion. He describes them as like a speed boat bouncing across waves—as if riding the current of air and skimming very close to the mountain tops. He could see that they were crescent-moon shaped. They were definitely not like a flying saucer in outline and the myth that these craft were "disc-like" is remarkably enduring but utterly false.

Arnold abandoned his search and landed at Yakima at around 4 pm. He went to the air company office, described his sighting and sketched the craft. The pilot noted how he timed them flying between two measurable points (Mount Rainier and Mount Adams). Their speed was well in excess of 1000 mph; although this estimate had involved a guess as to their distance and height.

One of the airline pilots called in to hear this tale suggested that they were "guided missiles" which he knew were under development at Moses Lake. Arnold shrugged at this, half accepting the theory, and got back into his plane to continue homeward to Pendleton, Oregon. Nobody was more surprised than he to find himself greeted there by a large crowd waiting for an air show but who had been alerted on the radio by someone at Yakima as to what he had seen above Mount Rainier.

FLYING SAUCERS

Arnold was keen to get home and hastily described the motion of the objects to a reporter as being "like saucers skipping across water," elaborating a little to explain how rocks could be bounced across the flat surface of a lake or pond. Understandably, the idea that the objects were *shaped* like saucers stuck firm from this description. Now infamous headlines were conjured up that Arnold had seen ''flying saucers,'' from which the erroneous impression of their saucer structure arose.

Several days later, after endless calls from the media and reports of people who had watched the sky and ''seen flying saucers,'' Arnold got a call from Dave Johnson, aviation editor with the *Idaho Statesman*. Johnson, a very knowledgeable aircraft expert, insisted there was no US ''secret'' craft like the ones that the Callair pilot had alleged. This was the first time that serious doubts appeared in the pilot's mind that his ''flying saucers'' had been earthly in origin.

Precisely what Kenneth Arnold saw that day remains in doubt. There have been good attempts to explain it as clouds, flocks of geese or reflections off the aircraft canopy (although Arnold says he had opened this up to rule out that idea because it had occurred to him at the time). The view that these craft may have been spaceships is barely more credible as an answer. A formation flight of nine alien starships is hard to comprehend.

Intriguingly, some of the sightings made in the 1947 wave *before* Arnold's well publicised report were also of multiple objects, although today these are extremely rare. The UFO mystery seems to mold itself like plasticine and change with time. Fact and fiction often intertwine in ways that can be very difficult to unwind. That is what seems to have happened here.

One of the cases that quickly followed Arnold occurred on 4 July 1947, just ten days after his Mount Rainier adventure. The new witnesses were Captain E.J. Smith and his co-pilot Ralph Stevens, taking United Airlines Flight 105 out of Boise, Idaho. They had spotted a formation of round objects (eventually nine in total) and had also shown them to stewardess Martie Morrow. This incident occurred above Emmett, Idaho, soon after take off.

At first the United crew had assumed the objects were military jets coming home from an Independence Day celebration, but their odd behavior soon ruled that out. They seemed to

FLI DALLAS   7-8-47   6-17 PM
DIRECTOR AND SAC, CINCINNATI   URGENT
FLYING DISC, INFORMATION CONCERNING.   MAJOR CURTAN, HEADQUARTERS
EIGHTH AIR FORCE, TELEPHONICALLY ADVISED THIS OFFICE THAT AN OBJECT
PURPORTING TO BE A FLYING DISC WAS RE COVERED NEAR ROSWELL, NEW
MEXICO, THIS DATE. THE DISC IS HEXAGONAL IN SHAPE AND WAS SUSPENDED
FROM A BALLON BY CABLE, WHICH BALLON WAS APPROXIMATELY TWENTY
FEET IN DIAMETER.   MAJOR CURTAN FURTHER ADVISED THAT THE OBJECT
FOUND RESEMBLES A HIGH ALTITUDE WEATHER BALLOON WITH A RADAR
REFLECTOR, BUT THAT TELEPHONIC CONVERSATION BETWEEN THEIR OFFICE
AND WRIGHT FIELD HAD NOT SOME OUT THIS BELIEF.   DISC AND
BALLOON BEING TRANSPORTED TO WRIGHT FIELD BY SPECIAL PLANE FOR EXAMIN
INFORMATION PROVIDED THIS OFFICE BECAUSE OF NATIONAL INTEREST IN CASE
AND FACT THAT NATIONAL BROADCASTING COMPANY, ASSOCIATED PRESS, AND
OTHERS ATTEMPTING TO BREAK STORY OF LOCATION OF DISC TODAY.   MAJOR
CURTAN ADVISED WOULD REQUEST WRIGHT FIELD TO ADVISE CINCINNATI
OFFICE RESULTS OF EXAMINATION.   NO FURTHER INVESTIGATION BEING
CONDUCTED.

                    HYLY
                    RECORDED
END
CXXXX ACK IN ORDER   EX-23
UA   9½ FBI CI HJU
DPI   HS
8-38 PM O
8-22 PM OM FBI WASH DC

blend and merge almost as if they were some kind of optical effect.

Arnold was on a fishing trip with his friend, Colonel Paul Wieland, who had just returned from the Nuremberg war trials. He dumped the colonel at Seattle airport on their way home as soon as he heard about this sighting and rushed to meet the United pilot. A bond between Kenneth Arnold and Captain E.J. Smith was formed that morning. It was to prove highly significant in the days to come.

A FLOOD OF MAIL

The latest media story about Arnold resulted in floods of letters reaching his home. Each one told Arnold of a sighting or offered a theory as to what was going on. Amidst the sackful of mail that Arnold received was one on 15 July from a man in Evanston, Illinois, called Ray Palmer. His headed paper said "Venture Press."

Arnold later reported that if he had known at the time that Palmer was a publisher of fringe stories about aliens, science fiction and underground monsters he would have run a mile and never replied, but he asked his friends and press contacts for advice and nobody had heard of Palmer or Venture Press.

Palmer had offered to pay Arnold for the right to publish his first-hand story, but this was not of interest to the pilot. He had by now freely submitted an official report to the Army

Opposite *On 8 July 1947, as Arnold began to collect UFO reports from western USA, one of the most remarkable of all was the alleged crash and retrieval of wreckage from a "disk" near Roswell, New Mexico. The public were told it was simply a balloon and the story fizzled out. This then secret memo, only released 30 years later, proves the origin of the debris had not been explained—but, as the FBI were informed, was shipped to Wright Field (now Wright Patterson Air Force Base), home of the Foreign Technology Division. Five months later this became the home of the US government's UFO investigation team.*

Air Force at Wright Patterson Air Force Base in Dayton, Ohio, believing this to be his patriotic duty. So he just sent a carbon copy of this onto the man at Venture Press without requesting money in return for its use. This was to set up the final link in a chain involving Arnold, Captain Smith and now magazine editor Palmer. The three were about to become embroiled in a most extraordinary affair.

Ray Palmer was a desperately enthusiastic 37-year-old. Since 1938 he had edited *Amazing Stories*, the world's first science fiction magazine. This had, for example, published wild tales and lurid drawings of scenes that would later become part of the UFO mythology. Later he set up the first ever serious magazine devoted to the paranormal. Known as *Fate*, it still exists today, and Arnold's first-hand account which Palmer had requested actually appeared in the very first issue.

Until his death in 1977 Palmer continued as something of an enigma. He was undoubtedly the first man to recognize the enormous public interest in flying saucers and the commercial opportunity they represented. Sadly, he was too much of a jack of all trades to benefit from his own foresight.

In his third letter inside a week to the reluctant UFO witness, dated 20 July, Ray Palmer told Arnold that he had received a report from two harbor patrolmen in Tacoma, Washington. Not only had they seen the by now commonplace formation of UFOs, but they had physical proof—bits of metal that had rained down upon them. Palmer wanted Arnold to fly immediately to Tacoma, investigate the case and collect samples to send onto him at Evanston. He offered to pay all expenses for this trip.

At the time, however, Arnold had other things on his mind. As a result of his letter to Wright Patterson, two military intelligence officers, Lieutenant Frank Brown and Captain William Davidson, had asked to come north to see him. Arnold felt honored to be singled out like this and agreed to meet with them at the Hotel Owyhee in Boise. They had flown there in an A-29 bomber "just to see me," as he later reported with pride and amazement.

SECRET INTELLIGENCE

After discussing his case with these intelligence officers Arnold suggested they also meet Captain Smith, whom he knew was due to land at Boise on a commercial flight that evening. They were glad to do so, saying Smith was "on their list." Back at the Arnold home, the two officers were offered any of the pile of his UFO mail to take for study. They did not seem interested in witness stories, taking those from societies expressing interest in starting to investigate "flying saucer" reports.

Before they flew off in their A-29 back to California, Brown and Davidson told Arnold to call if he had anything important to relate. They also politely advised, Arnold reports, "that it would probably be better for all concerned if I refused to discuss my experiences further with outsiders."

After debating what to do about the trip to Tacoma for some days, Arnold chose to test the water by asking for expenses from Ray Palmer up front. Inside 24 hours $200 was wired through—more than enough for a fairly lengthy trip to the coastal port. Arnold was not told by Palmer that his correspondent (Fred Crisman) had already written to Venture Press about the "Deros people" (a race of strange creatures supposedly living under the earth!). Had Arnold known this fact about the witness he may well not have flown to Tacoma.

But by now, according to British aviation writer Gerald Heard in his 1950 account of Arnold's story, the pilot had by chance received news of the Tacoma sighting from a further source. After a lecture to a luncheon club in his home town of Boise, Arnold was informed by an unknown member of the audience that there was a case that had occurred in Tacoma and this man happened to know one of the two witnesses (a harbor patrolman called Harold Dahl). The audience member thought Dahl reliable.

As a result, Arnold reports that on 29 July 1947 he took off "from a cow pasture near my home" and flew to the industrial coastal town of Tacoma to officially investigate his first UFO encounter. He was never to grasp the way in which his trip was effectively engineered for him by a series of coincidences—the Palmer letters, the stranger at his luncheon lecture who vouched for one of the Tacoma witnesses and who knew him by chance, and so on. In retrospect it was as if someone wanted to ensure that Arnold took this trip.

If so, his expedition west was to prove a frustrating, mystifying and ultimately tragic exercise—and one about which UFOlogists argue fiercely to this day.

TROUBLE IN TACOMA

Once the pilot reached Tacoma—a place he did not know well—Arnold had his first surprise. It proved very hard to book a room at any hotel. All said they were full. Nobody, not even Palmer knew he had been heading out that day. Yet when he phoned the grandest establishment in the city (the Hotel Winthrop)—more or less as a last resort—they already had a room reserved in his name. Arnold was baffled. He assumed that (by yet another coincidence) someone else named Kenneth Arnold had reserved the room but had not turned up. In any case, he accepted his good fortune.

Looking through the phone book in Room 502, he found only one man named Dahl with the right initials and so called him up to arrange an appointment. Dahl was not keen on talking when Arnold phoned him that night. He suggested that the pilot fly straight home and forget all about his investigation. But he soon relented and said that he would be with Arnold within half an hour. Even then, he again advised Arnold to reconsider, saying, "This flying saucer business is the most complicated thing that you have ever got mixed up in." But mindful of the $200 he was spending for somebody else, Arnold decided to press on.

Eventually, Dahl explained what had happened on the afternoon of 21 June—that is, three days *before* Arnold's own historic sighting. He had supposedly been out patrolling for the harbor board in Puget Sound near Maury Island, which is some three miles offshore. With him were two crew, his 15-

year-old son and their dog. Suddenly they spotted a formation of six objects shaped like doughnuts but with windows. One seemed in trouble and the other five were circling around it.

Unsure what might happen as the central UFO appeared to be dropping lower, they beached the boat and started to take photographs with the official harbor patrol camera. Then what looked like newspapers floated out of the central craft, fluttering down to the beach and into the sea. These turned out to be light thin pieces of white metal resembling aluminium. Unseen by them against the darkened sky, some rather more dangerous cargo was also being deposited onto the beach. This was heavy slag-like rock resembling the local lava outcrops. It was hot and caused the sea to steam when it struck. The party fled for the safety of some caves, but not before the dog was struck and killed and Dahl's son was hit and injured on the arm.

Eventually, the objects flew away and Dahl and his men collected some of the debris. His boat was damaged but they managed to get back to Tacoma, where the boy was taken to hospital. The dog was "buried at sea" on the return journey.

Dahl immediately told his superior, Fred Crisman, who did not believe him but took the metal fragments and the film from his crewman. This was processed and allegedly came out covered in spots "as if exposed to an X-ray machine." (These photographs were never seen by any investigators and seemingly were "lost" a few days later.) After seeing the debris, Crisman agreed to sail out next day and check for himself Dahl's claim that some "20 tons" of the stuff had rained down on the Maury Island shore.

A STRANGER CALLS

At 7 am on 22 June, a man arrived at the Dahl house and asked the patrolman to go out with him to breakfast. Dahl agreed thinking he was interested in purchasing salvage, a not uncommon practice. The man was dressed in black and aged about 40. He drove a dark sedan and took Dahl to a cafe in the upmarket part of town—which was odd, as those seeking salvage usually went dockside.

After they sat down and ordered breakfast the man proceeded to tell Dahl in stunning detail all about the UFO episode from the day before. It was so accurate it was as if he had been in the boat with them. The man in black pointed out that this was to prove that "I know a great deal more about this experience of yours than you will ever want to believe."

The stranger spoke in mysterious terms about how the encounter "should not have happened" but that if Dahl knew what was good for him and he loved his family he would keep quiet about the matter. There was a clear threat that if he did not do so bad things would follow, although nothing was specified. In any case, Dahl ignored the request and told many of the local dock workers.

By now Arnold was perplexed with this whole weird story and readily agreed to go with Dahl to his "secretary's house" to see the debris for himself. Arnold carefully noted the route taken because he intended to return alone in daylight. He also noted the details inside the rather seedy homestead.

Dahl's secretary was engaged in paperwork but the harborman eventually showed Arnold one of the lumps of dark metal "which I am using as an ash tray." Arnold's disappointment was immense. He recognized it immediately as a lump of ordinary lava rock and said so. Dahl shrugged, said he knew nothing about geology, and suggested they go to see the bits of white metal that Crisman had collected. He had obtained plenty of pieces, which were now in a box in his garage.

Arnold, however, was losing patience and his interest in the case was fast evaporating. He suspected he was being duped. But next morning at 9:30 Dahl and Crisman arrived unannounced at Arnold's hotel room. Crisman was anxious to "take command" of the situation and to tell the pilot all about his own sighting. This had occurred when Crisman went to Maury Island to collect the metal fragments that he had been told by Dahl were all over the beach front. As he took samples one of the objects had passed over the shore and he now had no doubt that Dahl was telling the truth.

HELP REQUIRED

After these revelations Arnold quickly decided he needed help, so he put through a call to Captain E.J. Smith to see if he was willing to take a few days off and join the investigation. Smith agreed and on 30 July Arnold flew the short hop from Tacoma to Seattle to pick up the United pilot. After his initial meeting with the two patrolmen, Smith was also worried that something did not seem right about this case. But he could not break the witness stories.

The concerns of Arnold and Smith deepened when Ted Morello, the head of United Press in Tacoma, called the Winthrop Hotel to say that something mightly odd was going on. An anonymous caller was phoning him supplying full accounts, virtually word for word, of what he said the two investigators and Dahl and Crisman were getting up to in the bedroom. Arnold had not announced his arrival in town to the press, but these accounts were remarkably accurate.

Although at first this suggested further evidence of a hoax, it soon clicked that some of the conversations had occurred when Arnold and Smith were alone. Despite a thorough search, no listening device was found in the hotel room. So how did the mystery caller know what was being said?

Morello reported that this man was in touch several more times in the days ahead. On at least one occasion the person was still on the line when the reporter phoned Arnold at the Winthrop and got him to "count noses" present in Room 502. Both Dahl and Crisman were present with Arnold and Smith at that moment and so it was clear that neither witness was the phantom caller, Morello confirmed that the voice seemed identical to the earlier calls.

Despite having their own plane, which could have flown low over the island to check the beach for scattered UFO debris, the two investigators never bothered to go and take a look across Puget Sound. However, British researcher Harold Wilkins reported in 1954 that he had a contact in Tacoma who had looked into this case for him. The man went to the beach some weeks later and no UFO debris was scattered there.

Of course the "spoiled film" was also requested from Dahl by Arnold. Dahl said Crisman had the film. Crisman said he would bring it. Then he said he could not find it. Finally he suggested it must be in his weekend cabin. But Arnold had long given up all expectation that he would ever see this evidence and declined to go into the mountains to hunt for it.

The exasperated UFOlogist decided he had only one option left: call the intelligence officers, Brown and Davidson. Perhaps their expertise could sort out this frustrating case. Arnold called the officers at Hamilton Field, as he had been asked to do. He was told to put the investigation on hold. Within two hours, despite it being late evening, Brown and Davidson arrived at the Winthrop. They had seconded a B-25 to fly them there. Dahl left the hotel before they came, handing Arnold a phone number where he might be contacted later. Crisman agreed to tell the story to the two men.

For some hours the two intelligence agents listened to the saga and examined the fragments. Then, according to Arnold, they suddenly lost interest. The two men said they would fly home immediately. Arnold offered to put up some beds in his room. As a pilot he knew the importance of resting before a flight. However, Brown and Davidson insisted that as 1 August was Air Force Day they had to have the plane back by morning. If true, this makes the fact that they flew so far on such a thin lead late on the 31st all the more hard to understand. However, leave to fly home the two officers did, taking with them a box full of metal fragments supplied by Crisman. It was after midnight when they headed back toward their B-25 at the local base, McChord Field.

DISASTER STRIKES

At breakfast the following morning Arnold, Smith and Crisman all learned some terrible news from the radio. A B-25 had crashed 20 minutes after take off from Tacoma at about 1:30 am. Although no details were available, the three men knew who had been aboard. Two airmen had died in the accident. Again, they knew just who these were.

Unsurprisingly, Arnold felt responsible for this tragedy. Brown and Davidson would not have been on that fatal plane ride but for him. He phoned Palmer in Illinois and told him he could have his $200 back as he was quitting the case. Palmer was sympathetic and urged them not to carry any of the metal they had collected on the plane trip home. Instead it should be posted to Illinois.

At the United Press office later that morning the two pilots were played an interview that had just been recorded by Morello with one of two survivors who escaped from the B-25 crash. This intensified the problems. The interviewee was an army man who had hitched a ride. He explained how the two pilots had loaded a heavy box onto the B-25 before take off (presumably the UFO wreckage), then soon after they became airborne one engine caught fire but the plane flew on without it.

The hitcher was then forced to parachute from the plane being pushed out of it by Brown. The engineer on board, Sargeant Mathews, also escaped in this way. But Brown and Davidson, both of whom had parachutes and so could have jumped free at any point, stayed aboard the plane. Why they did not get clear remains unknown. As the survivor parachuted to the ground eight minutes passed, and he saw the B-25 fly on above him. There was ample time for the pilot and co-pilot to get away and he had assumed that they *did* escape, only to be stunned by the news that they had died in the crash.

Arnold and Smith remained in town expecting to be called by McChord Field to answer questions about the tragic accident. Meanwhile, the phantom caller proved himself to United Press by revealing the names of the two dead intelligence agents well before the Army Air Force officially released the news.

Then Major George Sander of the intelligence unit at McChord confirmed to the United Press that "a somewhat secret cargo" was aboard the plane and told them that "no-

one was allowed to take photographs of the wreckage until
the material was removed and returned to McChord Field.''

ACCIDENT OR SABOTAGE?

Another riddle appeared when Ted Morello showed Arnold
and Smith a United Press teletype message received within
hours of the crash (it was not clear whether this was shortly
before or just after the accident, but it came to them before
names of the crash victims were released). This message carried a story about Dick Rankin, one of the most celebrated
stunt pilots in the USA.

Rankin had, in fact, had his own UFO encounter whilst
flying a few weeks beforehand. In the teletype message this
pilot revealed the astonishing claim that two intelligence officers named Brown and Davidson had interviewed him about
his encounter and that in his opinion they were very close to
learning the truth about the UFO mystery. As a result, he argued, he was sure that they were in danger. Somebody was
trying to kill them. Nobody seems to have ever discovered
why Rankin thought this.

The call to assist the Army Air Force with their inquiries
into the crash never came. By Sunday, 3 August, Smith had
had enough. He left the Winthrop refusing to tell Arnold where
he was going. Hours later he returned with Major Sander, the
McChord intelligence commander. Smith had been to the base
to give his story. Now he wanted Arnold to do the same.

Sander showed mild interest in the fragments strewn all over
the hotel room floor. He suggested he would have them tested
and added that in a couple of weeks the truth about the incident would be revealed to the two men. He inferred that they
had been victims of a hoax by Dahl and Crisman, who were
not even real harbor patrolmen. Until the Army Air Force intelligence told them otherwise, Arnold and Smith should remain silent as to what had happened, because the case was
under investigation and now out of their hands. In respect to
the two dead men they naturally agreed.

Despite his certainty that it was just a hoax, Sander was none the less wrapping up every scrap of debris on the hotel floor. When Arnold tried to take a small lump away as a souvenir the Major stopped him, saying, as if it were a passing thought, "we don't want to overlook one piece, do we."

Once finished, the Major drove Arnold and Smith to a site which he said would explain everything. It was a nearby smelleding works. He clearly knew where he was going, finding the right road and stopping by a pile of slag first time. Superficially this material looked similar to the "lava rock," but Sander would not let the men compare the fragments now locked away in his car boot.

THE MAN THAT NEVER WAS

After Major Sander had gone back to his base, Arnold decided to visit Dahl and drove Smith to the house where he was first shown the wreckage on the night of his arrival in Tacoma. Dahl had said he would be working there that weekend. Arnold was sure that he reached the same house, but it was deserted. In fact it looked as if it had been derelict for months. He tried calling Dahl on the phone number he had been given. There was no answer. Later, back in Boise, the operator insisted that no such number was listed in Tacoma. Dahl had vanished and was never traced again. It was as if he had been professionally relocated—a tactic commonly used by intelligence services.

Crisman had also disappeared, but the mystery caller phoned Ted Morello one last time to report that the alleged boss of the harbor patrol had been flown to Alaska aboard an Army bomber. This was never confirmed, but it was subsequently established that such a flight did indeed leave McChord Field on the very day stated. Crisman was not heard from again until many years later. Dahl, so far as we know, even left his family and business when he permanently disappeared. Indeed, Harold Wilkins reports in his 1954 account that he wrote to Crisman in Tacoma on 23 January 1951 but received the letter

back from the post office in the town. This indicated that all
attempts to trace anyone of that name had failed.

RESOLUTION

With the case and its hard evidence snatched from under their
noses, Smith and Arnold parted company and Arnold prepared
to fly home to Boise. He felt utterly shellshocked by the events
of the past week and could not make up his mind what had
really happened.

Given the tragic fate of Brown and Davidson, Kenneth Arnold checked his aircraft very carefully indeed. All went well
until he landed to refuel at Pendleton. Climbing up from the
runway on take-off the Callair engine failed. Having little forward speed catastrophe loomed, but fortune and skilled flying
prevailed and Arnold crash landed safely in fields dead ahead.

Investigation subsequently revealed a disturbing fact. Somebody had switched off the fuel valve. Without fuel the little
plane was doomed to fall out of the sky. If it had done so a
few seconds later there would have been no escape from the
impact. Arnold was lucky to be alive.

The US intelligence services did eventually publish an explanation for the Maury Island affair. They claimed that Dahl
and Crisman confessed under questioning after Arnold and
Smith had left town. The entire story was a hoax cooked up
by them. It began as a joke, rapidly got out of hand and resulted in tragedy. The UFO debris was simply a collection of
rock found on Maury Island. It was not smelted metal as
Sander had curiously tried to persuade the two pilots.

As for the phantom caller to United Press, this was Dahl or
Crisman playing tricks and the Man in Black simply did not
exist. They made it all up. The men were just poor salavage
crew sailors who saw their big chance to sell a story. On the
surface this sounds perfectly reasonable. The case did have
huge problems and even Arnold—who was convinced of the
reality of UFOs—began to suspect he was being hoodwinked
in some way.

In 1956 the former head of the US intelligence investigation into UFOs, Captain Edward Ruppelt wrote of the case and called it "the dirtiest hoax in the UFO history" and that Dahl and Crisman "should have disappeared into Puget Sound" given the deaths of Brown and Davidson. Whilst he claimed that the secret material aboard the B-25 was a file of intelligence reports and not the UFO debris (as had been previously assumed), he shed no light on why the intelligence officers failed to escape the blazing plane. The truth was never revealed to Arnold and Smith because the US government did not want to embarrass them. Although prosecution of Dahl and Crisman was considered it was not pursued, because no malice had been intended by the two tricksters.

This hoax explanation is the view that most cautious UFO researchers have accepted ever since. However, some do disagree. Kenneth Arnold knew something didn't add up but never bought the hoax explanation. In 1977, in one of his last public appearances before he died, he spoke at a conference celebrating 30 years of "flying saucers" and expressed his feelings that the hoax claim was itself the real fraud.

Indeed, Ray Palmer notes that when *Fate* magazine published the claims of the US government that Dahl and Crisman had confessed to a hoax the magazine received a letter signed by Crisman (seemingly his final communication) in which he threatened to sue for libel unless they retracted these "bogus" allegations.

WHO HOAXED WHOM?

New York journalist and UFO historian John Keel suggests, rather curiously, that there was a real incident in Puget Sound but that aliens and UFOs were never involved. Instead, the witnesses encountered an illegal dumping operation in which radioactive waste was being deposited on Maury Island. As such they fell foul of the intelligence community who warned them off and invented the hoax solution. But this seems to be little more than speculation on his part.

In whatever way we look at the case it is full of questions. Few have ever attempted to suggest that Arnold and Smith were part of any hoax—merely naive, at worst. But assuming that these two respected pilots were truthful (particularly Arnold), then we must wonder about the way in which room 502 became available or how Crisman or Dahl could have been the phantom caller to United Press when they were both present in the hotel whilst one of these calls was made.

Then there is the riddle of Major Sander and his expedition to the Tacoma smelting works. Why was he trying to persuade Arnold and Smith that this was the source of the fragments? Indeed, Palmer and Arnold had a crucial ace up their sleeves. Fragments of debris had already been sent to Illinois before the lid came down. Major Sander had failed to collect these and probably did not know of their existence. After the official report by the US Air Force published an analysis to show that the material was just lava rock found all over the coast, Palmer paid for a study of his fragments. They were not unusual, comprising iron, zinc, aluminium, copper and other elements. But there were high levels of calcium and titanium, which was unexpected, and they certainly did not appear to be the same lava rock that the US government were officially blaming for the hoax debris.

More questions pepper this baffling case. Why did Dick Rankin warn United Press that the two intelligence officers were in danger? Why did Brown and Davidson fly to Tacoma in such a hurry for a matter that was so readily explained and never important? If they were collecting other secret material (not the rock samples), is it pure coincidence that Arnold called them to Tacoma on the very night this was due to be ferried to California? Why did they not get out of the burning plane?

We might also want to know what happened to the house where Dahl had kept the fragments—or, indeed, to Dahl? And Arnold certainly needs to know how his fuel valve was switched off.

And then there is the MIB aspect to this story. If it were unique to this case then we could easily dismiss it as just another part of the hoax. But it fits the pattern of other cases so well. Yet Dahl's MIB story preceded all of those others in a proper UFO context, so this was no copycat hoax. As such, you do have to wonder how an invention came to match later reality so well.

In 1980 two experienced and reputable British researchers, Brian Burden and Bernard Delair of Contact UK, assessed the case and concluded that it was an elaborate intelligence operation and had been set up specifically to discredit Kenneth Arnold as the man who was then the most important UFO witness in the world. If his credibility was diminished, so then was the belief that UFOs were real.

If the Maury Island UFO incident was a hoax (and there is no persuasive evidence that a real UFO encounter ever occurred), then Arnold seems to have been the primary scapegoat. He was encouraged to go to investigate by both the Palmer letter and the mystery member of the audience at his Boise lecture. He was led into booking the room which may well have been bugged. Then he was taken by the nose into a messy affair which led to the deaths of the two intelligence officers who seemed to be pursuing UFO cases on a full-time basis in those early days.

That is, of course, assuming these men did really die and did not parachute from the plane unobserved and then "disappear," just as Dahl and his "safe house" seem to have done.

Naturally, this is all surmise and interpolation of evidence. Perhaps the case was a combination of coincidence, an ill thought-out practical joke that went disastrously wrong and a terrible tragedy that struck two of its innocent victims by sheer misfortune.

However, if not, and if Arnold was being targeted in this incredibly elaborate fashion—who was responsible for trying to discredit him in this way and why was it deemed necessary to go to such lengths to try to implicate the world's first UFO witness in such shady goings on?

Perhaps there are lessons to be learned for the whole confusing riddle of the Men in Black.

3

THE THREE MEN

The MIB story first came to popular attention thanks to a strange man called Albert Bender from Bridgeport, Connecticut. Aged 30, he already had a deep fascination for the occult and surrounded himself with magic memorabilia that he called his "chamber of horrors." In April 1952, responding to the growing public interest in UFOs after Kenneth Arnold's sighting, he set up what would become one of the world's first investigation groups. He was to pay dearly for this move.

Bender announced to his new members of the IFSB (International Flying Saucer Bureau) that they should welcome aliens rather than consider them hostile. This rapidly struck a chord with people and the group expanded in numbers at a prodigious rate during the summer and autumn of 1952.

During the five years since Arnold had made his sighting there had been mounting distrust of the way in which the US government was handling the flood of evidence. It was known that they had a secret investigation team based at Wright Patterson Air Force Base. This began to function in late December 1947 and, indeed, it is hard to know just who Brown and Davidson were working for when they had met with Arnold, Smith, Rankin and others several months earlier.

Wright Patterson was (and is) home to the "Foreign Technology Division"—where all intelligence connected with novel enemy aircraft would be assessed. So locating the newly created UFO project at this facility—whilst perfectly logical—

provoked understandable concern as to what the Pentagon *really* believed about these flying objects.

Paranoia was fuelled by retired US marine Donald Keyhoe, who still had many friends who were serving officers. Some were linked to the official UFO project at Wright Patterson. For most of its life this was code named Project Blue Book and handled many sightings from USAF pilots and miltary personnel. As a result, Keyhoe's contacts leaked data to him about important cases.

His first book (indeed the first ever book on UFOs) was called *Flying Saucers Are Real* and was a huge international hit in the spring of 1950. Although he jumped to a number of speculative conclusions about a massive cover-up of an alien invasion, Keyhoe showed that a lot of good evidence was being evaluated by the government. He had access to cases which were being kept from the public.

ROBERTSON IN A JAM

The reaction to Keyhoe's revelations (of which the creation of a UFO group by Bender was but one of several) deeply worried the intelligence community. From data released by the US Freedom of Information Act (1976), we know that the CIA were concerned about public interest in UFOs and feared that the USSR might invade America during a spurious wave of sightings that clogged up communication channels. To combat this they convened a meeting of top rank scientists.

This team met in Washington only a few months after Bender had launched his IFSB (and just as it was proving itself to be such a huge success with branches spreading out to encompass the UK, Australia and other English-speaking lands). For several days in January 1953 the CIA panel of scientists (chaired by atomic physicist Dr. H. P. Robertson) debated how to defuse public interest in UFOs. They had a real problem to combat which they were struggling to control.

Robertson made a number of recommendations. These included a policy of Air Force debunking of UFOs that would "result in a reduction in public interest in flying saucers." Cartoonists could make silly alien films so that the public would stop taking the subject seriously. Television, movies and media articles should be manipulated to change the perception of the average American. Celebrities could be recruited to tell stories of cases that had been explained so that the public accepted the view that UFOs were unimportant.

The panel of scientists also advised that a big potential threat was coming from the fledgling UFO groups (such as Bender's IFSB) because they had the ability to steer public opinion. The panel urged that "such groups . . . should be watched because of their potentially great influence on mass thinking if widespread sightings should occur." In other words, and quite incredibly, UFO activists like Bender were given the same degree of recognition by the CIA as foreign spy cells! As a result, intelligence operatives were advised that UFO groups and conferences should be monitored and routine surveillance of their leaders be mounted.

The continuing secrecy behind some intelligence files means that we still do not appreciate what specific moves were put into motion as a result of this panel. But they spoke of a plan that "within a year and a half to two years" should see the "dangers related to flying saucers . . . greatly reduced if not eliminated." So something was clearly done in response to the physicist's advice.

COOKING THE BOOKS

Released documents from 1953 and 1954 show delight expressed by the intelligence community at how these secret schemes were working. Project Blue Book was ordered to cook the books, doctor the figures and explain cases at all costs (even when in truth they were far from being explained). This dramatically cut the supposed number of UFOs but infuriated the head of Blue Book, who in 1953 was a very honorable intelligence officer called Captain Edward Ruppelt.

Ruppelt's no nonsense style was revealing the truth in many

significant cases and as a result not going down too well in the Pentagon. He soon quit the USAF in frustration and strongly affirmed UFO reality in his memoirs published in 1956, while speculating that he was a front man to an unseen cover-up.

Apart from this sleight of hand with the figures, there are grounds for suggesting that the sudden spate of absurd "contactee" stories that appeared during 1953 and 1954 were stimulated by the CIA. Out of nowhere came various amiable crackpots claiming that they had met friendly spacemen and been taken for rides on their starships to serve as representatives in some intergalactic federation.

Did US intelligence have a hand in planting these stories by getting agents to claim bizarre yarns which UFOlogists would eagerly promote? Even if the contactee movement happened by chance, these tales were just what Dr. Robertson ordered. They made those starting to take UFO data seriously begin to doubt their wisdom. Ruppelt was eventually forced to recant because of them and published a new version of his book in which he disowned his previous positive conclusions.

Given these things, we must wonder how Albert Bender's new UFO organisation was perceived by the intelligence agencies and what they chose to do about it. They surely must have monitored his progress and been desperate to defuse the impact he was having on popular opinion.

THE VISITATION

Only days after the Roberston Panel met in 1953, Bender appointed a man called Gray Barker to be director of investigations for the US branch of his IFSB. Barker certainly wrote in colorful prose and was not opposed to making things up if they sounded better than the truth. This I can vouch for from first hand experience based on a tale he published about me in 1983 which was about as credible as a novel by Enid Blyton.

Barker's propensity to embroider the truth may have been

Director, FBI, from SAC, San Francisco   September 4, 1947

RE: WEEKLY INTELLIGENCE CONFERENCE

Lt: ▓▓▓▓▓▓▓▓▓ again discussed the activities of the
Air Force in investigating the "flying disc" complaints, and also reported
an additional complaint of this nature which has been the subject of a
separate communication to the Bureau.

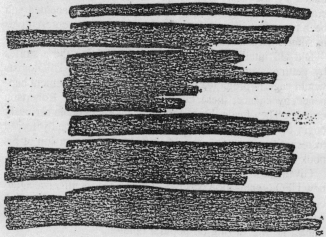

recognized by the CIA. Possibly this led them to single out the IFSB as a prime target in expectation that its new investigations' officer would color any attempted surveillance so vividly that it would limit the credibility of the group.

In September 1953 Bender shocked Barker by saying that he was quitting the UFO field and disbanding the IFSB. Three men had threatened his life if he did not do so. Their visit was so frightening that he was physically ill for several days. The following month, in the final issue of his IFSB magazine, Bender wrote, "The mystery of the flying saucer is no longer a mystery. The source is already known, but any information about this is being withheld by orders from a higher source . . . We advise those engaged in saucer work to please be very cautious."

With that he left the scene, although rumors were rife amongst those who chose to carry on. This included the Australian and British branches of the IFSB. The latter soon renamed itself the BFSB (British Flying Saucer Bureau) and continues in 1997, centered in Bristol. From here stories of other IFSB members being silenced followed. Edgar Jarrold, one of the leaders of the Australian Bureau, wrote only a month after Bender's departure that there were now only two possible answers to the UFO mystery: either they came from Mars (a popular idea of the day), or they were something more sinister which he was not allowed to discuss. He hinted at the latter.

After these comments Jarrold says his life was made a misery. A dark car kept appearing outside his office and he was watched from it by sinister figures. There were threatening phone calls, knocking sounds on the wall of his house and other events that terrified the UFOlogist. In early 1954 he was

Opposite *That secrecy is prolific when government discuss UFOs is self evident from this early report. It discusses the period when no official UFO project yet existed within the US Air Force but shows that the matter was the topic of covert agency meetings—the results of which remain obscured by censors' ink despite the existence of a Freedom of Information Act in the USA.*

even invited to meet with a senior Royal Australian Air Force figure and reputedly given secrets of the UFO. But Jarrold left the field after reputedly being pushed down an escalator in a Sydney department store by "unseen forces" and narrowly averting serious injury.

THE TRUTH ABOUT THE THREE MEN

Edgar Jarrold was one of Albert Bender's closest confidants in the IFSB. It is widely believed that Bender told him a good deal more than most about the three men who came to call. However, leading Australian UFOlogist Bill Chalker—whose reports on early Australian UFOlogy appear in Jerome Clark's mammoth *UFO Encyclopedia Project*—feels that there were personal problems in Jarrold's life and his later disappearance was readily explained by these.

In any case, the saga of these vanishing acts by early UFOlogists was told in graphic detail by Gray Barker in a 1956 book entitled *They Knew Too Much about Flying Saucers*. Bearing in mind the caveat about Barker's penchant for blending fact with fiction, his version of these events has to be treated with some caution. But it is allegedly based upon what Bender told him, soon after he was warned off by the three men. It has also been supported by others who knew the IFSB founder, including early leaders of the British branch.

According to these accounts Bender was told the answer to the UFO riddle by government confidants and had put this news in writing to another of his team. A few days later, in August 1953, three men turned up at his home. They were middle aged, all dressed in black and arrived in a dark car. They wore homburg style hats and one was holding the letter that Bender had just posted.

The mood of these visitors was very threatening. Two spoke during the interrogation and the third sat impassively by and said nothing during the whole meeting—simply staring at the UFOlogist in a strange way, which some have interpreted as an attempt at hypnotism. This is intriguingly similar to the behavior of the second man who visited Shirley Greenfield some 23 years later.

Bender was never in any doubt that these men were human and served as intelligence agents for the US government. They advised that the Pentagon had known the truth about UFOs for a couple of years but that it was a disturbing solution. It was simply not possible to reveal this answer to the world but, when the time was right, the facts would be released. Bender was led to believe that this would happen "within four years."

The UFO buff was also told by one of the MIB: "In our government we have the smartest men in the country. They cannot find a defense for [UFOs]. So how can you do anything about it?" But at other points during the grilling one MIB tried appealing to Bender's "honor as an American." When that did not work another warned that he could be sent to prison for treason.

Expressing amazement at the map of the USA on Bender's wall dotted with pins denoting sighting locations and the myriad home towns of the ever expanding team of IFSB investigators, one of the men said, "My God, but you are all over the place!" then expressed shock at his intelligence-gathering skills and insisted that they would have to take away his entire membership address list. They even wrote down serial numbers from his tape recorders.

Apart from all of this it was intimated to Bender that any of the "inside" sources who had confided information to him had somehow been moved out of the way and would not talk again. This was done by several different methods—including relocation or finding key government jobs to shut people up.

FROM EARTH OR FROM KAZIK?

After Barker first told this amazing story, Albert Bender was pursued by former IFSB members who were desperate to know "the real truth" about UFOs. The four-year deadline soon elapsed and unsurprisingly, no government revelation had come forth. But for continued pressure by Barker the time may never have been right. It seems fairly clear than when Bender finally agreed to "tell all" he did so under great duress and his heart was definitely not in it. For this reason, and because of the banality of Bender's ultimate "truth," there were many (Barker included) who felt they had been conned and the IFSB founder was still keeping the ultimate secret to himself. However, Bender's 1962 book (*Flying Saucers and the Three Men*), which Barker finally persuaded him to write, was to be the final "answer," according to the former IFSB leader

So disappointed was Barker that he effectively told his readers not to believe the new book. Certainly the version of Bender's 1953 encounter as told here is remarkably different from that initially reported by Barker six years earlier. Although the visit by the sinister figures was still described there was no longer any pretence that they were government agents. Bender now alleged they were really aliens in disguise. Indeed, Bender wrote of how the dark suited men turned into monstrous beings with hairy skin and glowing eyes even as they stood in his apartment.

Moreover, when Bender was sitting in a cinema one night one of the monsters had materialised right next to him, and terrible poltergeist attacks struck Bender's home, causing objects to move on their own and fires to break out. These horrific events led to his decision to quit.

When the visit by the "three men" eventually occurred they were very much more like satanic beings and formed out of blue clouds of smoke. Then Bender was "abducted" to the alien base in Antarctica where much nonsense was fed to him about their home world called Kazik. They had such advanced powers that they could explode all our atom bombs if they chose. But the aliens were only interested in extracting an element from sea water and shipping it home. Nobody must know about this task until their mission ended in 1960. When it did, Bender was finally free to tell all.

The response of Bender's many admirers to this final explanation was shock and dismay. Those being charitable said he was still forced to cover-up the real answer. Others saw him as deluded, if not crazy. Hardly anyone—not even those who had pressed him for years to come clean—believed a word of *Flying Saucers and the Three Men*. Nor was Bender especially interested in promoting his own epic. Soon afterwards he moved to the other side of the USA and made his phone number unlisted.

As for Gray Barker, in 1980 he spoke to UFOlogist Jerome Clark of the J. Allen Hynek Center for UFO Studies in one of his last interviews before his death. Regarding Bender's abduction by the aliens from Kazik, he stated his continuing disbelief of his lifelong friend: "If I'd been there in his room while he was in 'Antarctica' maybe I would have seen him lying in his bed in a trance."

Barker still felt that Bender had undergone a real experience in 1953 and that he may well have somehow brought about the wrath of the CIA or some other intelligence agency because he got close to the truth. This was certainly what Bender had implied to Barker and all other high ranking IFSB members in the days immediately after the alleged intimidation. The three men were humans, not aliens. They had arrived in a car, not a spaceship, and they had employed very down to earth silencing tactics, not spacenapped him through magic to their base in Antarctica.

The truth may remain shrouded forever. Was Albert Bender just deluded and his friend Barker desperate to find a conspiracy where there really was none? Or was Bender forced into inventing such a ridiculous tale about shape-changing aliens in order to hide the more human—and sinister—reality that some government agency *had* threatened his life?

4

THE 1950s:
MISSING IN ACTION

One of our biggest problems is that—almost by definition—if there are agents of intimidation and their scare tactics work, then people may be too frightened to testify about their encounters with them. So we cannot hope to have a full picture of MIB activity. However, another, type of infiltration was to become characteristic of the Men in Black and first surfaced in the wake of the Bender case.

PROOF ON SCREEN

Tom Drury had been a leading figure in the department of aviation on the island of Papua, New Guinea, then administratively part of Australia. On the sunny afternoon of 23 August 1953 he was filming some idyllic scenes on the beach road at Port Moresby. His wife and children were with him as he pointed his movie camera seaward. Mrs. Drury then noticed a part of the sky where a curious cloud was forming. Knowing about the weather was vital to an aviation expert and yet Drury had never seen anything like this white mist before. The cloud grew thicker and then a silver cigar shaped object seemed to emerge from it and streak skywards as fast as any rocket. It traveled far in excess of the speed of sound but there was no sonic boom—something that puzzled the witness even further.

Once back at the airport Drury was soon able to establish

that there were no aircraft, civil or military, in the area. The only other possibility was a missile. But the one place from where this could have been launched was Woomera in the Australian outback. Given that this was thousands of miles south of New Guinea and the object he had filmed was low on the horizon, this idea was considered impossible. In any event (as secret data was later to reveal) Woomera had no launches that day.

Once the film was processed it was clear that the deputy aviation director had captured the UFO very clearly. Given his influential position this evidence was highly prized. So he sent it to the department of civil aviation, who forwarded it to the government on 22 September for their analysis and advice. Air Force Intelligence told Drury that they were sending it onward to Washington—presumably to Project Blue Book. Although the Americans were allies this was still a curious decision and Drury assumed it occurred because the USA had the most experience in dealing with UFOs.

All went well until his footage was eventually returned by the government on 12 July 1954. It was intact—shots of the beach, a native boy spearing fish. But the frames depicting the silver bullet-like object emerging from the cloud had mysteriously disappeared. They had simply been cut from his film and their departure was not even mentioned by the Australian government. The cover letter with the film merely expresses disappointment that Air Force Intelligence could not resolve the case other than to note that Drury's footage contained a "blur of light."

THE HUNT IS ON

In 1982 industrial chemist and UFO investigator Bill Chalker was given a unique opportunity. As Australia was about to introduce a Freedom of Information Act the government were wary of the flood of requests for UFO documents. These had recently occurred in the USA after a similar law was passed. Since Chalker had shown himself to be a rational person the

Australian government decided to invite him to Canberra, where they gave him the opportunity to study and take copies of all the Air Force data on UFOs. The one proviso was that he make the evidence available to the rest of the UFO community and so ease the expected pressure of countless letters from UFO buffs. Needless to say, Chalker obliged and spent much time wading through thousands of files. One of his goals was to learn more about the Drury film.

There had been all sorts of stories about it circulating since the 1950s. The strangest involved Edgar Jarrold, Albert Bender's friend, who claimed MIB surveillance on his office and quit the field after his escapade on a Sydney escalator. Jarrold had alleged that he was the only UFOlogist who had seen the Drury film intact—or (as it transpired) was given some 94 still frames of the UFO extracted from it. This was reputedly before the evidence was sent to America and mysteriously disappeared.

Jarrold's sight of the footage had allegedly occurred when he was invited to the offices of Air Force Intelligence in Melbourne during the summer of 1954. This was by no less a person than the Aviation Minister, William McMahon (although evidence suggests Jarrold only saw a squadron leader from the intelligence staff when he got to Melbourne, and not the parliamentarian himself).

Of the stills that he was shown Jarrold wrote, shortly before he quit the field, that they conclusively depicted a ''shiny disc-like object whose behavior could by no widest stretching of the imagination be attributed to a bird, balloon [or] orthodox aircraft.''

Chalker discovered that the initial Air Force Intelligence file was opened on 30 October 1953 and labelled ''Photographs of unexplained aerial object over New Guinea forwarded by T. C. Drury.'' Its original classification was ''secret'' but this was subsequently overlaid with the motif ''lost.'' The file that Chalker got to see was one specially opened after the film had done its vanishing act so as to incorporate data presumably not lost from this otherwise missing archive.

CARRYING THE CAN AT CANBERRA

From his survey of the available files Chalker says that there was evidence that the Australian government in Canberra had treated the film in the context of possible enemy action over New Guinea and that "one consequence of this may have been manipulation of the UFO controversy by intelligence agencies." This wording sounds as if they were picking up tips from the practices of the CIA. Was this the real reason why the film went onto the USA? Did they fear its impact on shaping public opinion over UFOs given that it was of such good quality and taken by a highly credible witness? There was even an indication that the film was actually studied by the CIA when it reached America. This tends to suggest that the Drury case was an impressive one.

By the time Chalker began his inquiries in 1982 Drury was an elderly man but freely cooperated with the UFOlogist. He was quite philosophical, wondering if the necessary analysis work by so many different organisations had not simply consumed all of the frames with the UFO on them. He seemed not to blame anyone specifically in Canberra for its loss.

Drury also believed that ASIO (Australian Security Intelligence Organisation) had been involved in the case, although their primary interest was counter-espionage, rather like the CIA. Through detective work Chalker tracked down the two ASIO agents responsible for work in Port Moresby during 1953. Neither was willing to talk about the case, although one "hypothetically" noted that if they had been involved it would have only been in the capacity of a "courier" for the film.

A January 1973 memo in the Canberra government files was also from ASIO and discussed the case. This noted that, aside from the copy sent to the USA, the film was also forwarded to the RAF in Britain. My searches through UK government records in Kew have not revealed this copy of the Drury film or any report about it, although many significant British cases from this same period are not released by the Air Ministry, so the disappearance of the Drury film is hardly unexpected.

THE LOST FOOTAGE

Intriguingly, Chalker uncovered a problem with Jarrold's story, for the files contain a letter dated 2 December 1953 sent to him by the Department of Aviation. It seems that Jarrold had requested "contact prints" from Drury's film. The DoA did not deny its existence but reported that he would have to wait until the new year when the film was back from the USA for such copies to be made available. Either this was a stall tactic or it means that the original film was already at the Pentagon. If copies were sent to the USA and Britain (as implied in other records), we might expect the original footage to have remained in Australia. Indeed, the fact that the Australian government would even consider the release of irreplaceable evidence to a foreign country is itself worthy of note. Even so the existence of this note establishes that Jarrold did *not* see the film before it went to the USA.

Another curious file (dated early 1955) indicates that copies of stills from the film had been sold at "4/9 [about 25p] a pop" to UFOlogists. The Air Force record names both Edgar Jarrold and Fred Stone as recipients of these purchases. If true, they had evidence that not even the witness himself possessed by 1955, and it is difficult to understand how Air Force Intelligence could sell them still photographs at the same time as they were returning the film to Drury *minus* any shots with the UFO on it.

It does appear, however, to be true. Jarrold reported seeing stills in July 1954 when invited to Melbourne (even though Jarrold never mentioned having to pay for them). But what of the other man to get prints—Fred Stone? Interestingly, the secret files that Chalker copied contained a letter from Stone to Air Force Intelligence dating from 1973. In this he says several curious things.

For example, Stone implies that he was shown the film in late 1954 (*after* the copy minus the UFO footage had already been returned to Drury!). He met with Air Force Intelligence at their request for a private screening that was "much clearer to view," Stone wrote in his letter to Canberra twenty years later. He surmised this deterioration was due to "the use by the bodies of the USA Air Force, then their Navy dept, plus our own Air Force and Navy." Moreover, as of 1973 Stone intriguingly noted he had kept his "promise to the [intelligence] official at the time when I was interviewed in Melbourne regarding same and [the stills] have never been shown publicly."

There was one happy outcome from Chalker's discovery. Stone sent back copies of these stills to the Australian Air Force so that they could then copy them and at Bill Chalker's behest finally (after thirty years!) give some of his UFO images back to the man who took them—assuming his government would look after the evidence for him. Of course, these prints were dim and fuzzy. As Stone appears to suggest, they give no real flavor of the glory of the original footage. But where is that today?

MORE LOST FILM

Chalker further tells us that the archives depict several searches for the missing footage (usually when Air Force Intelligence were pressured to do so by UFOlogists). Scans in 1966 and 1973 were particularly evident. Although UFOlogists were fobbed off and told that the film had been "lost," Chalker reports that the following is the true conclusion in the files: "The upshot is that the 'excised' frames either are still in DAFI (Air Force Intelligence) archives, have been destroyed or (perish the thought) have been lost."

Stone was also involved in another case of three men driving across the Nullarbor Plain at Easter 1954. They were near Eucla on the border between Western Australia and South Australia when their car was chased for miles by a glowing UFO and they succeeded in taking many photographs with several different cameras, including close-up shots that revealed a structured craft.

Unfortunately, the men had stopped at the next town to report the sighting to the police. The air base at Woomera was called and the witnesses were detained until a helicopter landed, disgorging Air Force Intelligence officers to talk to them.

As a result of this intervention the photographers were warned that they must under no circumstances ever discuss the case. Their camera and film were confiscated by ASIO, who promised to return it after study. But when the camera was sent back the film was missing—except for one blurred shot. A cover note further advised the men that they must still obey orders and remain silent.

After Stone published news of this case five years later he was visited at home by an ASIO intelligence officer and himself warned into silence. Despite pressure from his colleagues Stone refused to be drawn into further discussion on the matter. As his 1973 letter to Canberra shows he was similarly compliant regarding the Drury evidence held in his possession for 20 years. But why should ASIO or Canberra be so desperate to silence witnesses and hide the best photographic evidence from public view?

Thankfully, one of Stone's colleagues, Colin McCarthy, continued to investigate and eventually found one of the witnesses who had filmed the UFO near Eucla. He was understandably reluctant to talk, but indicated that he had also been visited at home by an intimidating stranger who professed to be an ASIO agent. As the witness said, he ordered silence and "frightened the living **** out of me."

As proof of their sincerity this witness showed McCarthy the surviving photograph to illustrate that it was "next door to useless" (possibly the reason why it had been sent back to them). It was as if ASIO had hoped the three men would publish this photograph and, as a result, destroy their own credibility in the absence of the better photographic evidence which had been taken from them.

AGENTS OF SILENCE

The idea of intelligence agents visiting UFOlogists, perhaps infiltrating their groups in some way, seems ridiculous, but it was actually another of the options debated by the CIA panel in 1953. So we should not be surprised to see reports of it in operation.

There have been various claims. For example, Stan Seers of the Queensland Flying Saucer Bureau told how he was also seemingly approached in 1959. ASIO had occasionally requested help from UFO groups. Just as today, most UFOlogists would agree to share data. As Seers noted, it seems ridiculous that anything more covert should be necessary in view of this.

Nonetheless, a person claiming to be an ASIO intelligence agent requested a secret meeting with Seers in a car park. This man offered help (such as giving the UFOlogist a private hot line number to the prime minister!) if he agreed to pass on the best of his new cases. But when Seers revealed that he had raised this offer with his fellow members of the Queensland group for their support, the ASIO officer went crazy and threatened retribution. Several years of struggle followed during which a mysterious stranger attempted to play members off against one another through secret phone calls. The Queensland organisation found its effectiveness limited and Seers eventually quit.

Many of the leading UFO associations can tell stories about "odd" members, sometimes with openly admitted ties to intelligence agencies, the police or military units, who have played a curious role in that group's affairs. Often they seem not to do any real work but are always present when major cases are being discussed. The "spies in our midst" philosophy emerges from this but is often, perhaps, no more than paranoia. The fear that to take it seriously may imply delusional tendencies is why it is rarely discussed in UFO circles—but it is not without some degree of suspicious evidence. For obvious reasons, not least the laws of libel, UFO groups are reluctant to be very open in their discussions of these matters or the naming of any individuals.

5

1957:
MEN FROM GHARNASVARN

Thus far the vast majority of the evidence for MIB has been leading us toward one probable conclusion: These visitors appear to be humans working for an intelligence organisation and endeavouring to scare off witnesses, monitor UFO groups, perhaps infiltrate and confuse the situation and possibly even spirit away the best physical evidence—such as photographs.

You might wonder why any UFO enthusiast would even consider the possibility that MIB could be anything more exotic. Surely the theory that Men in Black are ''aliens in disguise'' stands very dubiously on the shaky foundations of Albert Bender's account regarding the metamorphic monsters from Kazik.

The following case, however, is certainly more credible than Bender's and is sufficiently well documented that we should take it seriously. It certainly puts the question of the MIB right back in the line of fire.

A TURNING POINT

Of immediate interest is the time frame for the start of this experience: November 1957. All eyes were then on outer space, because in early October the USSR had stunned the world (and especially America who had expected to beat them to it) when Sputnik 1 became the first artificial object to enter space. It was just a tiny lump of "bleeping" metal but ushered in a whole new era. Within a month, on 3 November, Sputnik 2 took the first life form from earth into space—Laika the dog. Its impact was even more remarkable.

During this period the UFO phenomenon also exhibited extraordinary activity. On 15 October the first alleged alien abduction was to occur when a Brazilian cowhand named Villas Boas was spacenapped from his tractor. This was a case that was to prove a turning point in the history of the phenomenon.

Perhaps even more significant was the incredible demonstration of "power" exhibited by the UFOs in the small Texas town of Levelland on the very night of the Sputnik 2 launch. Numerous cars and trucks were rendered useless as a dazzling object cavorted about the roadways stalling engines, switching off lights and generally scaring the local citizenship.

Even more dramatic was the truly incredible way in which UFOs penetrated top secret air space and manifested over the sites of two very critical locations. So far as can be told these occurred simultaneously—thousands of miles apart—and yet again were on that very night when earth was becoming a space-faring race for the first time in history, thanks to the sacrifice of Laika the dog.

The two sites singled out for these new UFO intrusions were the bunkers at Alamogordo in New Mexico, where the world's first atom bomb was exploded in 1945, and Maralinga in the Australian desert, where the world's most recent atomic blast—part of the UK government's antler series—had been detonated just three weeks before. Indeed this latter UFO hovered right over the marker point of the blast and was witnessed by many RAF personnel engaged in final "mopping up" operations—including Derek Murray, now with the Home Office. He told me, "I swear to you as a practicing Christian this was no dream, no illusion, no fairy story—but a solid craft of metallic construction."

All of these interconnected stories were reported inde dently of one another. They seem extremely time they all came together.

EVENTS IN AN ASTON VILLA

Britain was not to be left out of this vast jigsaw of evidence that linked North and South America with Australasia and Russia, for it was to generate its first true MIB encounter—although, interestingly, it is still widely thought of by UFO-logists as being an alien contact.

The events began on 16 November at Fentham Street in a large house within the district of Aston, Birmingham. This was a rambling terrace owned by Ron Appleton, a sheet metal worker, and his 27-year-old wife Cynthia. She was no mystic interested in UFOs. She had a one-year-old baby and a three-year-old daughter to care for. This was very much a full time occupation.

On that first fateful afternoon Cynthia reports that she suddenly felt strange and that a curious glow filled the room. The next thing she knew was that it was an hour later and she had no memory of what had transpired in between. We might quite reasonably suppose that as an overworked mother Cynthia simply fell asleep. However, during the later extraordinary events that were soon to unfold she was advised that this first experience had been a "failed attempt at contact."

The failure was rapidly overcome, because at 3 pm on 18 November Cynthia went into her upper level sitting room to check on her youngest daughter and noticed that the sky had turned an odd rosy pink color. She had little time to admire this early and unprecedented "sunset" before the room was filled with a terrible "heaviness" and the tingling like one gets prior to the onset of a thunderstorm. Cynthia's hair stood on end and her skin began to tickle. Although Mrs. Appleton had no idea what was happening to her she was, in fact, being swamped by some kind of electrical field the origin of which remains uncertain to this day.

As the now startled woman was taking on board these experiences, Cynthia also heard a whistling noise. It began slowly then rose in pitch until its high frequency was penetrating her skull. It only disappeared when a misty shape began to form by the fireplace. This wavered like a TV picture when first switched on but sharpened to the image of a most peculiar man.

Her immediate fear at this sight was diminishing rapidly. Indeed, only later did Cynthia appreciate that there was a kind of telepathic message entering her mind being impressed upon her subliminally in some way. This voice was repeating the words "Do not be afraid" and was having precisely the desired effect of calming her down.

The story of her meeting with this alien became known to the UFO community soon afterward and was briefly reported in *Flying Saucer Review*. I was fortunate to meet clinical psychologist Dr. John Dale, who had visited the Appletons on several occasions during 1958, and he allowed me to study his voluminous files on the case. These included new information forged from the friendship that he built up with the witness.

STRANGER IN CELLOPHANE

During this initial encounter Cynthia felt strange. It is wise to bear in mind the accounts of both Albert Bender and Shirley Greenfield concerning the "hypnotic" nature of their MIB experiences. Cynthia reports that "he seemed to have some control over me. I should say that it was like hypnosis."

The entity communicated telepathically that he came from another world called "Gharnasvarn" and that the people were friendly but still shunned open contact. Our scientists had built rockets to try to reach their home world but they would fail because we had to "travel with a sideways attitude" rather than "pull against the great force of gravity." Until earth stopped having wars these entities would only contact people like Cynthia who had the ability to communicate because of her unique brain with the correct tuning frequency.

The person was quite human-like, although with elongated features. His skin was pale and his hair blond. In hei~
stood over six feet tall. He was wearing a silve~
like cellophane or a plastic raincoat and with~

Cynthia later described him as best resembling a "Greek athlete."

At this point in the procedings the entity opened his arms wide like someone playing charades and miming a TV screen. Subsequently images appeared in thin air within the space that he had marked out. These showed to Cynthia scenes from Gharnasvarn. The "TV images" also depicted UFOs and atomic explosions.

From the notes about this event written by Dr. Dale in early 1958, one is left with the realization that Cynthia is describing a moving three-dimensional image or hologram. But there is a problem. Cynthia cannot have seen one of these. Indeed holograms had not been invented when the psychologist penned this report, and it was some years before a working prototype was demonstrated.

When the being finally disappeared (fading away just as he arrived), Cynthia noted that he had been standing on a piece of discarded newspaper. This had a scorch mark upon it. According to John Dale it resembled a lightning strike or small electrical discharge.

RETURN VISIT

It is easy to see from this account why the case is presented by UFOlogists as an alien contact. When it is discussed by them this first encounter from November 1957 is usually all that they report. By itself it seems to have little relevance to MIB cases. However, it cannot be taken by itself, for this was only one of eight visits that Cynthia Appleton was to receive from this entity.

On the second encounter, which happened on 7 January 1958, the man arrived in this same pyrotechnical fashion— literally appearing in her living room. This time he had no helmet and wore blond hair to shoulder length. With him was a similar colleague with shorter, curlier hair. On this occasion more was explained about her "special brainwaves" which ____ed the contact. Cynthia was also advised that their appearance in this way was a "projection" rather than a real visit. Despite this she tried to touch him and only felt a kind of "slime" in her fingers.

However, this spectacular method of appearance was not to continue. On all six subsequent occasions that the men from Gharnasvarn arrived at the Appleton house their mode of appearance was very different indeed. They came by car!

Most of these later visits took place between February and August 1958. Sometimes the first entity was alone and sometimes the second figure came too, but they were no longer dressed in silver cellophane costumes. They wore black business suits and old fashioned hats—classic MIB attire straight out of the Bender story. As Cynthia said, they knocked at the front door, evidently having walked down the streets of Birmingham without anyone having realized that they were not ordinary human beings.

On the first visit of this kind, in February 1958, her eldest daughter (now aged 4) was present and could testify to the peculiar events that followed. The blond-haired being said that he was injured in some way. His finger was burnt and first aid was necessary. Cynthia was asked to bring a bowl of hot water and bathe his hand. Then he injected himself from a small tube and finally sprayed some kind of jelly all over his hand. Moments later all trace of the burn disappeared. It was only after he had gone that a small piece of skin was found discarded in the washing bowl.

Cynthia followed the entity when he left her door this time. She saw him walk around the corner and get into a large black car that had tinted windows. It drove away immediately.

A CURE FOR CANCER

During the various visits throughout 1958 much new information was conveyed. Cynthia kept pointing out to her visitors that it was pointless telling her such things because they passed over her head due to her lack of scientific knowledge, but the entities were unmoved.

She was advised that time did not exist. It was a philosophical invention by mankind. We also failed to understand that all life was connected at some deep inner level, not separate as we assumed. Detailed scientific facts about the nature of atoms was then conveyed to her. She was told this was the basis to understand how to cure cancer—a disease that was caused when a body organ was shocked in some way during over use. Indeed a complex cure was outlined to her which involved changing the frequency rate of the vibrations of atoms at a sub-atomic level, but Cynthia struggled to remember the terms used when she tried to describe this to Dr. Dale.

The psychologist told me that aside from this science, real or imagined, Cynthia regaled him with information about a new device which the aliens had told her earth people were building. He later charted its progress. It was what we now call a laser, just coming to fruition in the laboratories of the day.

I asked Dr. Dale whether he ever saw the skin. He did. Cynthia had preserved it when he visited a few days after that particular encounter. She allowed Dr. Dale to take it home with him and be used his contacts at a Manchester university to gain access to a scanning electron microscope. The study of the residue was strange. Nothing about it was obviously extraterrestrial—nor was it human. The chemist who carried out the examination said that it most closely resembled animal skin—possibly a pig—but he could not positively identify it. This bizarre result only serves to deepen the mystery.

Many years later doctors were to discover how pig DNA was remarkably similar to the human equivalent and could be used to grow artificial organs for possible use in human transplants. But in 1958 that would have seemed like the most absurd science fiction.

CHILD OF THE STARS

After the final regular visit by the entities on 18 August 1958 there was one further encounter a month later. This was even more fantastic than those that had gone before. For now the blond haired man declared that Cynthia was going to have a baby. Moreover that whilst her husband would be the father this baby would (in some unexplained manner) be "of the race of Gharnasvarn." Quite precisely they told her that it would be a male child, that she should call it Michael, that it would be born at the very end of May 1959 and would have fair hair. It would weigh 7lbs 3 oz. Such claims seemed pure nonsense in an age when accurate predictions of that type were not possible.

In any case, Cynthia knew that she had not missed a period so could not be pregnant. By now, however, she had no reason to doubt the visitors from Gharnasvarn and so went to see her doctor. He confirmed that Mrs. Appleton was indeed going to have a baby. Yet when her visitor had told her this news she could only have been a matter of days past conception.

These facts were all put on record at the time. A church minister, the Reverend Tiley, had like Dr. Dale paid her several visits and was insistent that Mrs. Appleton was "a very trustworthy person." He added that he believed her story "from beginning to end." These comments were given to the local press as UFOlogists decided that they should now document the claim about the coming "space baby." This was done so that if it were to prove correct the skeptics would have great difficult explaining this evidence away. It was then picked up by the *People*, a national newspaper.

The child was duly born and was a boy with fair hair. The birth date was almost exactly when the man from Gharnasvarn had predicted. Its measured birth weight was only one ounce different from that suggested. After the birth Ron Appleton was asked for his comments and he said that if the alien returned he was going to make sure they understood that *he* was the father (although this was something that they had never disputed). Probably on the urgings of the media he was also quoted as saying that if they came back Cynthia should ask for some sort of intergalactic maintenance money.

So ended a truly extraordinary case. Dr. Dale kept in touch with the Appeltons for another year or so after the events concluded. The child grew normally. The visitors never returned—either by spaceship or by car—and life returned to its pleasant routine for the Appleton family. I have tried to trace them today—particularly Michael, who would now be approaching 40. I have had no success as yet, however, and can find no UFOlogists who have even attempted to follow through the story since about 1961.

Perhaps Michael Appleton is out there and will get in touch after reading this book. It would be fascinating to know if the man from Gharnasvarn ever made his presence known again.

6

1963:
FIELDS OF FOLLY

The UFO debate attracts quite an assortment of characters, some with rather extreme ideas and individual ways of conducting an investigation. These people can behave oddly, even irrationally, and it may be reasonable to suspect that *they* could get mistaken for an MIB by an understandably befuddled witness. As such, it is useful to compare the activities of such folk with the antics of MIB and see if this argument holds firm.

HOLE IN THE GROUND

A good case to examine occurred in Britain early on the morning of 16 July 1963 at Manor Farm in Charlton, Wiltshire. This was an area destined to become a focal point of odd goings on a quarter of a century later when the world was agog thanks to the many "crop circles" which filled the local landscape. Indeed in 1992 *Crop Watcher* magazine carried a report from Graham Brunt that he had even found circles on Manor Farm itself back in 1951.

Some more imaginative UFOlogists were looking toward an alien invasion (wrongly, in my opinion) as the cause for these crop marks, although two hoaxers later emerged to claim the phenomenon as their handiwork. No doubt these men did fake some circles, but they did not make all (or even most) of them.

I believe a weather effect was probably involved as well.

On that summer morning in 1963, however, the world was yet to hear of crop circles when at 6 am Leonard Joliffe, a dairy worker from the farm, heard a loud explosion. At first little was thought of it, but then a few hours later another Manor Farm worker entered the boundary between a potato field and barley crop to came upon the real source of the mystery: a big hole in the ground.

It was relatively shallow—just some 4 inches deep, as if scooped out by a spoon—but measured irregularly across a circular zone between 9 and 12 feet in diameter. Directly in the center was a vertical hole which appeared to be several feet deep and had radiating spoke marks leading from it. If a lightning strike was responsible for this it had dug the earth remarkably deep. It seemed more like an explosion had come from beneath—or possibly, that a heavy object had landed and created the trace.

ENTER THE MILITARY

Land owner Roy Blanchard was taking no chances. He called the police, who in turn rapidly summoned the army. Captain John Rogers from the Horsham unit of the bomb disposal squad arrived to take control.

After a preliminary inspection Rogers told the now waiting media that he was baffled. He discussed the problem with his superiors but confirmed there were no scorch or burn marks suggestive of an explosion. That appeared to scupper the early theory that a buried World War Two bomb had gone off thanks to chemical decay across the 20 years since it had been discarded by a fleeing enemy bomber. This sort of thing was not uncommon in many parts of Europe at the time.

Roy Blanchard pointed out some of the things that were intriguing the army but about which they had kept silent. His potato crop had not been exploded. It had vanished. There was no trace of it anywhere in or around the crater. Moreover, the small rocks in the soil were crushed to powder. He had no doubt that a very heavy object had landed from above. As a result, the speculation began that an alien spaceship might be buried beneath this hole in a field.

Interestingly, Blanchard told the *Flying Saucer Review* that military sources had approached him after he gave this interview and "warned me to be very careful what I said. I was told that it was not considered appropriate that I speak in public about such things." This is interesting because it again represents the cornerstone of the MIB philosophy, yet it undoubtedly applied here to forces from what we must assume was either the army or air ministry.

THE MAN FROM WOOMERA

By 18 July Captain Rogers had decided to gingerly drill a borehole into the crater and take magnetic readings to ascertain what might be down there. This only added to the mystery as the results suggested that there was a large metallic object underground. Not surprisingly, Rogers added, "We have never encountered anything like this before."

It was at this stage that Dr. Robert Randall appeared. His delightfully dotty ideas came to detract serious attention from the case. In retrospect UFOlogists wondered if that was the point. The press and TV channels featured him freely, stating that Randall was an astro-physicist at the Woomera rocket site in Australia. He was portrayed as part of the government team investigating the case.

One reason for this conclusion was a quote from army officer Sergeant James Reith, who told the *Daily Mail* that he had met Randall in Woomera and, "You can take his word as one of authority on these matters." He further advised the *Daily Express* that Randall had predicted the discovery of crystallised carbon inside the hole and the army team had promptly found just that! As a result, "his views are not to be ignored," the army man insisted. Randall had now said that molten metal was lurking below the surface and wreckage from a spaceship undercarriage was probably the cause.

This endorsement to the media ensured that Dr. Randall was treated as a government spokesperson. Although the army later suggested this was a misunderstanding, because of the absurdity of what the man from Woomera had to say, the story of the crater soon lost public support.

Randall argued that a three legged spaceship from "somewhere in the region of Uranus" was to blame. It had a 50-man crew and since it took two years for a voyage to earth was clearly due here once again after last appearing in Australia. The aliens were friendly but afraid of our abuse of atomic weapons.

Given all of the attention Randall was getting (even in responsible news sources), few checks were made about him. Yet Australia House could find no record of Dr. Randall, at Woomera or anywhere else. Checks were also made by UFO-logist Waveney Girvan. Randall *did* exist. He lived in nearby Tidworth and locals noted that he "studied cosmology."

When Girvan tracked Randall down (despite noting that "he became rather elusive" and soon vanished from the case), the scientist now said that the press misrepresented him. In fact he was a medical doctor, not an astro-physicist, and had merely lived at Woomera, not worked there. In view of the remote location of this secret outback base this seems rather odd. Later—when his house was besieged by media—a harrassed woman said that he was a medical doctor *and* a physicist with many degrees to his name. The university involved was checked. Again, nobody recalled Dr. Randall.

A METEORITE—OR NOT?

On 22 July, with the media now on the run thanks to the strange claims of Dr. Randall, Charlton's village bobby, Tony Penny, returned from holiday and reported that in the days leading up to the appearance of the crater (probably around 10 July) he had witnessed an orange ball of light crash from the sky toward the Blanchards' farm. At the time he had thought it a "shooting star."

This new twist alerted Patrick Moore, a famous amateur astronomer whose TV programme *The Sky At Night* was already popular in 1963. Moore went to Charlton to see the "metal object" when the army finally decided to dig it up. He no doubt expected to find a meteorite, which would be of great value to astronomers in learning about the solar system. After the excavation Moore was cited in *The Guardian* regarding a small lump of rock weighing half a pound which had been pulled up from beneath the hole. He explained that it was "almost certainly a meteorite"—although "shrimp sized"—and would have "turned itself into a very effective explosive" when it hit the ground. But tests were still necessary to verify that fact, as Moore naturally appreciated.

For the media, however, the game was finally over—Dr. Randall's spaceship from Uranus had been demolished. The combined effects of his wild theories and Patrick Moore's rational solution had killed off the story so far as press and public were concerned.

Unfortunately, the story was far from dead because the rock was not a meteorite, as many had understandably surmised and as the by now increasingly fraught military had no doubt dearly hoped. Indeed it is interesting that eyewitnesses tell of how—on the very day that this rock was dug up—two Air Force intelligence officers appeared in the field for the first time to survey the recovery operation.

The tiny size of the Charlton rock was not like the large metal object detected on site and about which one careless army man had let slip that their meters "went crazy." Waveney Girvan further learned that a meteorite which fell in Kansas in 1948 had left a crater six feet across, half the size of Charlton. But that falling rock had weighed in at over a ton—vastly more than this small lump now picked up from Wiltshire. Also, during the Kansas rock fall the crops had not been consumed and surface rocks were not turned to powder as in the Blanchard Farm. So the idea that a small bit of ore from space was the culprit in this case seemed to be losing its credibility.

WHAT FELL AT CHARLTON?

Girvan called up "Southern Command," who were coordinating the now week-old investigation. He says that the powers-that-be were reluctant to talk to him. Thankfully, Girvan, a respected aviation writer, knew the science editor at a national newspaper and put the problem across. This man used his contacts to trace the scientist who had analyzed the rock for the military—a Dr. F. G. Claringbull, head of mineralogy at the British Museum. He confirmed that the rock had proved to be "ordinary ironstone such as found naturally across southern England. It could not have caused the crater." The UFOlogist immediately phoned Southern Command, who reluctantly agreed that he was correct.

The army decided, however, that it was not their job to put right the press assumptions that the Charlton case had been solved. So Girvan made sure that *he* notified the Press Association and called all the newspapers who had covered the story. Had he not done so or not had the fortune to track down the truth, it seems as if it may never have emerged. The British government would have left Randall's daft ideas and his apparent official status to vie alongside the discovery of "the meteorite" as providing the only "truth" in the public domain.

Girvan himself rightly saw how lucky he had been and felt it signified an attempt at obfuscation. The media were not desperate to resurrect the story, even though it was now shown to be still enigmatic. Even Dr. Claringbull was moved to say that "there is more in this than meets the eye."

Briefed by the UFOlogists, Conservative MP Major Patrick Wall (later Sir Patrick and a key figure in the NATO defense committee) posed questions in the House on 29 July. In response, the Secretary of State for War John Godber (the equivalent of today's Minister of Defence) commented that Southern Command had found no evidence to explain the hole but admitted that the recovered rock "was not the cause of the crater."

Wall also perceptively asked what two Air Force Intelligence officers were doing sniffing about the site—to which he was fobbed off with no straight reply (a sure sign that there was something to hide), just the bland remark that nothing happened "which could justify further investigation by the air ministry." Officially Captain Rogers vacated the farm on 26 July and that was that.

TWISTS AND TURNS

Or, rather, that was not quite that. A month later the press brought the Charlton case back to life with stories supplied by a man called John Southern who alleged that he and two friends had faked the Charlton crater. He then demanded they retract this story. Southern explained that he was a researcher testing a theory that somebody faked the Charlton crater. His master plan was to claim that he had done it so that any real hoaxer would come forward. Nobody did and Southern was thus convinced that the crater was caused by some unknown source.

No newspaper carried his recantation, but Girvan tried to get the *Daily Mail* to do so. They declined, arguing that there was huge public interest in the case but that they did not want to be left "open for endless discussion" and prefered to stop the story there and then.

Interestingly, the very same weekend as the hoax revelation was first published Dr. Randall reappeared. He told the *Daily Sketch* that the Archbishop of Canterbury and Prime Minister Harold MacMillan were ignoring his warnings of an invasion from Uranus. MacMillan did have other things on his mind (the Profumo scandal for one), but Randall explained why he was so certain.

The man from Woomera had met a being from Uranus in Lammermuir, Scotland. The entity was dressed in a black suit (wearing black was essential to protect the Uranians from the sun as they tanned so easily). Uranus has 300 million inhabitants, he said, but as the man in black was warning the doctor about the coming invasion the foolhardy scientist tried to take off his spacesuit, whereupon the being spontaneously combusted, leaving mere ashes. ''It was very stupid of me,'' Dr. Randall told the paper. The physicist explained that his battle to convince the world was scuppered by the ''cranks'' associated with UFOlogy. He accused them of making ''the most ridiculous and unlikely statements.''

Was Randall a harmless eccentric who conned the army at Charlton into taking him seriously? In June 1964 UFOlogists reported that they had sent money to a company called Ce-Fu-X, with Randall associated. Ce-Fu-X promised to supply a radio frequency to let UFOlogists contact Men in Black on the planet Uranus, but nothing had yet been received for their money.

When challenged, Randall stood by his ''aliens from Uranus'' saga but seemed more interested in his ''cancer research laboratory'' and the ''amazing breakthrough'' he was just about to report from here. Needless to say, Dr. Randall, his laboratory and his breakthrough were not heard of again.

7

1964:
INTRUDER ON THE SHORE

Before I became a UFO researcher there was one case which had always intrigued me. Details were sketchy and nobody seemed to have carried out firsthand interviews. However, it had impressive evidence and seemed in need of further study. So in 1990 I decided to try to find the key witness—Jim Templeton—who at the time of the events 26 years before had been a fireman in what is now the county of Cumbria.

What he had to tell me proved absolutely stunning. The case was far stranger than I had ever realized and had an MIB sequel that was typically bizarre. I am virtually certain that Jim Templeton had no idea of the importance of this incident. To him it was just an odd sequel to the main events, and I suspect he had never even heard the term Men in Black.

How often do clues like this hide in cases that are virtually unexplored?

NO PICNIC ON THE MARSH

The case unfolded on a pleasant late spring day. Jim Templeton and his wife decided to go out onto Burgh Marsh to the north-west of Carlisle to spend Sunday, 24 May 1964, taking photographs with his Pentacon camera. With him were his two daughters, including five-year-old Elizabeth, wearing a new pink dress. After picking a bunch of spring flowers he positioned her on the grassy bank beside a creek and took several shots. Mrs. Templeton and his older daughter stood just behind them, watching the scene as Jim composed the picture.

Burgh Marsh is a desolate spot on the banks of the Solway Firth looking toward the famous village of Gretna Green in Scotland. It is tidal and so not the ideal spot for a stroll unless you know the area well. It also had a site where the Ministry of Defence were constructing Blue Streak rockets, striving to take Britain into space. A mile across the estuary was Chapel Cross nuclear power station, and a VLF radar site was west at Anthorn. It was a place of strategic interest to outside observers.

On the marsh that day there was not another soul about. The cows and sheep, however, were behaving oddly. The Templetons have rarely seen them act as they did, huddling together as if responding to some unseen force. The only other occasions Jim can recall seeing activity like this was in the immediate moments before a thunderstorm when the air is heavy with static. But there was no storm on that afternoon in 1964.

THE PUZZLE PICTURE

All of these things were fading to memory a week or so later when the Kodacolor X film was returned to the local chemist. Jim had been an experienced photographer for 30 years and taken official pictures on behalf of the fire brigade, so he well knew the basic skills. But he was utterly bemused when the young woman serving him said, "Jim, you have some nice photographs, but it is a pity that the best one of Elizabeth has been spoiled by that man in the background wearing a space suit."

Jim thought she was joking. He knew there had been no man in any shot—and definitely not one in a space suit. But when she pointed it out to him he saw exactly what she meant. A strange figure in a white suit—not unlike an astronaut's outfit—did appear to be standing behind Elizabeth's head.

It was not Jim's way to make an issue out of the photograph. Certainly he did not desire publicity from it. Instead he sought the assistance of the police and it was through them that the picture came to wider attention via the local paper, *The Cumberland News*.

When Superintendent Donald Roy of Carlisle Police saw the photograph he was puzzled. There was undoubtedly a man visible, but the definition was not quite right. He was at an angle to the vertical and, if one imagined where his legs ought to be (out of sight behind Elizabeth's head), these would not be on the ground. In fact the figure would be floating slightly. The strange being looked rather alien, drifting there ethereally.

Whilst admitting "I don't know the answer to this one," Superintendent Roy noted the lack of definition and striations across the image on the photo. This did look peculiar. An official file was opened and the film evidence was shipped off to the CID investigation lab in Penrith where Superintendent Tom Oldcorn took command. Unusually high profile police figures and resources were now being put to work on a matter which one might not expect to have attracted such attention.

ANALYSIS BEGINS

Kodak were also intrigued. The first thing that both they and the police wanted to eliminate was the possibility of a hoax. Making a double exposure would not be difficult for a man of Jim Templeton's expertise. However, it was rapidly concluded that this was highly improbable. Indeed I expect that anyone who spends time talking to the Templetons would also quickly decide that, whatever else might be involved, a hoax by this unassuming couple was certainly not it.

But there was another option. The man in shot has some resemblance with a fireman wearing a protective suit. Given Jim Templeton's line of work this was rather a coincidence. Had he taken a photograph of just such a person earlier in the film and the two images become accidentally superimposed during processing? Once more this idea failed to survive analysis attempts.

Jim had not taken such an earlier photograph. Whilst a double exposure was possible from two quite different films taken by two different photographers, it would be fantastically unlikely that the other photographer would have filmed a fireman and that this was then accidentally superimposed on a film taken *by* a fireman. Double exposures also leave telltale signs, and there were none visible in this case. The image behaves exactly as would a real person floating behind Elizabeth's head. That seemed the only viable option. But how was this "intruder" floating in midair if not by such an optical fluke? In the end Kodak admitted defeat and even offered "free film for life" as an incentive to any of their staff who could figure out how the image was formed. Nobody ever claimed the reward.

Meanwhile the police were investigating ever more wild ideas. A UFOlogist had suggested that an invisible spaceship might have been on the marsh and the alien phased in and out of reality so fast that the human eye could not see it whereas the camera shutter had succeeded. Jim Templeton's camera was set to a shutter speed of one hundredth of a second—just about fast enough to register things that the eye could not see. But the idea of an invisible alien popping in and out of visibility at a rapid oscillating frequency still seemed too ridiculous for any serious consideration.

THEORIES GALORE

The ideas of the police were no less weird. Locals had seen mirage effects on the marsh caused by hot weather. It could bend light rays and cause the sea from the estuary to appear as if it were in the sky. "It might well be that something has arisen from that," Superintendent Roy said, with less than overwhelming confidence.

Most commentators argued that the figure on the photograph is too obviously a man to be just some chance reflection. But what man, and why did nobody see him at the time? In the end, the police came around to the conclusion that a real person *was* in the photograph, somehow or another. It was the only explanation that made sense to their experts. They tried to get Jim to admit that his wife had accidentally intruded into his field of view—but she had not done so, and even if she had she was not dressed in a white astronaut's uniform or floating in the sky!

The police next attempted to propose that a streaker who had been known to frequent the marshes was to blame. As Mrs. Templeton told me, "I think I would have noticed a naked man running in front of us"—and, as Jim cut in to point out, "that man on the photograph is not naked."

Eventually the police also admitted defeat and in effect told Jim, "Sorry, we haven't a clue." Tom Oldcorn offered the official CID position in order to close their file. It was a masterpiece of understatement after several weeks of study. Oldcorn said "it must be some sort of freak picture."

OFFICIAL ENQUIRIES

Once the initial sources of investigation had given up on the matter there was a further brief flurry of interest in the photograph. On 11 June *The Cumberland News* called the Ministry of Defence in London to ask if they had an answer to offer. The MoD were interested in seeing a report. I have studied government archives for the period between May 1964 and March 1965 (now released into the public record). There is no sign of a report ever reaching Whitehall, but there are letters from UFOlogists asking about the case. The term "Cumberland Spaceman" is used. But there is no evidence of any investigation. Indeed, the implication is that the MoD had not even seen the actual shot. But if what happened next is the truth, then there *must* be more secret files somewhere else.

Possibly the most intriguing interest in the case came from Professor Sir Lawrence Bragg, one of Britain's most famous scientists of the day. As an atomic physicist he spent several days studying the evidence and promised to try to find an answer to this scientific riddle. So far as I can discover he never offered one—or if he did it went unpublished.

Throughout the years Jim Templeton has provided copies of his photograph to everyone who asked for them and still does so. He is still keen to find an explanation for this bizarre "spaceman" that came from nowhere. At no time has he ever shown a desire to gain money or fame. But he felt the need to remind me that his altruism did have its limits. "It would not really be fair to say I made nothing from the photograph," Jim cautioned. "I did get some foreign stamps for my daughter's album."

Having now seen dozens of different reproductions of the photograph—from black and white copies many generations from the original right through to the very first print still in Jim's possession—one thing has struck me about the evidence. The sharper the image the more obvious it is that a real person in a white suit is present in the shot. If this were a simple optical effect such an increase in clarity would very probably destroy that illusion. But a real man from *where?*

A team of Japanese researchers came up with the intriguing theory that the person in the shot is some sort of projection or hologram transmitted across the Solway Firth from Chapel Cross power station. This would, therefore, be a worker at the atomic energy plant going about his business and seen in the photograph through some freak of nature. That such a fluke might occur is hard to judge, of course, since it has no precedent. But we might note how projections or holograms seem to be involved in other cases—such as the first encounter of Cynthia Appleton in Birmingham (see p. 62).

Unfortunately, there is a big problem with this theory. Checks were made with Chapel Cross and there were no staff working in fire-resistant suits on that Sunday. So, if some kind of projection had occurred as was suggested, then it was an image transmitted through *time* as well as space!

THE MIB APPEAR

Whatever the truth about this photograph, we do know that those mysterious visitors—the MIB—were decidely intrigued by it and were soon to play their hand in this dramatic story.

About the end of June, when the furor had begun to die away, Mrs. Templeton took a phone call from a well-spoken man who said that he "investigated these things" (by now a familiar opening gambit when the MIB appear). He wanted Jim to discuss the case in detail and her husband, as usual, readily accepted the suggestion.

As requested, the man came to the house a couple of days later along with a colleague. Mrs. Templeton recalls them well. "They were extremely well dressed in black suits and looked very officious. They appeared very courteous but were somewhat off hand. They drove a large dark Jaguar car. It was very shiny as if new. But there was something rather odd about them."

Jim recalls that they never once, during the hour or so that he was with them, used names in reference to one another. Instead they called each other by numbers (Number 9 and Number 11). This fitted the image of secret agents that was popular in the culture of the day—the use of numbers and letters instead of names in both the James Bond movies and TV series such *The Prisoner*.

They did flash identity cards, which neither Mr. or Mrs. Templeton got to study for any length of time. But these stated that the men were from some government unit. Jim said to me, "I really cannot understand why people from our own government had to act like this. I was happy to cooperate completely. I would have answered any questions. It just wasn't necessary." He has always felt aggrieved that these two men from the Ministry of Defence (as he is sure they had to be) chose to behave so oddly.

And the oddness continued, for they asked Jim to take them to the site. He drove with them in their new car and they left it by the marshes and walked out toward the spot where the

photograph was taken. It was then that the strange nature of
the questions they asked really began.

INTERROGATION

"What was the weather like on that day?" they made quite a
point of asking. He had to respond in precise detail. Nothing
less would do.

Then the two men were intensely curious about the wildlife.
They insisted he describe in some depth how the sheep and
cows had behaved. They also wanted to know if he had noticed any birds during the taking of the photograph and
whether there had been any ambient sounds on the marsh during this period—wind in the trees, distant traffic, that sort of
thing.

Such questions baffled Jim. He had expected to be asked
about the camera and the film, not of things that he could
barely appreciate as relevant.

Then the mood changed drastically. "Suddenly they said to
me—now show me where the man was of whom you took the
picture?"

"What man?" Jim replied.

"The man who was standing there when you took the photograph."

"But there was no man. I did not see anyone."

"Really?" they said, looking quizzical, as if they did not
believe him. Jim says that it was as if they were upping the
stakes and trying to force him into admitting a hoax.

Of course, Jim stuck to his guns. "I told them there was no
man and they looked at one another and then said, 'Oh,
right'—and with that just marched off across the grass. Before
I had my wits about me they were halfway back to the car. I
could not catch up with them. They got in and drove off,
leaving me stranded on the marsh. There was no public transport out there. I had to walk five miles home."

It is no wonder Jim Templeton is baffled by the actions of
people who claimed to be from a UFO investigation unit of

the British MoD. Why would they treat him in this manner? If they were from a government unit it is one which officially does not exist and whose files are not available to the British public. The law states that all such records should now be available as more than 30 years have passed since these two men called on Jim and his wife. The only reason they can be retained is if they are deemed to affect national security. But why would an innocent photograph of a strange floating man do that?

ROCKET MAN

A few weeks after this visit Jim took another strange photograph on the marsh. It depicts a streak of light climbing into the sky, not unlike a rocket launch. Again, he saw nothing at the time, and rockets were not actually launched from this site. To my eyes the blur of light resembles some sort of lens flare with sunlight bouncing off the camera. But this is merely a guess.

The fire service also asked Jim to give a talk about his adventure and he readily agreed. In order to illustrate this he went to Burgh Marsh with his camera loaded with slide film. His intention was to take transparencies to show during his lecture. This was to bring a further mystery when the slide film was returned minus all the shots taken on Burgh Marsh.

Needless to say Jim reported the matter to the police—who, no doubt a little wearily, agreed to investigate again. They came back to him soon after and intimated that there was nothing they could do. The film had been seconded by the government for some sort of investigation and that was all that could be said. Jim pressed further and was merely advised that during a rocket launch around the time "when you took that photograph of the man" some automatic cameras had recorded "more or less the same thing." The launch was aborted as a result. "Now can you see why they need to have your film?" Jim *could* see. He asked no further questions and was happy to cooperate with any investigation, but he never heard anything further from the government about this mysterious event.

When I first heard this new part of the story from Jim at his home one winter's day in 1996, my credibility threshold was stretched toward breaking point. I had never seen reference to this amazing claim in connection with Jim's photograph and no matter how convincing the Templetons were—and they were *very* convincing—the idea that a British rocket launch in Australia was called off because a spaceman paraded before the camera shortly before takeoff seemed rather *too* incredible. But at least such an event made some kind of sense out of the apparent Ministry of Defence interest.

If indeed the weirdly behaving MIB were government agents, as Jim had presumed them to be, they would undoubtedly have been concerned about the possibility that Britain's attempt to enter the space race was being watched by unknown forces.

I have chased up this aspect of the story in an effort to see how much of it can be verified. As it turned out, a surprising amount was correct.

RETURN TO WOOMERA

The Public Record Office carries hundreds of documents in a correspondence file from a department of the Air Ministry set up in the early 1960s to investigate UFOs. Its primary job was to receive reports from the public and write back to reassure them that all was well. Only rarely did the data contain any evidence of actual investigations carried out into the sighting. They *never* involved site visits by strangely acting men such as those reported by Shirley Greenfield or Jim Templeton.

There were occasional references in these files to cases passed on from this MoD unit to the DSTI (Directorate of Scientific and Technical Intelligence). This was a department in which military strategists and government scientists worked together to assess intelligence data, somewhat like the Foreign Technology Division at Wright Patterson in the USA. The role of the DSTI in UFO study in Britain will be discussed in a later chapter, for their files, which are exempt from release onto the Public Record, may hold the key to the MIB mystery.

What you *can* find at Kew regarding problems with a Woomera "rocket launch" is very intriguing. It comes in the form of letters exchanged with a member of the public who asked for the MoD opinion about this very story. They were evidently aware of the matter saying that they would secure the evidence, and there is a note implying that film was later examined and found to show a lens flare.

Huge gaps occur in this record. There is no analysis of the film or stills from it on the public archive. Indeed, no trace exists indicating where the MoD get the suggestion that the footage shows a lens flare. On a previous case (a promotional shot of a new Vulcan bomber taken at Coningsby Air Base in Lincolnshire on 12 December 1963) there is a full analysis report and copies of the photograph on the Public Record at Kew. The spindle-shaped object beside the plane is without doubt a lens flare, just as the MoD conclude. But the existence of this complete record in the Kew archives debating a case from just a few months earlier makes the omission of similar data about the "rocket launch" film all the more frustrating. One must wonder where the files on this have gone.

Nevertheless, Jim Templeton was partially correct. A camera at a rocket launch had apparently recorded something strange around the time that his photograph was taken. So my next step was to try to find out precisely what occurred. Sadly, the scanty data at Kew makes this a problem.

The BBC were a big help. They had an extensive library of British rocket launches, from which I discovered that we were talking about a Blue Streak test at Woomera in Australia. This is fascinating. Woomera features yet again in one of these MIB cases. What is more, Jim Templeton took his photograph near where the Blue Streak missiles were actually being built around the very time that a similar picture was apparently secured at the site from which the missiles were then being launched 10,000 miles away. This certainly explains why the MoD found Jim's photograph of interest.

Unfortunately, whilst countless shots of Blue Streak

launches from Woomera are on the BBC archives, the relevant launch footage has gone walkabout from the files. It is indicated in the BBC archive at White City in London that the BBC did once have a copy, but the phrase "Can missing" suggests that at some time during the intervening years this footage has been removed—just as the data is absent from the Public Record at Kew. This suggests more than a coincidence at work.

I next tried to discover if there was anything about the incident on the Australian government files. But Bill Chalker found nothing in the Camberra records about film footage from a Blue Streak launch—particularly one with the count suddenly aborted because a "spaceman" had intruded into shot.

DISCOVERY

However, there *is* some film footage of a strange object taken at Woomera. I eventually managed to trace a still from Pathe Newsreel footage. The still is said to be a pale reflection of the original film itself (which nobody seems to have today), but it shows an object beside the launch pad and was recorded by cameras in the lead-up to a Blue Streak mission. The object is a lozenge-shaped halo of light amidst a cloudy vapor. It is certainly not a "spaceman" like the figure on Burgh Marsh. Indeed, it much more resembles the "blur of light" that Jim Templeton subsequently filmed here. The Blue Streak missile is clearly taking off in the shot, and so this launch was evidently not aborted.

If this is the footage over which all the fuss has been made, I can see why the MoD have concluded that it was a lens flare. This may well be the case, although this launch was in daylight and there is no obvious ground light. Lens flares more often occur at night when bright lights bounce inside the camera optics. It is possible for sunlight to create the same effect, and whilst the sun is not evidently visible in the launch film it was apparently low on the horizon at the time.

This Blue Streak launch at Woomera occurred at 9:14 A.M. on 5 June 1964—12 days *after* Jim Templeton took his photograph. According to aviation writer and UFOlogist Waveney Girvan—who says that he saw the film at a private screening in 1964—the color original footage of the launch depicts the object very clearly, and the UFO seems to be on the ground right beside the missile before take off. Although the idea of a lens flare was mooted to Girvan, he claims that the photographers at Woomera said that the camera was protected with a hood to shield against the sun as this is always very strong in the Australian desert. So the camera operators did not think the object was a lens flare.

A MYSTERY STILL

We may never have answers to the many questions that surround this case. Was it just a series of freak coincidences that linked the extraordinary Templeton "spaceman" photo and film of a Blue Streak launch? Were both events explicable as some optical effect, or were darker forces somehow at work? Fortunately, we do not need to resolve these issues, fascinating as they are, because our main purpose is to decide who were the visitors that came to see Jim Templeton.

What really matters is that *someone* took sufficient interest in his evidence to go to bizarre lengths in their follow-up. Once again, these strangers demonstrated knowledge about UFOs that caused them to pose unusual questions that imply they were not just UFO buffs. Again they reacted in peculiar fashion when faced with the refusal of the witness to be bullied into accepting an ordinary explanation.

Evidently these people also knew about the incident at Woomera and saw—as we can now see—that there are remarkable links between the two incidents which may well have *forced* a security agency to act. And whoever these vis-

Office Memorandum · UNITED STATES GOVERNMENT

TO   : DIRECTOR, FBI   DATE: March 22, 1949

FROM   : SAC, SAN ANTONIO

SUBJECT: PROTECTION OF VITAL INSTALLATIONS
          BUREAU FILE 65-58300

Re San Antonio letter to the Director dated January 31, 1949, which outlined
discussion had at recent weekly Intelligence Conferences of G-2, OII, CSI and
FBI in the Fourth Army Area concerning "Unidentified Aircraft" or "Unidentified
Aerial Phenomena" otherwise known as "flying discs", "Flying saucers" and "balls
of fire". It is repeated that this matter is considered secret by Intelligence
Officers of both the Army and the Air Force.

G-2, 4th Army, has now advised that the above matter is now termed "Unconven-
tional Aircraft" and investigations concerning such matters have been given
the name "Project Grudge".

G-2, 4th Army, advised on February 16, 1949, a conference was held at Los
Alamos, New Mexico, to consider the so-called "Green fire ball phenomena"
which began about December 5, 1948. It was brought out this question has been
classified "secret" and that investigation is now the primary responsibility
of the U.S. Air Force, Air Materiel Command, T-2.

██████████ of the University of New Mexico, discussed one siting which
he himself had made which was termed the "Starvation peak incident" and described the following characteristics which indicated that the phenomenon
could not be classified as a normal meteorite fall.

1. There was an initial bright light (no period of intensity increase)
   and constant intensity during the duration of the phenomenon.

2. Yellow green color about 5200 Angstroms.

3. Essentially horizontal path.

4. Trajectory traversed at constant angular velocity.

5. Duration about two seconds.

6. No accompanying noise.

RECORDED COPY

JEJ:md
2 cc: El Paso (100-4562)
2 cc: Dallas
 " ", Houston
 " " Little Rock
 " " Oklahoma City

Apr. 4 1949

- 1 -

itors were, they had the ability to confiscate film evidence. These are recurring themes throughout our investigation of the MIB and may well be vital to our understanding of who these strange men are.

Opposite *Are MIB particularly active when witnesses experience something linked to a defense establishment? The evidence points this way. Jim Templeton was near a plant building rockets. We have already discussed two previous cases where the Woomera launch site was involved. Yet as early as 1949 intelligence agencies were concerned by the apparent connection between UFO cases and "vital installations"—ie secret military research sites. This memo, released under the US Freedom of Information Act of 1977, shows the high level scientific concern about these matters. The University of New Mexico scientist whose name is censored from this memo is Professor Lincoln La Paz—a leading meteor expert and space science researcher of the day.*

8

1965–1967:
IMPOSTERS

Jim Templeton was not the only person to find himself faced with mystery visitors after taking a strange photograph. In fact this has become one of the most predictable times when the MIB tend to strike. It happened again just a year afterwards in the USA.

HIGHWAY ROBBERY

On 3 August 1965 former police officer (and once FBI trainee) Rex Heflin was doing his job as a highways inspector for Orange County, California. He was concerned about some trees that were obscuring clear sight of a sign warning motorists of a railway that crossed the road ahead. Sensing the urgency, he attempted to contact his Santa Ana base but the radio was unexpectedly dead.

As he continued to struggle to make contact he saw an object appear out of the corner of his eye. He watched it move across his path, traversing the road at a height of about 150 feet. It was approaching mid-day, and yet the road was surprisingly quiet. So he grabbed his Polaroid 101 camera and took a photograph of the hat-shaped craft with a flattened base as it moved through the sky. Heflin took two more pictures through his windscreen before it was gone. At closest approach he claims there was a rotating beam of light coming from the underside of the object. It was also "wobbling" like a gyroscope in its course. After it disappeared a ring of smoke was left in the sky and Heflin chased along the highway, taking a fourth photograph before that also faded away.

The case was not promoted by Rex Heflin. He was convinced the object was an experimental aircraft from a nearby Marine base and was simply intrigued by its shape. As such, he merely showed the photographs around to his friends and one of these—a local chemist—put them on display, from which they found their way into the local Santa Ana newspaper. The paper added that it took some time to persuade the photographer to let them use his pictures. He was not pressing to tell the story. However, UFO investigators were soon onto the case.

These UFOlogists had needed the original prints for study as polaroid images have no negatives. Heflin explained that he did not have them because NORAD had taken them away. NORAD (North American Air Defense) is the radar and defense unit that operates satellite surveillance to protect the USA. It monitors many military objects in earth orbit, but its interest in this case was odd.

Even before they arrived on the scene Heflin had been asked to loan his photographs to the military staff at the Marine base. He did so without quibble and received them back very quickly. So when a man arrived at his house and announced that he was with "North American Defense Command G-2" (their intelligence unit) who needed to see the photograph, Heflin did not flinch. He still believed that he had filmed a secret aircraft and this was part of the routine follow-through.

The man was in an ordinary dark business suit but carried a colored folder which was filled with numerous papers, supposedly giving proof of his identity. As a result the witness did not request a receipt, expecting that the government would hand his pictures back when they were finished.

This was a big mistake, for NORAD denied any knowledge of the mystery visitor as soon as Heflin politely inquired about the non return of his pictures. Indeed their Chief of Staff, Major General Magee, said in his written reply; "For your information NORAD does not have the responsibility for evaluation of UFOs and therefore would not knowingly be in the business of collecting UFO pictures for evaluation.'' He added that official UFO investigation was carried out by the US Air Force.

CONTROVERSY MOUNTS

It was not until 23 September that the USAF—in the form of a Captain Reichmuth from Los Angeles—arranged a four-hour interview with Heflin. Once again he cooperated fully.

However, Project Blue Book quickly concluded that this case was a hoax. They did so on a number of seemingly impressive pieces of evidence. USAF photo analysts noticed that the differences in focus between background and UFO implied that the hat shape was only about a foot or so across. They also found that Heflin did not discuss the smoke-ring photograph with anybody for some weeks. When challenged about this the witness rather curiously claimed that ''three photographs were enough for one day.'' Perhaps even more importantly, there are numerous clouds in the background of the smoke-ring shot. The sky in the other photographs seems clear, matching conditions on 3 August.

Heflin has utterly denied charges of a hoax. In his defense was the chief photographer for the local paper, who saw the originals before these vanished. The Air Force only received second or third generation shots to work with. The Santa Ana photographer insisted the originals were sharp and did not show variation in focus as the USAF allege.

Professional photographer Ralph Rankow also studied first generation prints in his investigation as the photographic consultant to the UFO group NICAP. He says that it is very difficult to get a background out of focus whilst foreground images are sharp using the type of camera Heflin operated to film highway traffic problems. Rankow supported the view of the *Santa Ana Register* that the prints were in focus, thus indicating that the object was large and at some distance from the lens.

Not all UFOlogists were convinced by this. Aviation historian Charles Gibbs-Smith posed numerous pertinent questions which Rankow partially answered. However, one of the critical debates centered on the strong sunlight which placed shadows of telegraph poles on the highway in the first photograph. Rankow claims that if the UFO was a model a foot or two across dangling in front of the car windscreen—as the USAF eventually concluded—then its shadow should by necessity be visible on the road surface. But it is not. This, he contends, proves that the object is further away and higher in altitude and thus much larger than the model being proposed.

In 1967 the University of Colorado began a two-year project, under the directorship of Dr. Edward Condon, studying the best UFO data in the Project Blue Book archives. The Heflin case was one of under 70 that they chose to assess in depth. Their study of the photographs further compounded the problems. Whilst the report lists the sighting as being one of around 38 percent that they ultimately rated "unexplained," the detailed analysis by Dr. William Hartmann terms the evidence "inconclusive."

Although the project coordinator, Robert Low, who interviewed Heflin on the Santa Ana highway, seemed impressed and described the case as "one of the best four or five" photographic cases on record, Hartmann reasonably pointed out that the only data which would allow judgment of the object's size, etc, was the witness testimony. Rex Heflin's case and the debate following it featured in *Flying Saucer Review*.

MIB OFFICIALLY RECOGNISED

During the early stages of the Condon team's investigation, Heflin was to claim a second MIB experience. He says that during this 1967 visit two men arrived in a dark car with a peculiar violet glow coming from behind its darkened windows. Someone appeared to be seated within, but it was not

DEPARTMENT OF THE AIR FORCE
OFFICE OF THE CHIEF OF STAFF
UNITED STATES AIR FORCE
WASHINGTON DC 20330

1 March 1967

AFCCS

Impersonations of Air Force Officers

to

ADC	AFSC	HQCOMD USAF	SAC
AFCS	ATC	CAC	TAC
AFLC	AU	MAC	USAFSS

Information, not verifiable, has reached Hq USAF that persons claiming to represent the Air Force or other Defense establishments have contacted citizens who have sighted unidentified flying objects. In one reported case an individual in civilian clothes, who represented himself as a member of NORAD, demanded and received photos belonging to a private citizen. In another, a person in an Air Force uniform approached local police and other citizens who had sighted a UFO, assembled them in a school room and told them that they did not see what they thought they saw and that they should not talk to anyone about the sighting. All military and civilian personnel and particularly Information Officers and UFO Investigating Officers who hear of such reports should immediately notify their local OSI offices.

HEWITT T. WHELESS, Lt General, USAF
Assistant Vice Chief of Staff

possible to make out any details. That person remained in the car whilst two Air Force uniformed intelligence officers got out and asked to interview Heflin.

The two air men reputedly asked odd questions, such as what the cameraman thought of then recent stories about ships and aircraft vanishing amidst the so-called Bermuda Triangle. Heflin claims that some kind of electrical equipment must have been brought into the house by the two men because his radio set (which had been left on in the background during the interview) was emitting strange "popping" sounds throughout. It had not done this before and did not do so again after the men left. Their demeanour was "threatening," but they made no actual demands of him.

In the light of his initial experience with the bogus man from NORAD, Heflin insisted on taking the full names and ranks of these two intelligence officers. None the less, the USAF later denied sending anyone to see Heflin, and when UFOlogists checked government records no officers of the names given were listed.

Regardless of the true nature of Heflin's photographs, his MIB claims were to have some effect on government policy. They were taken quite seriously by the Pentagon and led to direct action being initiated. In fact, on 1 March 1967 Lieutenant General Hewitt Wheless, Assistant Vice Chief of Staff at the Air Force in Washington no less, circulated a memo to all staff headed "Impersonations of Air Force Officers." This was very precise in its orders.

The memo briefly outlined Heflin's story of the NORAD imposter (naming no names) and a further case in which it reported that "a person in an Air Force uniform approached local police and other citizens who had sighted a UFO, assembled them in a school room and told them that they did not

Opposite An Air Force memo from 1967 in which staff are requested to collate data on the growing spate of MIB stories—where witnesses in the USA claimed to have been visited by bogus "intelligence officers."

see what they thought they saw and that they should not talk to anyone about the sighting.''

At the close of the Wheless memo all Air Force personnel hearing of such MIB visits by purported staff from the USAF ''or other defense establishments'' were urged to report the incident to the OSI—the Air Force special intelligence investigation unit.

THE MAJOR ARRIVES

As seen from this Air Force memo, Heflin's case was far from unique. Indeed it was merely the best documented of many similar MIB stories that occurred throughout the USA between 1965 and 1967. Because cases such as the Jim Templeton story were not known even to the UFO community, it was widely (but incorrectly) assumed that such episodes were unique to America.

A typically odd event is reported by New York journalist John Keel. In November 1966 two women at Owatonna, Minnesota spotted strange twinkling lights above a field. Suddenly one light swooped down low and one of the women collapsed onto her knees and started talking in a robotic voice as if something were transmitting through her vocal chords. She was acting as a ''Direct Voice Medium'' (a Spiritualist term— where the dead supposedly use a person's voice to convey a message) or, more commonly amidst today's new age community, as a ''channeler'' of some kind of cosmic wisdom. But this 1966 contact was more comic than cosmic.'' What— is—your—time—cycle?'' the voice asked followed by a series of questions indicating that the woman (or whomever was supposedly communicating through her) did not understand the concept of time. The UFO then promptly shot up into the sky and vanished.

After this weird episode, Mrs. Butler (the woman who heard the voice) said that she was plagued with strange phone calls in the middle of the night when nobody was at the end of the line and there were odd noises on her radio set, not unlike those described by Rex Heflin. This was a familiar pattern in the cases that Keel was by now uncovering.

Then Mrs. Butler ventured that she had had a "strange visitor." The man was wearing a dark suit and clothing that seemed brand new. His complexion was olive and his hair was dark and long—too long, she thought, for the Air Force officer that he claimed to be. He identified himself as Major Richard French and said he was interested in UFOs. Then he drove off in a brand new Mustang car.

Next day Major French was back claiming that his stomach was hurting him. As a home remedy Mrs. Butler advised he try "Jell-O" (jelly). She brought him a bowl and sat agape as he literally tried to drink it like soup!

After regaining her senses at the ludicrous sight, she explained the concept of eating to the man and he eventually left. But the Butlers were so puzzled they took down his car registration number. The vehicle turned out to be a hire car from Minneapolis. There was also a Richard French in the USAF but he denied "pestering" the Butlers and the USAF proved his case by showing French's identification. The real Richard French bore no resemblance to the man who called at their home.

MOTHMAN

Keel's most amazing (and disturbing) series of MIB cases centered on the town of Point Pleasant, West Virginia. This is on the banks of the Ohio River and linked by the Silver Bridge, which was a lifeline to the community. That word was soon to ring very hollow.

On 15 December 1966, 18-year-old Roger Scarberry, his wife Linda and their friends Steve and Mary Mallette were driving in a part of town known as the TNT area. This place was so called because it housed disused bunkers and munitions plants left over from the war.

Suddenly a figure appeared on the road behind them and appeared to chase the car. A terrifying scene followed in which this apparition pursued the four witnesses for some minutes. Man-like but about seven feet tall, it appeared to have bat-like wings and uttered a high pitched noise. Its eyes glowed coal red. The terrified youths fled at speed, escaping its clutches and reaching the sheriff's office in town. Deputy Millard Halstead took down their story and said later he had known them all their lives and they were genuinely scared. He went back with them to the plant but nothing was visible. However, when he tried to use his car radio it just emitted a high pitched squeal.

Next day the stories were circulating around the community and a name had been coined by the media for this monster. They called it "mothman." Numerous witnesses began to see it, including Connie Carpenter, who had a daylight vision of something "big and gray that flew."

By the time Keel arrived in Point Pleasant in mid-December, UFOs were being seen regularly in the town especially over the TNT area. He visited the site and wandered the abandoned power plants and byways above the underground tunnels.

Here Keel found what he thought was a beam of ultrasonic radiation emitted from some unseen source. It was creating a "zone," and if you walked through this spot your senses were heightened subconsciously and provoked into a marked fear reaction. Once you walked out of the range of this beam these symptoms vanished.

After Keel had interviewed many of the witnesses and returned to New York, odd things started to happen to these people. They included poltergeist effects around their homes. It was some months before one of the witnesses said in passing in a letter to Keel, "As I told your secretary when she was here." Keel was baffled. He had no secretary. It turned out that many of the witnesses had been approached by a blond woman claiming to work with John Keel. Armed with a clip board she gained entry into their homes and posed odd questions about the UFO sightings—always off-key ones, notably things about the personal lives and health of the witnesses after their encounter. As Keel put it, these were not the sort of questions the average UFO buff would think to ask.

This mystery woman was not the only stranger in town. Black cars plagued the area disgorging men claiming to be social welfare workers and asking questions about the children in the house. Other times they just asked for some water—a feature often found in UFO landing cases where aliens made the same request in monotonous fashion.

On 22 February 1967 witness Connie Carpenter was walking to high school when a dark car that looked old fashioned in style but was shiny as if brand new pulled up ahead of her. A deeply suntanned man with black hair got out as if about to ask directions and then tried to grab Connie and pull her into the car. She managed to escape and run home. Seven hours later a note was pushed under her door reading, "Be careful girl. I can get you yet." Police had to maintain a round-the-clock watch on her but nothing further happened.

This was typical of the off-beat, intimidating incidents that were affecting the mothman and UFO witnesses in the Point Pleasant area.

MR. APOL

Between 30 March and 6 April 1967 Keel visited Point Pleasant again to do more research and was escorted by Mary Hyre the local reporter who had coordinated much of the news gathering on the flap. In this period they saw several strange red lights and other UFOs over the town and the river—including one which "transformed" into an aircraft in front of their eyes.

Keel, Roger Scarberry and Steve Mallette also came upon a black Cadillac parked in the shadows on the TNT site. They approached a man who was sitting inside and seemed to be monitoring the situation, dictating notes into a microphone. He refused to answer any questions and just grunted.

Throughout the summer more witnesses suffered odd experiences. Cars and trucks parked for hours outside their homes in remote spots as if "on surveillance." Several reported how an "Indian" or "Hawaiian" complexioned man in a dark suit stopped them in the street, sometimes taking surprise photographs and running off. Even Keel had such an experience whilst walking on the streets of Manhattan. He also received phone calls asking him to go to Long Island, where he encountered strangers in dark cars who warned him to quit his investigations or else.

A woman called Jane had a similarly frightening encounter in June back in Point Pleasant. After her UFO sighting a strange woman told her that she had been selected for contact. She was then followed by a black Cadillac that drew up alongside her in the street, out of which stepped a very suntanned man wearing a dark suit and sunglasses. He told her his name was Apol.

Apol turned up at her house on 12 June and requested water "to take some pills"—then he gave Jane three of these capsules, one of which was for her "to have analyzed and assure herself it was safe." Surprisingly she obliged and swallowed one, as if under some kind of spell. This gave her a blinding headache and affected her vision temporarily. When later tested by Keel the drug was a sulphur compound similar to those used to treat urinary infections.

On 16 June a man called at Jane's home claiming to be "Colonel John Dalton." He wanted her to come to his Air Force base so he could ask questions and persisted when she declined. So she requested the address of his office, at which point he abruptly changed tactics and said he would come to see her. He came the next day, moments after her parents had gone out.

Colonel Dalton had a younger lieutenant with him, and they proceded to pressure the witness to tell them all about the "flying saucers in the area," as well as the strangers she had recently met. The mood was very threatening. Once it failed to work they produced a form full of questions about her medical history and personal life, such as how her grandmother had died. Jane understandably looked critically at this bizarre form and so they suggested she just sign it rather than read it through. When she refused the two men simply walked out and drove off in a blue station wagon.

MORE UNPLEASANTNESS IN POINT PLEASANT

Another witness, Jaye Paro, claimed she was then abducted by a man in a black Cadillac that drew up alongside her in the street. There were flashing lights on the dashboard that seemed to hypnotise her. The inside of the shiny vehicle smelled like a hospital. At one point a pungent smelling bottle was held under Jaye's nose and she was asked all sorts of questions which washed over her and made no sense. Finally, she was dropped off in the street at the point where she was picked up.

Soon afterwards Apol was back in action, making predictions about the political turmoil in the Middle East which Jane was asked to pass onto Keel. When the events began to happen Keel rushed to Point Pleasant to hypnotise the woman and attempt to get her to describe the mystery man in more detail. To his surprise he found himself talking directly to Apol, who claimed to be in his Cadillac nearby using Jane's vocal chords to communicate with the UFOlogist. He warned Keel that Robert Kennedy was in grave danger and predicted a plane crash (which Keel says happened soon afterwards). Kennedy was also to die at the hands of an assassin's bullet, but not until some time later.

In late July and into August 1967 Keel started to receive a flood of mystery phone calls (many of which he tape recorded). Some were from a man claiming to be Apol. They offered predictions sometimes couched in biblical language and speaking of a murder attempt on the Pope and "days of darkness" that would follow. When some of the prophecies (such as an earthquake in Turkey) occurred, while others, for example the papal assassination, did not, Keel was left floundering, wondering why he was being toyed with in this way.

By October Keel had received countless calls from Apol. The being said that he was trapped in time, forced to jump about from past to future (in our sense) because of the difference between linear time and the time he faced in his own "dimension." This was how "predictions" were possible.

From such conversations and various other messages given to UFO witnesses it was clear that a "big event" was coming soon. This would involve a power blackout in the northeastern USA and the date was clearly set out—15 December 1967. Keel was by now quite sure that this incident was going to happen. But what could he do to stop it?

The journalist was also getting further warnings about a disaster on the Ohio River in which many would be hurt. The messages implied an explosion at a factory, and so he wrote to Mary Hyre warning her of this on 3 November. But he advised Mary to be circumspect in whom she told.

PROPHECY

On 15 December at 5:45 P.M. John Keel was sitting in his Manhattan apartment, watching President Johnson switch on the Christmas tree lights at the White House. The Apol messages had inferred that the "visitors" would prove themselves by making the prophesied blackout start as the switch was thrown. Nothing happened. It seemed that Apol had lied yet again.

Then a news flash came on the TV. The Silver Bridge at Point Pleasant had collapsed. A rush hour traffic jam at 5:04 P.M. had backed up lines of cars. The old steel suspension bridge had swayed beneath their weight and then crashed into the Ohio River, taking dozens of vehicles with it.

More than 40 people died that night—including several of the witnesses to the UFOs, mothmen and strange intruders that had plagued the town for the past 13 months. They included some who had been visited by Men in Black.

Keel was shellshocked by all of this. Could he have prevented the tragedy? he was forever to wonder. One thing he did know. The phenomenon, whatever it was, acted in a deliberately deceptive manner. Disguise, confusion and mischiefmaking were all part of its repertoire.

9

1972-1977:
HIDDEN DEPTHS

Following our discoveries so far it would seem well worth-while to explore the background to other cases and see whether hidden depths lurk beneath the surface. The truth emerges very strongly. MIB visitations are far more common than we might imagine.

ALONE ON THE MOORS

On the night of 16 August 1972 Sandra Taylor—then a professional dancer—had been working in the north-east of England. Peter was a successful building contractor and could arrange his schedule to bring her home when she would be working until very late. At 2 A.M. on that mild summer night they were returning through the North Yorkshire Pennines, heading toward the Taylors' smart home near Manchester Airport. It was then that the strange things began to happen.

They were not exactly sure where they were as they had by-passed York and were seemingly not far from the base at Menwith Hill. This is a sensitive electronic surveillance site operated by the NSA (National Security Agency)—one of America's most secret defense organisations. UFO sightings have inundated local villages such as Darley and it is very well guarded.

About 10 miles north, between Thirsk and Ripon, the car radio began to act strangely. This was playing light music to keep Peter awake on the winding roads, as he had driven a long way that day. Now the reception was filling with static and losing the signal.

Soon after this happened the couple saw a weird object off to their left. It appeared to be landing in a small copse. A few moments later the road carried them into a position where they could note that it had landed in fields beside them. By now Peter had slowed to a crawl so they could watch the thing carefully.

Most peculiar was the object's color—a very bright fluorescent green—''like those socks you used to be able to buy,'' Peter added. Sandra confirmed that it was melon-shaped and very large. Indeed she kept pointing out to us that she had no idea UFOs were supposed to be that shape. As far as she knew from her limited awareness, UFOs were supposed to look like ''flying saucers.''

Reconstruction with the witnesses indicated that the object was at least 30 feet across and perhaps 50 feet from the car. The Taylors were in a little convoy of vehicles, with two cars ahead and one behind. In fact the lead vehicle was a police car.

According to the Taylors, the occupants of all four cars must have seen the UFO. It was impossible to miss. All appeared to slow down to a stop. But at no time did anybody apparently get out of these vehicles, something that in retrospect seems odd—especially when a door began to appear in the side of the craft.

This was a vivid blue/white. Peter likened to it a brilliant but oddly slow motion flashbulb. Sandra says it was ''like a sunbed lamp,'' suggesting that it might have been ultra-violet. It began as a dot and opened up ''like an old-fashioned TV set in reverse,'' spreading into a ''T'' shape several feet high. It simply formed in the side of the object without sign of seams or openings.

The Oz Factor

"You know—that was strange," Sandra said. "There was no noise. Even the trees. Not even normal night noises."

Peter suddenly realized that she was right—an eerie stillness had come over the whole area when they had stopped the car. Although they did not know it at the time, this effect (known to UFOlogists as the Oz Factor) is commonly reported at the onset of close encounters. It seems to mark a boundary between different realities where laws of time and space diverge.

"That was the weirdest part," Peter added, recalling now that it began as Sandra tried to get out of the door. "I felt a compulsion to do that," she remembered. "Something just made me want to get out. So I opened the door and started to step into the night to head toward that thing. Peter was dragging me back."

Her husband grimaced at the memory of the awesome silence. "There is always something, even at night. Birds twittering. Rustling. But nothing was doing nothing that night."

Sandra described the scene as Peter dragged her forcibly back inside. "I remember his exact words—'sod this for a game of soldiers.'" They drove away at high speed, leaving the object still in the field, and they do not even recall passing the police car. Their next memory is of the road ahead being clear.

Roy Sandbach and I got the impression as we interviewed the couple that there was more to this story than they could recall. If half an hour of memory was missing, who would notice that fact late at night? As Peter said, "When you see something like this you don't spend time looking at clocks."

Mrs. Taylor has experienced a number of paranormal phenomena, including the sighting of an apparition (seemingly the ghost of an old woman that used to live nearby). This is the sort of clue that often suggests deeper aspects to a case, which lie undiscovered in the subconscious mind of a witness.

Missing Time

A few weeks later Peter was driving his brand new Ford home from a contract job when its engine and lights began to falter. This happened on two successive nights. These "vehicle interference" events always happened at the same spot, as he was driving through the small village of Daresbury in Cheshire. Peter's car was in perfect mechanical order and soon recovered, but on a third run home—the very next night—the engine stalled and the lights went out completely. This time it did not recover.

Daresbury is the birthplace of fantasy writer Charles Dodgson (Lewis Carroll). It is right in the heart of a zone of repeated witness claims about all manner of weird events that have occurred here for many years. This fact had not been publicised in 1972, but researchers now call it "Wonderland" after Carroll's famous children's story where a girl called Alice enters a magical dimension. Apparitions, car engine failures and alien contacts have all been reported and similar locations traced around the world. The term "window area" is often used, as they seem to be windows to another reality.

It was 7:30 pm on that third night and Peter Taylor was in a rush to get home. But suddenly he found himself on an unfamiliar road and completely lost. Astonishingly, he was now near Preston in Lancashire—40 miles to the north of Daresbury. Stopping at the first call box, he phoned Sandra with the news. She also told him that it was 9:30 pm—two hours later than his previous memory.

Return Home

On the night of 17 August 1972, as the Taylors drove home and tried to forget about the UFO they had just seen, they eventually arrived in south Manchester. It was the middle of the night and they were shocked to find a police car waiting for them at the door. It was parked outside their house in the quiet little suburban side avenue.

Two officers were in the patrol car, and their first question was: "Have you anything to report?" The Taylors had no intention of talking about the UFO, so they denied that they had, whereupon they were asked more penetrating questions. Where had they been? Why were they trying to enter a house at this time of night? Eventually, in an obvious state of shock, the couple were allowed into their own front door.

Sandra has always ascribed this incident to coincidence. The police car just happened to be there and was reasonably suspicious of their late arrival. Peter is sure that the officers knew about the UFO sighting, presuming that the police car in Yorkshire must have taken down their license plate number and called through to Manchester.

Despite not getting to bed until after 4 am, Sandra says that she was up at 7:30, wide awake and "on a high." She was absolutely full of an odd euphoria. Sandra wanted to tell the world, although Peter had deep reservations. He felt it was better to say nothing. Sandra insisted, however, and phoned the police. Two officers arrived that morning—itself unusual, as police are not often fast at the investigation of ordinary UFO sightings, especially if they happen 60 miles off their patch. As Sandra says, "They seemed to know about what had happened already."

Anticipating the answer, the police asked, "Other cars were there, weren't they?" Then they added that York police were investigating the matter and had informed them that the object was just a large tent. "Do you want to change your story in the light of that?" they questioned. Sandra told them, "I am not blind. I have very good eyesight and I know what I saw." The police made a few notes and left.

A week later a story appeared in the Stockport paper with the heading "Heald Green Couple Flees in Terror!" Reading on to see if this referred to anybody the Taylors knew, they were astonished to see that the couple who were supposed to have fled in terror were themselves. At no time had they spoken to the press. They could only assume that the police had given them the story.

Men from the Ministry

Because the local press article had carried their address, the Taylors received numerous phone calls from UFO societies. The police also called to say that the national press wanted to feature the story. Sandra had flown to Gibraltar to dance in a cabaret and Peter was left to cope on his own, but the police said they would arrange a "press call" on one day, gathering all of the reporters together at the Taylor house.

Several reporters arrived, from both national papers and locals. The police officer despatched to supervise events even made the tea as Peter Taylor brought the press together in his lounge and arranged a rota so that they could use the phone in the hall to call in their stories. In all my years of UFO investigation I have never known such a procedure to be implemented.

However, the press conference was aborted before it got properly underway by a ring at the doorbell. Peter answered to find himself confronted by two official looking men who had arrrived in a large black car. It looked brand new. They wore dark suits and carried a card with the words Ministry of Defence on top. This they flashed in identification, although one man did all the talking.

The two strangers led Peter away from the reporters into an empty room and told him, "Look, it is in your interests that you do not talk to anyone about this experience." Peter needed little persuasion. But, as he pointed out, it was rather difficult to avoid as the press were all around them.

"Leave that to me," he was told, whereupon the Man from the Ministry promptly asked them all to leave. There were one or two murmurs of dissent, but Peter did not fully understand how they were removed so easily. Checking with local reporters I was told that they could only imagine leaving so readily in these circumstances if it were advised that an "exclusive deal" had been signed. So did this Man in Black pretend to be a rival journalist?

Once on his own Peter was quizzed in depth about the UFO. He found it odd that—unlike all the reporters and UFOlogists who wanted to hear the whole story—the MoD were just interested in the T-shaped door in the side of the object and the way that it had opened up. "The man kept asking me to tell them about this again and again and over and over in as much detail as I could recall," Peter says. "It was really strange."

WANDERLUST

Another case which followed a similar pattern involved a man whom I will call Billy Doyle. He was a fascinating character. A strict Catholic, he struggled to accommodate his experience within his faith, but good humor and a no nonsense retelling of the events compensated admirably. I have never met a witness more reluctant to color his testimony and who kept saying "that is all I saw—I cannot tell you more than that because I would be lying."

Billy was born in the Silver Mine Mountains of Ireland and recalls how his mother had a close encounter "with a funny thing like a big cigar" that hovered over their ramshackle homestead in 1944. Also around this time Billy had the first of his psychic experiences (seeing an apparition of a woman on a railway track when his school friends insisted that nobody was there).

Doyle then set off "around the world to seek my fortune," he said with an ironic grin. He had once walked across the Nullarbor Plain in Australia (scene of dramatic UFO encounters, as you have read) and worked on four continents. He had been everything from a miner to a barman and earned a crust in a rich variety of ways before moving to England to settle.

In October 1972 (only six weeks after the Taylors' encounter) Billy was employed in the still room at a small seaside hotel in Eastbourne, Sussex. His job was to make tea and coffee for the guests and his love of the sea kept his wanderlust at bay for several years.

Billy set off at about 7:30 pm for a customary walk over the golf links toward Beachy Head. This famous sheer cliff beauty spot is said to be the "suicide capital" of England but is enjoyed by millions for less disturbing reasons. He walked for about 90 minutes in the chill air. It was pitch dark now and he began to make his way back toward the hotel. To do so involved a short cut, ducking under a wire fence protecting the golf links, but as he continued on his path something odd happened. Rolling mist or thick cloud came in from the sea and rapidly enveloped the area in such a way that visibility was reduced to a few feet. As the fields were unlit, everything was plunged into blackness. It had also become eerily still and silent. The Oz Factor had struck again.

Bunkered

Billy certainly knew the dangers of the clifftops. Wisely he decided not to try to pick his way home for fear of taking a wrong turn and crashing over the cliff edge. He stopped in his tracks and began to plan his next move. If conditions did not improve, he was even willing to sleep in the sandy bunker.

Billy never got the chance to make that decision, for a huge "star" suddenly appeared from out of the mist above the English Channel. He assumed it was a search and rescue helicopter. As the glow approached and settled on the ground ahead of him he noted, "It had a remarkable violet/blue glow to it." This sounds very familiar.

The stunned witness insists, "It was like a solid thing. It came down like it could see and knew where to land. Like a helicopter would. But this was not a helicopter. It was a mass of lights—the most wonderful colors. Just like those in an arcade. They moved about and were so penetrating that they sort of attracted my attention. Especially the greens and reds. They were beautiful."

We tried to persuade him to describe the shape, but Billy refused to claim that it was a craft or ship. He simply said that it was multiple lights shining through the mist and radiating like a rainbow.

"I could not see the shape properly," he reminded us. "Because the glow from these moving lights was so intense. If I tried to fill in the shape that might have been behind them I would not be honest."

It was "moving, rotating, flashing" and spanned an area of sky several times larger than the full moon. He added: "I was sure I was dead. This was the gateway to heaven. I said to myself—well, Billy, that's your lot."

Once the initial shock was over Billy noticed that he was getting physical sensations from the object. "My skin was tingling like it was charged or something and my hair was standing on end. I know they say that in horror stories to frighten you, but this was true. My hair was really sticking up." Presumably he was being bathed in a field of electrostatic energy generated by the object.

Suddenly a voice filled Billy Doyle's head. "It spoke in an English you have never heard—clear, precise, not a trace of Irish about it. It was friendly, yet persuasive. It just probed into my head and made me believe it. 'Do not be afraid' are the only words I can precisely recall. It kept repeating them." Yet again this is something we have come across in many other cases.

Captured

As if in a trance, Billy says, he was lured toward the object. He reports, "I walked toward the lights because the voice made me. I kept repeating to myself—out loud, in my head, I don't know—it's all right. I'm safe. Then everything changed."

This change occurred instantly. He has no memory of a switch. One moment Billy was walking across the grass toward the lights in a daze, the next it had gone and there was a hard, solid surface beneath his feet. He did a quick double take and looked around. Somehow he was on a road and he was walking right up the middle of it. Everything was clear. The mist had gone. Indeed it seems as if this effect was localised to the spot where Billy had been that night.

Thinking it was still around 9:00 pm and so traffic could well be about, Billy quickly stepped off the highway and onto the pavement. "Not even a lunatic walks in the center of the road like I was doing," he says, still baffled by how this came about.

After regaining his bearings (which took him about ten minutes) Billy realized that he was on a street about three quarters of a mile from the golf course. He could not understand how he had got so far. Once oriented it was only another five minute walk to the hotel, but he was puzzled to meet the night porter at the door, as this man normally did not come on until late. Then he saw that they had stopped serving coffee, even though trays were usually set out until 1 am.

In fact it was now about 1:30 in the morning. Even allowing for all the walking Billy did that night, between three and four hours of memory are unaccounted for. His face revealed that he was stunned by these revelations and the porter asked Billy if he was all right. "I saw a star," was all he could think to reply. "Right—and were there camels too?" came the response.

After a good night's sleep, Billy awoke determined. He marched into the police station, demanded an interview and asked, "Have you got one of those things that can tell whether you are lying?"

The bored desk sergeant looked up and asked Billy what he was talking about. He started to explain that he had seen a UFO, at which point he was cut short with a wave of the officer's hand. "I suggest you go to see your doctor—or a psychiatrist. We have better things to do here." Then he was sent packing.

Billy gave up at this point. He decided that nobody was going to believe him. So his story was not reported by the media. Only the night porter and the police desk sergeant had been told.

Yet, about two weeks later, a man arrived at the hotel and asked to see Billy Doyle. He flashed a card at the reception to indicate he was with the police at which point, of course, he was directed to see the witness straight away. Billy says that he claimed to be some sort of "special officer" with the

"CID" but would not be drawn to say more. He was there to investigate Billy's UFO sighting.

The two men relocated to an empty room and the stranger asked Billy to tell his story. After he had finished the stranger said, "What would you say if I asked you not to report this? That it was a government matter?" Billy replied that he would agree, naturally. He was not interested in breaking secrets. The man nodded in return, as if satisfied with the answer, but did not insist on silence. Instead he simply reasoned with Billy, saying, "You do realize that nobody will ever believe your story. I suggest that you keep it to yourself."

At this point Billy began to wonder just who this man could be and how he came to know so much about him. He had not paid much attention to the stranger's appearance, but says that the visitor was dressed in a smart suit. He certainly looked very impressive and yet skirted around all questions of his origin, refusing to specify exactly where he had come from.

When Billy pointed out that nobody could know his identity—"as I did not get the chance to leave my name and address with the police, because the sergeant threw me out before I got that far"—then the "officer" suddenly came up with a new explanation for his knowledge.

"He told me that he had been checking door locks in the local hotels one night when he had seen a light in the sky. He then heard the sergeant say that a man from one of the hotels had come in to the station and reported a UFO, so now he took it upon himself to trace me. It had taken him two weeks to check every hotel looking for the right man, but eventually he got here."

This story satisfied the witness at the time and it was only rather later that the oddness of it all occurred to him. As he told me, "It is a bit strange that a man like him would go to so much trouble to find me. Besides which I could not find anyone who worked at another hotel who had been asked questions trying to track me down. And in any case, what would a special investigator with the CID be doing going around late at night checking locks? The bobbies on the beat do that, don't they?"

ABDUCTED

A truly extraordinary case was investigated by researchers Andy Collins and Barry King in October 1976, four years after it had occurred. Their detailed report was stunning. In the years since there have been a number of encounters with similar features, particularly in the USA. But this British case cannot have acted as their catalyst because it received no media publicity at all.

The witness was a 37-year-old woman who had moved to England with her husband from Turin, Italy, in 1963. We will call her Mrs. Verona. Her husband was 16 years her senior. They settled down in Taunton, Somerset, and he worked for himself doing odd jobs. They appeared to be an ordinary family with no thought of UFOs.

On 16 October 1973 the daughter of a friend called on Mrs. Verona to ask if she would drive to Wellington because the friend's mother was ill. Mrs. Verona agreed, but a series of coincidental delays prevented her trip for more than four hours. However, she had promised to go, so at 10:45 P.M. she set off for the half-hour drive.

On a country road near Langton Budville, about 15 minutes later, Mrs. Verona spotted a light beside the road. Almost immediately her 1967 mini car began to falter. The lights flickered, the engine spluttered and it coasted to a halt. After fruitlessly trying to restart the vehicle she reluctantly got out into the darkness and lifted the bonnet, hoping it was a simple fault that she could rectify. The dome shaped object was still in the field and she could also now hear a high pitched humming sound.

Fearful at her isolation (not a car having passed in some time to offer hope of rescue), Mrs. Verona slammed down the car hood and turned to plan her next move. Suddenly a heavy hand touched her shoulder. Looking around she found that a six-foot-tall figure in a metal suit was standing beside her. The woman lost consciousness, possibly fainting with shock.

Mrs. Verona awoke inside a well lit room on a flat table or bed. She was naked and covered by a blue blanket. Everything was icy cold. Her ankles and wrists were attached to the side of the metal by thick bands preventing her escape. All around were odd pieces of equipment and directly above her were two clear tubes pointing down at her body.

Before she had time to take this all in three men entered the room through an unseen door. They looked like ordinary humans of modest height but were covered in masks and gowns like surgeons. Two stood to one side and the third did all the work, communicating in some way (seemingly by telepathy and in words you might predict) "Do not be afraid." The robot was a "trained retrieval device" used by them to "collect samples" from outside. It was a "non-thinking intelligence."

The man brought several little cubes, placed them on a rail beside the bed and moved them up and down. They glowed different colors as he did so. He also moved a small hand-held object over her body and it glowed dimmer and brighter in the process. Then a small knife was used to cut a nail sample and a little tube painlessly extracted some blood from her arm.

Next the blanket was removed and one of the clear tubes descended onto her groin. A suction pressure was felt and this created discomfort, but not great pain. It felt as if fluid was being extracted from inside her body. Noting that Mrs. Verona was shivering, the cubes were removed from the rail and placed on the floor and a blanket put back across her body. Then all three men left the room.

The Nightmare

For some minutes Mrs. Verona was left alone in her nightmare, only able to move her head and feeling sick and with a sore throat as if she had just had an anaesthetic. Eventually one of the men returned, removed the blanket, stared at her lower body without obvious emotion and stuck a long needle or pin into her thigh. She felt no pain but her body started to go numb almost immediately.

The entity then silently raped Mrs. Verona. She was unable to scream or to move throughout. When he was completed he scrubbed her body with a blue cloth and left. Just before she lost consciousness for the final time she saw the men return and start to remove the pin and the straps that were restraining her body.

Mrs. Verona awoke by her car on the road. The UFO had gone. She felt very weak and was terrified. She scrambled into the mini, regained her composure somewhat and tried to start the engine. It did so first time. All thought of driving onto Wellington was abandoned. She went home to find her husband waiting up for her and clearly worried. It was 2:30 am, meaning that at least a couple of hours of memory is missing.

At first Mrs. Verona did not want to tell her husband what had happened. But he could see her distress. There was no way that she could hide from him the fact that something awful had happened. As the night wore on she confessed the truth, and a shocked Mr. Verona was very understanding. He suggested that they should put it all behind them and not try to tell people because nobody would believe such a story. She agreed, only breaking that decision years later after it had preyed on her mind so much that she felt she just "had to tell somebody or I would explode."

Callers

About eight weeks later (and when nobody else yet knew about it), the Veronas began to receive peculiar phone calls. About six of them were made during the next few months. They were never long in duration, just 30 seconds or so being typical. The calls repeated the same message again and again, almost as if they were some kind of post-hypnotic command. They could have been pre-recorded and played down the line as no real conversation ever ensued.

At the same time letters arrived. These had a local Taunton postmark but, like the calls, were anonymous. They carried very similar messages to the phone calls. Each was handwritten, on plain notepaper, just a few lines long and signed "From a Friend." Mrs. Verona's husband made her burn them. The gist of all these contacts was simple: "You must forget what happened to you in October. You should not tell anybody about it.''

Then the two strangers arrived. Mr. Verona was present as well and according to the witnesses they ''seemed like ordinary enough men.'' They looked so similar to one another that ''they might have been father and son,'' one being in his 40s and the other around 25. They both wore dark framed glasses. The younger one was tall and had a short beard. The older of the two was more stocky and bald. Neither wore the traditional dark suit, although the younger had on a black jacket. Their clothing was rather old fashioned.

When greeted at the door the older one (who did nearly all the talking) said, ''It is wise that you should let us in because we have to discuss a private matter.'' This set the faint tone of weirdness that surrounded the men. Both Mr. and Mrs. Verona say ''there was something very odd'' about them.

Once inside the house the couple was stunned to hear the entire close encounter described in detail (more detail, in fact, than Mrs. Verona could remember). The man then said, ''If you value your health, welfare and sanity you must not report this matter to anybody.'' The warning was conveyed politely.

Mrs. Verona says that the voice of the bald man sounded like the one on the phone, but she could not be certain. He was asked if he was responsible for these calls and the letter, but this was bluntly denied. Indeed the men refused to answer any direct questions or to give any names. Nor would they say who they were or how they knew so much about the UFO encounter.

The men returned several more times. Mrs. Verona says that after the initial visit she tried to stop them from coming into the house ''but I felt compelled to let them through the door.'' This matches the strange way in which the Greenfield family allowed their visitors to ''take over'' their house and lead an interrogation despite not wanting this to continue.

Both visitors came several more times during 1974 and sporadically after that until the investigators were first contacted in 1977. Mr. Verona was present during several of the visits and very quickly announced that he would call the police. ''It would be very unwise of you to do that," he was told. "Unpleasant things will happen if you do."

As a result of this threat (again uttered with impeccable manners), the Veronas agreed to tolerate the occasional visits as they were never in themselves unpleasant experiences. They wanted to try to forget and had never intended to go public with their story. These MIB attempts to silence them were, if anything, ensuring that the story was kept firmly in their minds.

During the various visits the two men would simply explain reasons why silence was necessary. These included comments such as, "It is not in this country's best interests to part with too much information. It is best to leave well alone. You are not supposed to let any of this out to anybody but if you do then you will be branded as a lunatic. These things just happen. There is no control over them. Sometimes they go beyond a certain point and this happens. Please leave well alone."

At some of the visits a curious thing was noticed. A large dark car—"like those used by diplomats" as Mrs. Verona described it—would drive past their window several times at very slow speed, as if cruising the area waiting (or, indeed, as if making sure that the Veronas saw it). Its windows were tinted and at night (when most visits occurred) it only carried dim sidelights. The men left by getting into the back seat, although at other times when they had not left it made a point of drawing up to the front of the house, opening its side door for a few seconds and then closing it again without anybody getting in or out. Then it drove away. Like many aspects of the MIB mystery this overt "display mode" of behavior seems to have guaranteed maximum attention was paid to the event.

On their penultimate visit, the younger visitor said in an impassioned plea, "Keep quiet for a while and no harm will come to you. Everything will be brought out into the open soon and the whole world will know about them. They come in peace and harmony and are worried about your high technology and low intelligence."

It was at this point that the decision was taken by the Veronas to report the events to a UFO network. The MIB claimed awareness of this decision, during one final visit after King and Collins had first established contact. The two men expressed gratitude that the couple had kept the story quiet for so long, even appeared relieved that it was finally coming out into the open and advised that they would not be coming back to see the witnesses any more. They did not do so.

DRAMA IN DYFED

Britain's biggest ever UFO flap—the spring 1977 wave—produced over 300 sightings between February and May. Most of the "window areas" (areas of high paranormal activity) were active but an unexpected one grabbed much of the media attention—the lonely West Wales coastal region of Dyfed north of Milford Haven.

Leading UFO group BUFORA was fortunate in having local vet Randall Jones Pugh to chase up the many sightings. He wrote a book, *The Dyfed Enigma* (with Ted Holliday), which is a straight telling of cases. It missed out the more sensational elements (including the MIB). Other writers, notably Peter Paget (a popularist UFO writer) and Clive Harold (a journalist), produced more dramatic versions of the same events, leading to much confusion.

One man who made a re-investigation to try to sort out these problems was amiable skeptic Hilary Evans. He was particularly scathing of the way the MIB story appeared in most accounts. But as recently as 1996 another of the key features of the Coombs' story (a silver suited alien looking at them through a house window) has been claimed as a hoax. A member of the local Round Table charity said that he dressed up in a "spacesuit" and has come forward in retirement to admit his dirty deed.

The version of the case that follows has thus had to take all of these problems into account.

Ripping Yarns at Ripperston

The Coombs family had a whole series of UFO sightings during the spring, including being chased in their car by balls of light on lonely roads. Pauline Coombs was at the focus of many of the events, which included poltergeist and ESP phenomena.

Some of the stories centered on the herd of dairy cattle which Billy Coombs and two other workers looked after for the owner of Ripperston Farm. These were alleged to have been "teleported" from barns or from one field to another, leaving no physical evidence of their movement.

Then, on 6 June (or 7 June, depending upon which version of the story you accept), Pauline was driving home from market (or a Queen's Jubilee party where she had left the younger children). She was either bringing some of the children home from the shopping trip or on her own in the car. As you can see, resolving even the most basic facts about this incident is a real problem.

Reportedly her eldest son, Clinton, greeted his mother at the door. He was hiding upstairs at first and took much persuasion to come out, being distressed about two men that had just been to visit. Clinton was certain that Pauline must have seen these men as she arrived by the one road into the farm which ran straight for half a mile and only allowed one car to pass at a time. Since the visitors had left by this route just seconds before, she could not have missed them. But Pauline had seen nobody.

Later it was discovered that the strangers had first appeared at their neighbor's cottage. This little house was rented by Brian and Caroline Klass. Caroline was a local nurse and recalls seeing a flashy metallic-colored car suddenly parked outside. She had not heard it arrive. According to Clinton it was very futuristic. Two men were inside, one of whom stayed there throughout whilst the second got out and walked about. He inspected the dairy equipment at the back of the farm and moved at incredible speed, as if traveling from one place to another instantaneously (although he was never seen to do this).

Caroline and Clinton described both men as looking identical, with pointed chins, high foreheads and pentrating eyes. Their skin had a waxy look to it. Both wore dark suits.

When Caroline Klass first approached the man outside her cottage he reportedly asked for Pauline Coombs. She asked investigators, "But how could he have known that I was not her?" Yet very different conclusions were offered by various researchers about these visitors.

Clive Harold paints a melodramatic portrait of Pauline deciding the visitors were not human and attempting to convince her reluctant neighbor. This is offered through reported word-for-word conversations that he must be reconstructing with a degree of artistic license. Peter Paget seems more aware of the MIB tradition and refers to other cases of intimidation (although none of this was evident from the men in the silver car that visited Ripperston Farm).

On the other hand, Hilary Evans visited Dyfed four years later to investigate the case on behalf of the magazine *The Unexplained*. The Coombs had by then moved to a new address, and he also met Rose Glanville only very briefly. She was a key witness to a UFO that landed outside nearby Haven Fort Hotel and whose story is amongst the most impressive in the wave.

Evans accuses both Paget and Harold of "uncritical reporting and sensationalist presentation" and thinks the Men in Black were ordinary people. The reason is that, Evans claims, Mrs. Klass now reported that they did not have a foreign accent, were not uncannily alike, and the car, whilst unusual, was just a car. In fact all peculiarities were more limited than implied. Most telling of all, she claimed that their first question had been to ask if *she* was Mrs. Coombs, and they did not miraculously know that she was not. She even had an explanation for why Pauline Coombs did not pass their car on her way in. The men had said they were going to another village, and Mrs. Klass had directed them there by a short cut.

There is no way to tell which of these versions of the MIB

story is the correct one, although Hilary Evans is a seasoned investigator and I am sure he is reporting what he was told. The same may well be true of Peter Paget and Clive Harold. The real point is that the story took on a life of its own, and this MIB visit readily changed just by placing a new emphasis upon the details.

STRANGERS IN TOWN

Many MIB stories are in essence simply about a strange visitor who asks seemingly odd questions and knows things he ought not to know. Yet in the wake of any UFO episode strangers may well be in town from the countless UFO societies out to chase up witnesses, and some of their members can certainly be considered a little odd in their behavior.

So we need to be careful, especially in circumstances such as the Dyfed flap where the MIB visits followed after weeks of press publicity about local UFOs. This is not always the case (Mrs. Verona's visitors are not so easy to explain, for instance), but we should be prepared to look for down to earth origins for any "mysterious visitor."

That said, Peter Paget offers an interesting twist. He claims that Caroline Klass and Clinton Coombs were not the only ones to see these two men. On what appears to have been the same day Francine Glanville, the receptionist at the Haven Fort Hotel, says that they paid a call there as well.

According to this report the car arrived "silently"—that is, it was just there when Francine looked up. She found this odd, as even bicycles can be heard on the gravel track. She was unable to describe the type of vehicle but found it odd. As for the men, she spoke of their smooth, fine white skin and probing eyes. They had artistic fingers that were very delicate and they possessed extremely good manners—but not a foreign accent, it seems.

Perhaps there were strangers in town after all.

10

1980–1988:
MEN OF MYSTERY

From the evidence to date we have built up a picture of the Men in Black that is chilling in its consistency. There really do appear to be intimidators out there threatening ordinary people who simply have the misfortune to experience a close encounter.

We are also moving chronologically toward the modern day in order to demonstrate that this phenomenon is happening here and now and clearly requires some sort of explanation.

The following set of cases comes from the decade of the 1980s and represents the MIB in its more modern guise. It will be interesting to compare these stories with the earlier reports so that we can judge whether these mysterious intruders have updated their act or are still performing the same old tricks. Either way, they are as terrifying as ever to the unfortunate victims of their appearance.

THE ONE THAT GOT AWAY

This may well be an example of a "near miss," an MIB encounter about which we were unable to learn the full truth—a case where the intimidators did their job successfully. As such it might well reflect many other cases which we know almost nothing about.

On 31 August 1980 Beryl Hollins*, living at Golborne near Wigan in Lancashire, was not feeling too well. So as not to disturb her husband she was sleeping on the settee when she was woken at 2 am by what looked like flames flickering through the lounge curtains. Fearing a fire, she went to investigate and discovered an amazing sight over some trees near a reservoir.

A rounded gray object with a dark band and a triangle of "bumps" was hovering in the sky. Sparks or flames were emerging from it and a misty pink glow filled the air all around. As she watched this phenomenon a probe dropped from its base and was lowered amidst the trees. After a few moments it was raised back up into the main object and this sped away toward the south.

Fortunately, Mrs. Edna Procter and her adult daughter, Edith, also spotted the object from about half a mile away. They saw the mist and sparks but described the UFO as more rectangular in shape (possibly because they saw it from a different perspective). They even noted a glowing window.

The story made a few lines in the local paper, largely as a result of the Procters' sighting. UFO group NARO investigated and investigator Peter Hough paid the witnesses a visit. Whilst the Procters' sighting was quite straightforward, that of Mrs. Hollins was certainly not.

The Balloon Goes Up

There had been a number of hoaxes carried out by youths in Lancashire shortly beforehand. They created home-made hot air balloons with candles and plastic bags. The candles heated the air inside the bag, causing it to rise and glow, and as the plastic melted a trail of sparks was dropped toward the ground. In the dark, these things were very strange to observe. However, that possibility was quickly rejected as an answer to this case. The Procters saw the object hovering for about 15 minutes before Beryl Hollins was woken by its glow.

*Beryl Hollins is a pseudonym

The other possibility was rather more difficult to determine. We had noticed that a number of reports from central Lancashire featured a small craft with a triangle of lights or protrusions on them. These had been occurring since the mid 1970s and there are even some similarities with Shirley Greenfield's Bolton sighting in 1976 (see p. 8). Our speculation was that a ''drone'' (a sort of sophisticated remote controlled aircraft) was being secretly built, possibly using a prototype electric motor in order to fly almost silently. This would be regarded as the basis for today's stealth technology.

It seemed odd that this would be flown near Wigan instead of some remote location, but we had suspicions that the technology itself came from this area. Also, those who were test flying in the dead of night might be aware that, even if seen, it would likely be reported as a UFO and this would ensure an element of secrecy. Most serious aviation commentators would disregard such a sighting.

It is worth noting that triangular UFOs are still being reported in the same area during the 1990s. Reports from Southport, Wigan, Bolton, Blackpool and Lancaster are widely believed to be a modern stealth test craft being perfected at the British Aerospace plant at Warton near Preston. This has the acronym HALO (High Agility, Low Observability).

British Aerospace were still denying this in early 1997, but the US government similarly denied the existence of their stealth aircraft even whilst they were being flown across Nevada and California. Interestingly, they too were mindful of the motto ''If we are spotted they will think it is a flying saucer and so not pay too much attention to us.''

The President's Man

Of course, if something like this is cavorting about the skies of Lancashire using microwave power one can well understand why ''Men in Black'' (assuming that MIB are really government agents) would pay a call on witnesses such as Shirley Greenfield. Did they also frighten off Beryl Hollins?

After the press story, Peter Hough contacted Mrs. Hollins

on 14 September. He was impressed with her helpfulness. But when he pressed to ask if other investigators had been in touch he was not prepared for her reply. The woman explained that just a few days after the sighting a man had called her from Jodrell Bank, the famous radio telescope in Cheshire. He had wanted to investigate her case. This man said that he was a scientist, but when she asked this stranger how he had got her phone number he simply said, "Don't worry—it was from a very good source."

A week later, on 21 September, Peter Hough returned to visit Mrs. Hollins and she seemed troubled. The man had called again, and this time he had been more forthright in his views. First, he gave his name, which Beryl did not recognize. She said that he had an American accent and professed to be literally alongside Jimmy Carter one day before he became President and when he had witnessed a UFO in the Georgia skies. UFOlogists know this case but believe it was a bright planet seen under unusual atmospheric conditions.

The mystery man warned Mrs. Hollins that she must not associate with the "cranks" within the UFO investigator field. Such people would call her but she should ignore them. He also later told her that he would like Beryl to visit Jodrell and answer some questions before various scientists. Several other witnesses were being invited. Naturally she agreed, thinking nothing odd about such a request.

However, Peter Hough knew that there was something very wrong. Without being too alarmist he warned Beryl to be careful and demand proof of identity when this man turned up again.

Don't Bank on Jodrell

Beryl Hollins noted that the scientist was coming to collect her in a car at 1:30 pm on 8 October. Her husband had agreed to be in when he arrived and Beryl also said that a neighbour, a former policewoman, would go with her—just in case Peter's doubts were valid.

There were very good reasons why NARO was suspicious

of this mystery caller, aside from the obvious MIB connotations. We knew very well that Jodrell Bank did not investigate UFO sightings, because we did this job for them! For many years they have channelled witnesses through to my phone number. The scientific staff had made clear their reasons for not wishing to get involved in UFO study. Indeed, when NARO decided to organise a UFO event as part of a nation-wide charity appeal, Jodrell Bank took some persuasion to agree to help us out by making facilities available. There was much academic pressure on the scientists not to associate with "nutty" UFOlogists, and only our good rapport with Jodrell over the years saved the day. Staff knew of our objectivity.

So, when Beryl Hollins told us of her mystery caller we were virtually certain that nobody from Jodrell Bank was truly responsible. Moreover, the name that she gave for this man (which we did not immediately recognize) turned out to be a leading astronomer at the site. The science center were genuinely perplexed and emphatically denied that they would invite UFO witnesses to visit.

As a result, Peter Hough "staked out" the end of Mrs. Hollins' quiet cul-de-sac on the afternoon of the planned appointment. No car or visitor arrived. Fifteen minutes after the scheduled appearance by the man from Jodrell, Peter walked up to the house. Nobody answered. Yet looking through the curtains he could see that there was an electric fire blazing in the lounge with a large dog in front of it, and the radio or TV set was switched on very loudly. The house appeared to be deserted.

Peter made several phone calls to Mrs. Hollins to find out what happened, but her friendly, helpful nature had undergone a dramatic transformation. On the first occasion she pretended to be someone else. During further calls, until the investigator gave up, she refused to comment. It was obvious that she was too frightened to speak to us.

A New Approach

In August 1982 (almost two years later) I phoned Mrs. Hollins, presuming she would not recognize my name and that time might have eased the situation. I asked if she would be interviewed for a new book that I was writing—in effect a ruse on my part. She agreed without obvious hesitation and so I set up an appointment to visit her and asked Peter Hough to accompany me.

When we arrived at the house there was a sudden crash (as if someone were fleeing out of the back door), but again no answer. Peter and I went to the back of the house. The dog was in a shed but the back door was swinging open. I pushed it gently aside and there were clear signs of recent occupation in the kitchen. Fresh toast was even on the cooker grill. Despite calling out loudly several times there was no answer and, of course, we had to respect Mrs. Hollins' privacy and go home.

Later that day I phoned her. She claimed she had to leave the house to visit someone in hospital, but it was evident that she was not keen on arranging another meeting. So we had to let the case rest at this unsatisfactory juncture and we still have no idea why Mrs. Hollins behaved as she did.

It would be easy to assume that this whole story was a hoax. If Mrs. Hollins was the only witness that would be the safest option, even if there is no clear reason for it. The problem is the independent testimony from the Procter women, who were not connected with Mrs. Hollins in any way. This makes it virtually certain that something really was seen over Golborne that night. If so, then what on earth went on afterwards, and why was Mrs. Hollins singled out for this apparent intimidation?

A REAL LIFE X FILE

To the surprise of many, the Canadian city of Vancouver, British Columbia is where the hit TV series *The X Files* is filmed.

On 2 October 1981 a real life case occurred at Victoria on Vancouver Island that might well have been scripted for Mulder and Scully. It was well investigated by linguistics professor Dr. P. Edwards and involved a man called Grant Breiland, who ran a neighborhood home watch security operation. The other witness was a filling station attendant whom Dr. Edwards only identifies as N.B.

At 9:30 pm that chilly evening Grant and his mother were saying goodbye to his sister who was driving home. Then Grant spotted a huge white light in the sky. Despite pointing it out none of the other witnesses (including a boy riding past on a bicycle) could see the object. Frustrated, Grant went to get his CB radio and sent out a message to appeal for other witnesses. N.B.—then on Mount Tolmie, some 3 miles away— radioed back that he could see the object. The two men swapped notes.

Grant now went indoors to get his camera—a Pentax SLR fitted with a 400 mm zoom lens. Through this he could plainly see that the UFO was like an upturned basin with a flat top surrounded by lights and radiating beams of energy. He took one photograph before the object headed away, making a curious sideways flip not unlike a priest motioning the sign of a cross.

Seven hours later there was a strange electrical storm in the town which caused street lamps to extinguish for a few seconds. Only one clap of thunder was heard. But both Grant and N.B. developed severe pounding headaches about this same time. They discovered this fact when N.B. turned up at Grant's door to talk about the previous night and the sighting. They had exchanged addresses by radio.

Meeting in the Mall

On Monday 5 October Grant went to a local shopping center, K Mart, to collect a part for his radio and meet with a friend as pre-arranged. But the part had not arrived and his friend did not show up. When he called from the shop pay phone he discovered that his friend had just broken his arm and could not come. After putting down the receiver, Grant noticed something distinctly odd. There were no people milling about the shop or using the vending machines beside the phone. He had never seen this busy store so empty, as it was usually packed, mostly with youngsters.

Stranger still were two men standing by the phone, staring at the witness after he concluded his call. But they did not go to use the phone. They just kept looking at Grant. Both stood as if to attention with arms by their side and motionless. They wore very dark blue (almost black) suits and their faces were peculiar, with no visible eyebrows and yet very dark eyes that stared fixedly without ever blinking. Both also had very suntanned complexions—"like after a holiday in Hawaii," as Grant phrased it. Their whole appearance was very mechanical.

One of the men said, in a stiff voice, "What is your name?" to which Grant said he would not tell. That man never spoke again, all conversation being handled by his near twin.

"Where do you live?" the other man asked. Again Grant said he would not tell them.

"What is your number?" was the next question—Grant pointing out that he did not say *phone* number, just number.

After several more seconds of staring the two men turned around as if joined at the hip and marched off like robots across K Mart and outside down a wheelchair access ramp. Grant followed them and stood in the pouring rain as they walked in the same stiff manner toward the edge of a mud drenched field upon which new building work was about to start. They never once looked back.

Suddenly Grant heard a voice that sounded like someone calling his name. He turned around but nobody was there. Indeed the street was devoid of people and cars, quite unlike it normally is at that time of day. The voice called twice more and when he looked back the figures were now marching straight into the mud soaked field, heading for nowhere except a wall. He turned again at hearing the last call, and when he looked back just a second later the men had gone. There was nowhere they could have run to or any place to hide, he claims. Dr. Edwards confirmed this on his visit. Grant walked into the field but soon got bogged down by the mud. Although he left prints everywhere, there were no traces of the two mystery men.

That night Grant had a vivid dream in which he followed the men across the field and they grabbed him. He next recalled being in a white room interrogated by them about his sighting. When he denied telling anyone else they accused him of being a liar and said he would be sorry if he failed to cooperate. Of his evidence they told him to "forget it—destroy it." This photograph has not been made public. Next morning, whilst showering, Grant found a strange red mark on his thigh.

Second Appearance

Later that day (6 October) N.B. contacted him to report that two men had approached him at his filling station. This was about three hours before Grant had met them in K Mart. N.B. described the strangers as wearing dark suits and having very blond, almost white, hair. Although they had no car they asked for some "petrol" (the normal usage would have been the American word "gas"). One man remained silent throughout as the other did all the talking. N.B. found a can to fill and asked what type of car they drove and whether they needed leaded or unleaded fuel. The man said "I do not know." When asked for a name to complete a receipt, the stranger said "We cannot give a name."

The men paid with a ten dollar bill and N.B. gave them change. He noticed in doing so that they seemed to have no fingernails and that they stared at the coins as if they had never seen anything like them before. At this the men marched off together with a very stiff gait, carrying the can down the street and disappearing around a distant corner. Fifteen minutes later they returned with the can and said, before departing, "Where do you live in this fine city?" N.B. gave his district but not full address.

After the men had left he went to put the can away and found to his amazement that it was still completely full. After hearing of Grant's subsequent meeting with what seems to be the same men N.B. decided to "heed the warning" and pull out of any cooperation with the investigation.

VANCOUVER AGAIN

Whilst the photograph seemingly suppressed here by the MIB has never appeared, it is worth noting that just 72 hours after this bizarre encounter one of the most highly regarded UFO photographs taken during modern times was secured only a few miles away.

Mrs. Hannah McRoberts, niece of one of Canada's leading nuclear engineers, was at a picnic spot near Kelsey Bay to the north of Vancouver Island. It was the sunny day of 8 October 1981. She was taking photographs of the mountain scenery (the same range from which N.B. watched his UFO less than six days earlier). Her camera was a Mamiya SLR with standard 55mm lens loaded with 100 ASA color film. Hannah had taken several shots before a curious cloud appeared over one peak, looking almost like a volcanic eruption of steam.

With her eyes fixed on this sight she took the photograph and got back to her family, seeing nothing else at the time. But when the prints were developed a small plate-like object is clearly visible next to the cloud above the mountain top. Enlargement shows it to be quite spectacular.

Many studies have been made of this case (reported to the planetarium in Vancouver and passed to UFOlogist William Allen). Experts have been impressed, especially as other shots on the roll fit the witness's story. When fakery is involved the rest of the film often contains failed hoax attempts, such as hub caps cast into the air where the camera did not quite make them look like a proper UFO. This object is sharp and clear and appears to resemble an upside down version of the thing that Grant Breiland says he saw through his camera lens. Of course, we might well ask why the MIB did not try to stop this photograph from being published!

WHERE HAVE ALL THE WITNESSES GONE?

Any UFOlogist will tell you that one of their greatest sources of frustration is the way in which witnesses often do not pursue an investigation but just give up. Studies have shown that if a witness contacts an investigator, the press, or some establishment such as Jodrell Bank or Vancouver planetarium, in order to report a sighting, they very often go no further and simply stop talking.

Investigators will usually send them a report form to fill in, providing basic details of their sighting. Under 25 percent of witnesses return these records. Even when postage is included the return rate still barely rises above one in three.

Of course, there is an inbuilt reluctance amongst most of us to fill out forms, and this must explain part of the shortfall. But it has occurred to researchers that when witnesses go to so much trouble, as they often do, to find somewhere suitable to report a sighting, then their decision not to proceed with the inquiry after first contact is all the more notable.

We cannot prove that intimidation by MIB has anything to do with this problem, although if there are occasions where warnings are issued to witnesses, as the many stories in this book seem to suggest, then a large failure rate in continued witness interest may be anticipated.

In situations such as the story of Beryl Hollins from Golborne we *may* see this process at work. But one case from the USA is even more illustrative and might be an example of what goes on far more often than we care to imagine in circumstances where we hardly ever learn the truth.

THE MAN IN BROWN

Researcher Joe Nyman from Massachussets provided details of this case when I met him in Boston. He has chosen to protect the witness (Marie) by hiding the location (eastern sea-board USA is all I can say about that). But we know that in September 1983 she saw a UFO at close quarters and, after much effort to find an investigator, finally established contact with Jules Vaillancourt, who worked with the biggest UFO organisation in the world—MUFON (Mutual UFO Network)—headquartered in Texas.

Jules phoned the witness and she described her sighting to him. Then he sent her the standard report questionnaire, as UFO groups all over the world are doing every day. This form was not received back. Because UFOlogists are usually working in their spare time and without any funding, Jules—like most of us—did not pursue the matter beyond that point. He assumed that Marie had simply chosen not to fill out the form. Perhaps she was worried about her friends or family laughing if the story got into print somewhere. There could be any number of explanations. But the truth was very different and discovered by mere chance.

Five years later Marie had another sighting and wrote to Jules to ask if he would come to see her. Luckily, he was still at the same address and the letter reached him. Fortunately, he persuaded Joe Nyman and Martha Munroe, who lived closer to the witness, to pay her a visit. That meeting was set up for January 1989.

After talking generally for some time with Marie and her husband, they were asked casually why they had never re-turned the MUFON form. Not only did they insist that they had sent this back but they added that the man who sent it to them—Jules Vaillancourt—had come to see them to discuss its content. Vaillancourt confirmed that he had never been to meet with the witness and had not received any MUFON form.

This puzzle was now explored in more detail, and it emerged that in May 1984 a man claiming to be Jules Vaill-ancourt had phoned Marie and asked to come around "to discuss her form" a few days after they had posted it. Mike gave a detailed description of the man—gray hair, old-fashioned shoes, brown suit, mustache and with an "official" look to him. He said that he lived in Ashburnham, which was the town to which they had sent the form. Moreover, he had with him the form they posted and the envelope and made a point of showing this to the couple, so they had no reason to doubt that he was who he said he was. This man arrived in a dark gray Mercedes car.

Regression

Eventually Martha Munroe separately hypnotised both Marie and Mike to find out more about the visit by this Man in Brown, duplicating the work done earlier with Shirley Green-field in the UK (although we had not published details of that session).

Both witnesses well described the events of the day without being able to hear what one another was saying under hypnosis. Mike recalled how he had asked "Jules" if he wanted a drink, at which point he heard a voice in his mind saying "This is none of your business. Keep out!"—so Mike left Marie all alone to her "interview." She recalled feeling dizzy as she sat looking at the visitor.

Both witnesses say that "Jules" had barged into the house and sat straight down directly opposite Marie, staring at her. He painstakingly went through the details of her form, but when she suggested that they go to the spot where the UFO had hovered (only a few hundreds yards away) he rather oddly declined and abruptly left the house.

Marie and Mike were independently shown a photograph containing several MUFON investigators, one of whom was the real Jules Vaillancourt. Both failed to spot him. In fact the real Jules is physically quite different from their description and has never driven a gray Mercedes.

In a later regression Mike was to claim that he now rec-ognized the figure. It was a hooded "alien face" that he re-called seeing during a childhood dream. Nyman and Munroe note that they cannot judge the credibility of this recall but can attest to the apparent fear exhibited by Mike when he made this recognition under hypnosis. "He seemed to suddenly jump six inches off the couch, causing confusion and fright among those at the session," the investigator reports.

NEW AGE TRAVELLERS

One of the better known abductees in American UFO circles today is Christa Tilton from Tulsa, Oklahoma. She edits her own magazine, which describes the many encounters she has allegedly undergone with the "grays"—a form of small, large-headed being that many American witnesses profess to meet during their spacenappings. Such beings are far less common in cases outside the USA.

Christa Tilton claims an intriguing MIB encounter in May 1987, at about the time when her abductions were underway. She had gone walking with her friend Barbara in Boynton Canyon near Sedona, Arizona, an area claimed to possess incredible "spiritual energies" and where the thriving New Age community from nearby Phoenix has one of its most important settlements.

As Barbara walked higher up a mountain Christa stayed under the shade of a tree. Soon she heard a car engine on the road below, but paid no attention until she realized that the engine was not switching off. Finally turning to look at it, she saw "the weirdest black car I had ever seen." It was an old-fashioned limo that was "so shiny I could see my reflection in it." Everything about it was black.

Suddenly the rear door opened and a man, dressed all in black, peered out and rotated very mechanically as if he were a robot, gesturing to Christa that she should follow. Screaming to Barbara, now well up the hillside, the abductee jumped into her car and pursued the limo. It headed off toward what seemed to be a military compound with a guard at the gate.

By the time Christa arrived here the black car had vanished and the guard denied he had seen such a vehicle. Feeling rather scared, the witness drove off back toward her friend, only to find the black limo blocking her path ahead. From this angle it was possible to see inside the car. There were two men, both in black and wearing sunglasses, although that in itself was not unusual in the hot desert sun. Rolling down the window on her car, she heard the man say to her ''The time is all wrong,'' before mumbling something about the local topography in words she did not fully understand.

It was only at this point that Christa says she realized that this car was not an ordinary limousine. As it sped off in a flurry of dust, she cursed the fact that she had not used her fully loaded camera draped around her neck. Chasing after the black limo, Christa got close enough to take a photograph, but as she pressed the shutter on her Canon nothing happened. A sign flashed on its viewfinder saying ''out of film.'' The camera would not work. The strange car had by now completely disappeared. Later she found there was film in the camera.

ON ILKLEY MOOR

Probably the strangest MIB case—indeed just about *the* strangest case of any type—with which I have ever been involved began for me on 4 December 1987. That day I received a letter with a Leeds postmark from a man who told me he was a former police officer. I have agreed to use the name Philip Spencer to protect his real identity (known only to about half a dozen UFOlogists).

Spencer told me that he had been walking over Ilkey Moor at 7:45 A.M. on 1 December. He was going to visit a relative and had with him his Prinz Mastermatic camera loaded with 400 ASA Kodak film. His plan was to take some pictures of the townscape in the valley below. He had been heading for the village of East Morton when he saw a strange figure on the rocks ahead. It had a dark green cast and a large head. It appeared to gesture to him then and he quickly snapped a photograph before it scuttled around an outcrop and disappeared. Philip followed and was just in time to see a disc-like object shoot into the sky—although, sadly, he was too stunned to film that.

Abandoning his plans he returned to civilisation, expecting it to be around 8:15 am. But the church clock showed it to be 10 am. After trying to use up his film on local buildings he soon realized it was futile and left several shots untaken. Then he got the bus into Keighley, found a one-hour photo processing shop and had his film developed. The picture of the strange entity came out.

Little Green Men

After regaining his composure Philip went to the library two days later to look for a UFO group to contact. He found my address in one of my books and wrote his letter, but provided a box number hundreds of miles away rather than a local Yorkshire address or phone number for my reply.

When I received this letter I was immediately impressed. Spencer came across as a rationalist. I talked the matter through with fellow researcher Peter Hough and replied to the box number address, but I also attempted to trace the witness in Yorkshire (where his letter implied that he lived). I had his real name, of course, and he was listed by directory inquiries in the relevant town. I called the number to learn that he had left that very same week and no forwarding number or address was available. Consequently all that I could do was hope that Philip would reply to my letter, in which I had stressed the importance of proper testing of the photographic evidence.

I was never to receive a reply to my letter and remain puzzled by the logic of his later explanation—that he got frustrated with the delay that he had introduced by giving a box number far from where he lived. After receiving my suggestion for photographic analysis work Spencer instead found somebody else to contact. This other UFOlogist was Arthur Tomlinson, whose phone number was not unlisted (as mine was).

By chance Arthur mentioned his recent call from Philip Spencer to Peter Hough when they chatted on the phone around the turn of the year. Peter had just seen the letter sent to me and quickly realized this was the same case. He told me what was happening and also persuaded Arthur to let him go to meet with the witness on Ilkley Moor. Once he had my phone number Philip Spencer talked to me on the phone and Peter and I planned what to do next.

Analysis Begins

From these initial contacts Peter and I agreed that Philip Spencer was remarkably laid back. He seemed utterly disinterested in any publicity or making money from his photograph. He knew it was the sort of thing for which tabloids would pay dearly, but he exhibited a total lack of desire for attention (and to this day has refused to appear on TV or radio and has given no newspaper interviews). More than that, I got the impression that he lacked the sort of emotional tie to the case that one ought to expect of someone who had secured such dramatic evidence. But perhaps that was just his way.

When I eventually met Philip he seemed a persuasive chap who was always willing to assist. Peter was by now befriending him. Indeed Spencer had even assigned the copyright of his photograph to his new friend, saying that this freed him from having to talk in public whilst it allowed any necessary research to be carried out. The witness said that he wished to shun public association with his "little green man" story because it might affect his career prospects. This seemed reasonable enough.

Most of the investigation of this case was carried out by Peter Hough. He arranged, for example, for electrical engineer Dr. Edward Spooner at the UMIST university in Manchester to examine Spencer's compass. The witness claimed that it had reversed polarity after the encounter (pointing south instead of north). Peter also persuaded Liz Kelly of the Radiological Protection Board to make a site survey on Ilkley Moor where the UFO had been spotted. Ways to reverse the compass polarity were found (although none were simple) and there were no magnetic anomalies detected at the site on Ilkley Moor.

On 11 January 1988 Peter and I started work on the photograph by taking it to Tony Marshall, a professional wildlife photographer in Sheffield. We wanted to establish whether the small greenish figure had attributes of life. There was indeed a small entity with a large head standing on the rocks in the picture, but there was no way to tell just by looking at the fuzzy photograph whether this was a model or a child dressed up in a rubber suit, let alone a real alien.

Marshall was unconvinced. He told us that he suspected the figure was a small bendy doll, but perspective tests on the site would establish whether the object was really of doll size. It was not.

Other important things emerged from this initial study. Spencer had provided the entire roll of film (as we had requested). This fitted his story, because it showed landscape shots that were taken before the alien photograph and a series of buildings immediately afterwards, just as if he were indeed attempting to quickly use up the roll to get it processed. These other photographs were generally sharp. The alien shot was very fuzzy and dark. This might have made sense had the picture been taken at about 7:45 am—as the witness story alleged—whilst using the high ASA rated stock. Unfortunately, we could soon establish that the sky line above the hills was too light. This photograph was definitely taken at least an hour after the time reported if the date was indeed 1 December.

Further study of the film was undertaken by the Kodak laboratories in Hemel Hempstead (who established it was not trick photography but a real object on the moors—although not, of course, what that real object was). They also found it underexposed by two stops, making the computer enhancement they hoped to attempt virtually impossible.

Peter Hough took comparative shots on site from which we could prove that the entity was about four and a half feet tall—although, again, not if it was a model or child dressed up like an alien.

Explanations

By this stage Peter Hough and I were really baffled about this case. Frankly, I thought it had to be a hoax. After all, it was a shot of the almost apochryphal "little green man," which, despite the media laughter, never occurs in real UFO cases. The witness also seemed just too disinterested in his photographic scoop of the century. I had to agree with Peter (who by now knew Philip Spencer very well) that any motive for a hoax was difficult to define, since fame and fortune were not involved.

I wondered for some time if this was a "set up"—a sort of test by a psychology student or even a skeptical science group. Had they faked this picture with its obvious sensational overtones just to see how UFOlogy would respond? When my reply to Philip Spencer had indicated caution, did he seek another group that might not subject the matter to quite so much rigorous analysis? But as the years pass this theory becomes more difficult to sustain. A decade later and Philip Spencer stands by his story and nobody has come forward to report on the folly of the UFO movement in the wake of how it has handled this case. If it is a test, then what are they waiting for?

Spacenapped

By now Philip Spencer had agreed to meet with a clinical psychologist, Jim Singleton. Two sessions were held in March 1988, at the second of which Spencer was hypnotically regressed. Again I found him oddly remote during his hypnotic testimony. Perhaps more importantly, Singleton *was* impressed. He was certain that the witness was describing an experience that he believed had really happened.

The new memory to plug the missing time "explained" several things. For example, inside the UFO (where he was predictably spacenapped by the green creatures) Philip allegedly encountered a strong pulsing magnetic field which attracted his camera and compass. More importantly, his story now included the claim that the photograph was taken *after* the 90 minute time lapse had ended. As such, it was now after 9 am, not 7:45 am as he had thought—perhaps explaining why the sky in the photograph was too light.

Checks with folklore of the Ilkley Moor area by researchers such as Nigel Mortimer found records of a similar entity being seen in and around the White Wells area. That this location has some associations with witchcraft and magic is also suggested by a trip that Peter and I made to the site in 1994. Someone had built a large symbolic cairn of stones on the knoll behind which the entity fled.

To be honest, I still do not know what to make of this case. There are questions about it which still bother me. One newspaper (possibly peeved that the witness was not interested in giving an interview) has "exposed" the truth, alleging that an insurance salesman had recognized himself as the alien. He was riding a bike, wearing a blue anorak and carrying a briefcase!

Aside from the fact that any study of the original negatives shows this theory to be ridiculous, the salesman was interviewed by Peter Hough. He did ride over the moors to visit farmers but had not done so on the date in question and never set off that early in the morning. He seemed to regard the issue as a good joke.

I met with optical physicist Dr. Bruce Maccabee in the USA to discuss the plan to have computer enhancement work conducted but it was impossible, much to his disappointment given the potential of this case. The fuzziness of the high ASA rated film meant that enhancing the grain brings images in which your imagination sees things that are not really there.

Jefferson and Davies

This is an extraordinary case. I could still not discount a hoax by someone, somewhere; although the logic behind such a venture is hard to figure out. On the other hand, it might be a genuine alien contact—whatever one of those proves to be! Either way, like so many other cases where dramatic photographic evidence is involved, it attracted the MIB.

During the first week of the NARO investigation, on 15 January 1988, and just four days after Peter and I had taken the film to Tony Marshall in Sheffield, Philip called Peter late at night. He explained that two men had been to see him that day. They were from the Ministry of Defence.

We found this hard to credit for a number of reasons. At that point only Peter Hough, Arthur Tomlinson, his DIGAP colleague Steve Balon and myself knew of the case and—more importantly—the real identity of the witness. There had been no publicity whatsoever for the case and the MoD simply could not have then known about it through any normal means.

Yet Spencer claimed that the two men arrived at 8:30 pm and stayed for 50 minutes. Neither he nor his wife (who confirmed that she had been present) saw how they had arrived. They were in their early 40s, wore smart business suits and flashed photo identity cards that had the MoD symbol on top. The cards also carried their names. One man was called David Jefferson, the other was Davies (neither witness could recall the first name, as he remained silent whilst Jefferson did all the talking).

Jefferson and Davies acted strangely. They seemed perplexed by the electric fire which was in the room and wanted to know how it worked, asking several questions. It was a perfectly ordinary fire that ought not to have caused such a reaction. They said that they had come to interview the witness about his sighting but did not explain how they had traced him. Spencer admitted he had been too stunned to ask. He told them about the sighting but never mentioned the photograph. They knew of it and asked him for the negative. He stated that it was "with a friend." In fact, Peter Hough had it at his house. At this revelation and without asking who the friend was, they simply got up and left.

When Philip Spencer had called Peter following this visit, he was clearly upset. He said that the case was getting out of hand and if so many people knew who he was the press might call him next. Peter had a hard job talking him round from abandoning the investigation.

At 8:55 the next morning, 16 January, Spencer called Hough again. Now he claimed that the Mirror Group Newspapers had just called. They had his real name and address and were going to carry a story. After they rang off he called the newspaper's Manchester office himself. He asked to speak to the man writing the story about a UFO photograph to try to stop it from getting published. The news switchboard said they knew of no such story.

Peter called me in desperation. Spencer was asking for the negative back and insisting that we must have alerted the press. He added that it was too dangerous to continue. Because Hough had to go out that morning, I had to seek to keep the witness on side. Immediately I phoned both the London and Manchester offices of Mirror Group Newspapers. By all accounts this would have been within an hour of their call to Spencer and within 30 minutes of his call back. Nobody knew a thing about a "story regarding a UFO photograph" (as specific as I dared to be), nor would anyone admit to receiving a call from Spencer about this same matter. With the newshounds now begging me to tell them more about a story they must have sensed was interesting, I got off the line quickly and phoned the witness.

Philip Spencer confirmed what Peter had reported, but seemed to be appreciably more calm. I had less difficulty than I anticipated persuading him to let the investigation continue, although he did reiterate his demand for no publicity. I purposefully tried to egg him into seeing the vast sums of money that could be made from his picture—simply to see if he would bite and not because there was any intention to promote this case as yet. As expected, he did not show the least interest in making money. He expressed the desire that we use his photograph to find out what was going on.

If Spencer is honestly reporting these events during this 12-hour period in January 1988, then what are to make of it? Who visited him and how did they find where he was? Who called him pretending to be from a tabloid newspaper when it is quite clear that this paper did not have the story? Otherwise, they would surely have published the case—something they never did.

Presuming somebody did phone Spencer, were they playing on his deepest fear—the publicity that might upset his search for a new job? Perhaps this was a more subtle form of intimidation, as by then the case was too far gone to stop by merely warning the witness to say nothing.

The MoD Position

Whatever the truth, Peter Hough—after much effort—got the MoD to admit in writing that they did not send anybody around to see the witness on that day. They even insisted that the design for the photo identity card—which Spencer had described from memory—was not the correct one in use.

It is worth noting that this denial came from Air Staff 2A—the secretarial unit in Whitehall that receives UFO reports from the public and whose head between 1992 and 1994 was Nick Pope, a man who has become celebrated through his 1996 book announcing a belief in alien UFOs.

Air Staff 2A did not claim that no element of the British government might be able to send people around to see a witness, only that *they* did not. It is also interesting that, despite several written requests from Peter Hough, they failed to confirm or deny whether the MoD had intelligence officers working for them in 1988 with the names of Jefferson and Davies.

On the other hand, of course, if you were going to invent two identities for MIB with overtones of Americana, then what better than Jefferson and Davies, harking back to a former US President?

11

FOREIGN AFFAIRS

Although I have reported incidents from Australia and Canada, most of the reports of MIB activity to date have come from the USA and Britain. There are good reasons for this. America simply has more UFOs than anywhere else and so, inevitably, MIB encounters are more common as well. Britain, on the other hand, is where my first hand investigations are centered, and it is important when dealing with evidence of this type that I report first hand wherever possible.

It would be wrong, however, to assume that MIB events do not happen elsewhere. They are definitely less common—or at least they are less frequently reported—but they do exist.

ITALIAN JOB

At 3 A.M. on 24 July 1952 (some sources say it was 25 July) Carlo Rossi was fishing in the River Serchio near San Pietro a Vico. The unfortunate man then in his fifties, had only one arm following a railway accident, but he still enjoyed these expeditions.

Attracted by a light above the deep water, Rossi saw a strange object hovering low over the river. This was like a flattened cotton reel with rotors on top and it emitted orange and blue flashes. A tube was descending into the river and seemed to be sucking up water. There are interesting comparisons here with the object that Beryl Hollins saw over the Wigan reservoir some 28 years later (see p. 125).

As Rossi watched this strange sight a human-like figure appeared in an opening atop the object. After apparently spotting the fisherman he pointed him out to another unseen figure that was inside the UFO. Understandably concerned, the witness fled, scrambling down the river embankment up which he had climbed for a better view. A beam of green light passed over his head to mar his escape and he felt an electric tingling sensation like strong pins and needles. Throwing himself to the ground the witness was able to see the craft rising upwards and vanishing in the direction of Viareggio.

The baffled fisherman decided not to talk about his sighting, but on 15 September he arrived at his regular spot on the bank in late afternoon to find a stranger waiting to greet him. He was dressed in dark blue and had very angular features. His eyes were penetrating. Although the man spoke Italian he had a heavy accent like one a Scandinavian might use. The man asked Rossi if he had ever seen "an aircraft or other flying object over the river." Sensing menace from the stranger, the witness denied that he had done so, whereupon he was offered a cigarette. The fisherman had never seen one like it before. It had a gold mark on the side. But as soon as he started to smoke he began to feel dizzy and nauseous. At this point the stranger snatched it from him, tore it up, threw it into the river and hurried off.

Fearing that someone was trying to silence him, Rossi went to the Public Prosecutor's office in the town of Lucca and swore out a statement of his UFO encounter. This incident occurred before the Albert Bender saga about the three Men in Black (see p. 42). and so certainly pre-dates almost all modern examples.

CHINESE PUZZLE

Finding an MIB case in China was unexpected, as until very recently the Communist state frowned upon the reporting of even the most straightforward UFO sightings. But there are examples. One of the most fascinating comes from 1963 and involves Li Jing-Yang, a security guard who at the time lived in some miners' housing on the outskirts of Yangquan in Shansi Province.

Jing-Yang was with a group of youngsters who saw a strange object hovering in the sky. It looked like two plates placed on top of each other and so closely tied that they appeared sealed together. Because news of UFOs from the West was strictly forbidden, these boys had never come across anything like it before and assumed that it was a novel type of aircraft.

The next day, as Jing-Yang was walking down the street, he was approached by a strange man who was dressed all in black clothing. He was tall, had peculiar facial features and walked in a mechanical fashion, almost like a robot. Several passers-by were attracted by his curious gait.

This man singled out the youth and began to talk, although Jing-Yang says he was acting like a ventriloquist and his mouth was not opening as the words came out. He asked the boy if he had seen a disc in the sky, to which he agreed that he had. The man then pointed to the exact position where it had appeared and said, "That is where you saw it." The boy nodded.

Looking at him fixedly, the man announced, "You must not tell anyone that you saw this thing. Do you understand?" The man grabbed the arm of a perplexed Jing-Yang and refused to let him pass until he consented. Finally, agreeing that he would maintain his silence, the grip was released and the terrified witness was free to leave. He saw the man trundle off down the street, still walking stiffly, and then suddenly vanish into thin air as he turned toward a corner. Jing-Yang only agreed to talk 20 years later when the Chinese UFO Society in a less restrictive political regime sought out witnesses. All of these attributes are common aspects of the MIB found in western cases.

FRENCH CONNECTION

In France an intriguing story centered on the town of Draguinan (literally "dragon town") amidst another "window
area" which has spawned dozens of close encounters. Loom-
ing above it is the somber Le Malmont ("the evil mountain"),
rife with legends of demons and monsters.

On 19 October 1973 Gabriel Demogue and his girlfriend
rode up this 1500 foot high hill on their motorcycle to enjoy
the spectacular view across the south of France. In the evening
gloom an orange ball of light appeared and crossed their path,
disappearing over a rise up ahead. Rather perturbed by this,
the couple drove back to town. Four friends to whom Gabriel
told this strange story then jumped into their cars and decided
to set off to investigate.

Once on top of the mountain, by a lookout point with a
stone table that surveyed the valley below, they heard some
strange whistling/screeching noises and felt waves of heat pass
over. There was also a red light coming toward them which
resolved into a glow on the chest of a tall dark figure.

Panic erupted as three of these black figures surrounded the
two cars brought by the party. Two of the witnesses were able
to drive off at high speed, but the others found that their car
engine had failed. They were trapped on the top of Le Malmont with three men dressed in black suits who stood right
next to them and were clearly intent on nothing good.

Suddenly one of the men called out at the beings, "Are you
good or are you bad? In response, a symphony of cries and
whistling noises erupted from the entities. Terrified by this,
the witness managed to escape by pushing the car down the
slope, the momentum providing a jump start.

As a result of this very direct warning to leave Le Malmont
by three Men in Black, these intrepid UFO investigators quit
all pretence of any future research. When J. Chasseigne tried
to follow up the case he had great difficulty finding two of the
witnesses and persuading them to talk about their nightmare.

A MEXICAN WAVE

One of the most intriguing MIB accounts comes from a wave of UFO activity in Mexico. I am grateful to UFOlogists Jerome Clark and Richard Heiden who conducted the interviews with 23-year-old pilot Carlos de los Santos Montiel.

On 3 May 1975 Carlos was flying his Piper light aircraft on approach to Mexico City when it began to shudder. Baffled, he looked around to see what was wrong and spotted a small gray disc on his wingtip. Looking to the other side a second disc was flying parallel with him on that wing as well. Then he saw, to his horror, that a third was coming head on toward him.

Desperately Carlos tried to pull the plane up from this collision course but the controls did not respond. The disc, measuring about 10 feet across, flew directly beneath him, so close that it bumped his undercarriage in doing so. The Piper was now not under the pilot's control and yet still, paradoxically, it was flying normally.

Shrieking into the radio, the pilot reported these events to Mexico City Airport air traffic control, who helped to guide him to a safe landing. By now the Piper was responding to his commands and returning to normal operation.

There was never any question of his story being doubted, because Mexico City control had tracked the three UFOs on radar even as he spoke with them. Air Traffic Control operator Emilio Estanol explained that these objects made a 270 degree turn at a speed of 518 mph—all within a turning radius of just 3 miles. This was considerably less distance than a normal aircraft flying at that speed would require. The G forces involved would be tremendous.

Carlos was investigated, given medical and psychological evaluations and treated for shock following his ordeal. But he was pronounced fit to fly again. The case became much discussed by the Mexican press, and in mid-May Pedro Ferriz, a celebrated TV presenter and believer in extraterrestrial UFOs, persuaded Carlos to appear on his show to tell his story.

Driving on the highway toward the Mexico City studio, Carlos noticed that two black limousines ("like a diplomat's car") had appeared, and these now hemmed in his own car. One was driving in front and the other closely followed him behind. Both were so shiny and new that they looked as if they were on the road for the first time. Within minutes these vehicles had forced him toward the side of the road, where he had to pull up to avoid their close attentions

Both cars stopped just ahead and four men jumped out. They were tall, had a Norse appearance (blond hair, blue eyes and pale skins) and wore dark suits. One put his hand on the door to prevent Carlos getting out. Another spoke in a robotic voice (but in Spanish): "Look, boy, if you value your life and your family's too, don't talk anymore about this sighting of yours."

The four men then jumped back into their cars and sped off, before Carlos had time to think. Once he did think, he made up his mind quickly to turn around and drive home, abandoning all plans to give the TV interview that day.

In mid-June Dr. J. Allen Hynek, the noted astrophysicist and American UFO researcher, was passing through Mexico and asked to meet with the pilot. Carlos had already been reassured by Ferriz that the strange men were really "aliens," although his own view tended more toward CIA operatives. But Ferriz noted that from many cases in UFO literature their threats were empty and the pilot had nothing to fear. So Carlos agreed to talk with Hynek. After an initial talk the scientist was impressed and invited Carlos to breakfast with him at his hotel the next day for a further discussion on the case.

On his way to the hotel the pilot had to call at the offices of Mexicana Airlines, where he was applying for a job. Heading from here to meet Hynek, he was intercepted again by one of the men dressed in black. This man accosted Carlos on the steps of Hynek's hotel and said curtly, "You were already warned once. You are not to talk about your experience."

The witness protested that he was just having breakfast and Hynek was trying to help him figure out what happened during the sighting—about which, of course, people knew by now in any case. But the MIB pushed him bodily backward, saying,

"Look, I don't wan't you to make problems for yourself. Why did you leave your house at six this morning? Do you work for Mexicana Airlines? Get out of here now and do not come back."

Unsurprisingly, Carlos did precisely that, although when the MIB failed to fulfil his threats the pilot gradually started to feel able to talk about his experience and was never to be bothered by these strange men again with their voluble but hollow intimidations.

When he talked to Clark and Heiden in 1977, Carlos claimed not to have heard about MIB stories from the USA until *after* he had reported the incident. But he added that two things really struck him about the men: the fact that they were so pale in complexion, and that at no time did he see any of them blink. They just stared fixedly ahead.

BACK IN THE USA

In May 1968 UFO investigator John Robinson was probing a series of local incidents in New Jersey. These involved witnesses to UFOs and other assorted phenomena and culminated in visits by three strangers to one of the witnesses—George Smyth, then living in the town of Elizabeth. Indeed Smyth eventually received calls telling him bluntly not to attend a forthcoming UFO conference in Cleveland that he was planning to visit, that he should cease research into his case forthwith and end contact with a number of well known UFOlogists, including Robinson.

The men who had stood outside Smyth's house were readily identified by his description. They were three of the UFOlogists that he was later told by phone not to contact—John Keel, Gray Barker and James Moseley—all leading lights in the field of research into MIBs.

But there were two problems with this. These three UFOlogists had been nowhere near the house in question on the day of their apparent "visit." Also, the license plate of a dark car that had stopped the witness as he walked down the street simply did not exist.

As this saga was developing toward its conclusion, John Robinson and his wife Mary found that they were now the targets of intimidation at their home in Jersey City. A large dark car was parked outside and a strange man seemed to be watching them. This only occurred after Robinson had gone to work and when Mary, shortly afterward, left to go shopping. It happened on four successive days. John Robinson concluded that the stranger intended to warn him off by scaring his wife, suspecting that he might be less easily intimidated given his awareness of the MIB evidence.

That night he called James Moseley in Manhattan to report the matter, and when Mary went out the following morning the black car and the man were not there for the first time that week. But soon after, on returning from the shops, she noticed Moseley standing on a street corner behaving very oddly, waving his arms about as if directing traffic.

Mary Robinson puzzled over this unusual sight for a few minutes but decided he was trying to "draw out" the mysterious watcher by making sure that he was seen by all who passed by. Evidently this was done without success, as the black car was still not there as she entered her house. It had struck her as odd that he was out in the morning as he was known not to be an early riser.

Having forgotten something at the shops, Mary had to return a few minutes afterward. Both on her outward trip from the market and her return a few minutes later Moseley was still on the street corner. So, once back inside, she started to prepare to cater for her visitor, sure that Moseley would pop in for a cup of coffee and a chat before returning to New York. Then came the big surprise. The phone rang. It was Moseley. He was still at home in Manhattan, almost an hour away from Jersey City, and could not possibly have been on the street corner. Yet she had just seen him there *three* times.

On 18 May Moseley and his colleague, Timothy Green Beckley, another New York researcher interested in MIB, asked if they could come over to talk to the Robinsons about these events. Moseley brought a camera and when they reached the house the black Cadillac was parked outside a disused factory opposite the Robinsons, just as it had been earlier in the month. The strange man in a black frock coat and old fashioned hat was also standing in the doorway again, staring at the UFOlogist's home. Moseley and Beckley drove around the block three times. On the third occasion the man and the car had vanished. But during the first run-by they took two photographs of the strange man.

This is the only known photographic evidence obtained during an MIB visitation.

12

GRAND DECEPTIONS

From time to time we have mentioned the possibility that Men in Black stories may result from a hoax. This is something that we cannot ignore, although it need not mean that the witness invents a bogus visitation. There could be people intent on persuading us that MIB are real by acting out the legend based on the literature—presumably, jokers from the fringes of the UFO community. Whilst this may seem a somewhat absurd idea, we have to examine it carefully before interpreting the MIB data in more remarkable fashion.

GET OUT OF TOWN

In October 1973 there was a major wave of UFO sightings, mostly in the southern states of the USA. Cases included the alleged abduction of two fishermen by wrinkly-skinned entities who spacenapped the terrified witnesses from a wharf at Pascagoula, Mississippi.

There was also a little reported case of a motorist who observed a silver-suited figure walking along the side of the highway. It was little reported, because the case quickly proved to be a hoax, cashing in on all the previous media publicity. Yet it might have been the inspiration for what was to happen just a few days later at Falkville, Alabama. Local police chief Jeff Greenhaw received a call late on 17 October to describe a flashing UFO reported by an anonymous woman. She directed him to the site, but when he got there no UFO was to be seen. Nor, indeed, was there any sign of the caller. Instead, a figure in a silver suit stood by the roadside and glinted in the light from the patrol car.

Greenhaw, aware of all the recent UFO activity, as most people in the country would have been by then, took out his camera used to film accident scenes and snapped some photographs of the alien. These simply show someone—or something—in a silver suit. The entity then fled down a rutted, muddy side road, desperate to escape the police. Greenhaw attempted to give chase but lost the figure in the dark.

After the news of his sighting emerged, the police chief was subjected to a campaign, evidently designed to hound him out of town. His trailer home was burnt down by persons unknown. He received hate calls. After a series of further attacks it was soon mutually agreed that Greenhaw should leave office, although there never seems to have been any indication that he was not good at his job.

This Alabama police chief was surely the victim of a vendetta using the UFO mystery as a weapon to gain his removal from office. He was set up for a fall by someone who wanted him out of the job. The phone call was part of the plot, but other more drastic steps were used to follow through.

Such an incident has to infer the possibility that MIB visitations might on occasion be used by vindictive people in situations where an individual needs to be discredited for unexplained reasons.

CEASE UFO STUDY—OR ELSE!

In 1980 there was an excellent UFO group in Wiltshire known as SCUFORI. It was small but dedicated to serious research and determined to solve cases whenever it could. This six-man team was to have one quite remarkable brush with the MIB in a story of extraordinary determination.

It began on 18 August of that year when member Charlie

Affleck found a shrivelled plastic bag on his doorstep. It appeared to have been heated or even melted, but inside was a piece of paper with words written in yellow fluorescent ink, stating "Cease UFO Study. Do not meddle or else."

SCUFORI, being rational, ignored the threat, but a further letter soon arrived by post. In similar ink and style it said, "Beware. We are watching you all. Do not interfere. We will meet."

Within a week several group members began to receive phone calls. Up to 30 of these were eventually to be made, to all members of the group. After the first few came in most were tape recorded. An electronically synthesised voice was issuing various threatening messages.

After a harrowing trip to a wooded area at the behest of the calls (where group members heard gunshots that thankfully turned out to be a local landowner engaged in late night hunting!), SCUFORI decided to approach the Swindon police. Sadly, they could offer no help

Soon the scale of the threats began escalating. There was talk of destroying homes of the SCUFORI members—even death threats. The UFOlogists went back to the police hoping that with such clear evidence documented in writing and on tape the authorities would surely act. But the Swindon police insisted that unless any of the threats were actually carried out by the MIB they were powerless. They even refused a seemingly reasonable request to trace the origin of the frequent phone calls—something that would probably have been possible.

Detective Work

Forced to do their own detective work, SCUFORI realized that the inside knowledge displayed by the MIB suggested he might be a member of their group. Whilst all six of them trusted each other and each seemed genuinely baffled by the events, they soon realized that only one member had received no calls whenever anybody else was present. Then they realized that he had found messages and tapes on the ground "by fortune'' when the rest had missed them completely.

Suspicion now centered on this man, but they were sure that he would deny it all if confronted and the mystery would then never be resolved. On 1 December this member—possibly now alerted to the suspicions of his colleagues—claimed that he was stopped by a man dressed in black whilst walking to the group meeting. He allegedly touched the UFOlogist's arm near the pocket in which he was carrying the tape containing the MIB phone messages. This was melted to a frazzle.

Now determined to trap their phantom MIB, the group built a remarkable surveillance device and planted it at the rural meeting site chosen by their intimidator. This involved a camera and flash within a steel box buried in the ground with a concrete base. A trip mechanism would trigger if a tape message left for the MIB was collected. The camera and a flash would fire and the steel shutter would immediately come down, protecting the incriminating photograph that had just been taken. The concrete base made the construction so heavy that nobody could dig it up and carry it away.

This ingenuity was rewarded. A tape was left and the MIB did go to collect it. Furious efforts had been made to open the steel shutter. He clearly knew that he had been photographed and the concrete base had even been dug out and dragged several yards across the field. But the trap had worked. The evidence was still inside its protective sheath.

The photographic proof vindicated the group's suspicions. One of their own members had engaged in weeks of this sometimes vicious campaign to try to force them out of existence. But why? The man insisted that he was genuinely being harrassed by an MIB who had threatened that his own life would be made unpleasant unless he assured that SCUFORI closed down. Of course, if the group had been any less rational then this might well have been the outcome. Fortunately, the Swindon team were too sensible to be caught out.

THE APEN MYSTERY

If you think that the four months of antagonism faced by SCU-FORI represents a one-off within the UFO field, you would be wrong. There is an even more fantastic MIB-style vendetta against UFOlogy waged by a mysterious organisation calling itself APEN. (A full account of the APEN affair was published in 1986 in a series of articles for the now defunct magazine *The Unknown*.)

They made their presence felt in spring 1974 when I received a one hour cassette tape with an American voice announcing that he was J.T. Anderson, supreme commander of APEN (Aerial Phenomena Enquiry Network). That first APEN tape was full of TV and radio broadcasts on UFOs. Other voices from APEN intruded during the tape. They uttered short messages that were powerful, such as, "Beware—UFOs can be hostile!" There was also news that APEN Unit 23 was being set up to probe harrassment of UFOlogists by MIB. Aside from this odd mixture of advice, information, threats and bizarre organisational structure, the tape opened with the chimes of Big Ben, an extract from a German wartime propoganda broadcast and a Nazi party marching tune played loudly.

Most of us assumed that this was all a joke. But then the letters started to arrive. Between December 1974 and April 1975 I got several. Leaders of UFO groups in northern Britain got their own versions. The letters were on headed stationery but there was no address to reply to, as there had not been with the tapes. Nobody had any way to contact APEN. It was one-way traffic.

Frankly, the format of these typewritten letters was absurd. They were filled with pseudo-bureaucratic language such as "Code = 7= Case no 174L 74-71/349 ST. Classification now = Jasmine = Clearance date 02 DE 74." It all seemed very childish.

Suspecting that someone was trying to create disruption by targetting local groups who were then trying to work together, we mutually agreed to ignore APEN, hoping that if they failed to get attention they would eventually give up. However, APEN continued to send material to UFOlogists—including a startling report on a UFO landing case from January 1974 in north Wales.

The Landing

A good deal of information was offered about a supposed alien contact in which a "discoid, domed ball and tripod undercarriage" UFO had come down and entities from it had contacted a Mr. W. He was described as a retired professional army engineer, aged 58, with a wife and son (aged 25) living with him at his "large Welsh farmhouse at the base of the hill." The aliens were, quite incredibly, said to have given Mr. W the ex-directory telephone number of APEN and told him to contact them and them alone.

The rest of this absurd report lists demands for immediate assistance from APEN control—a "Land Rover (low wheel base), Theodolite, Stroboscope, Infra Red/Ultra Violet sensors and five walky-talkies." Four more APEN operatives are requested (at least one of whom is to be female) and facilities for regression hypnosis were required. Much as I was wont to dismiss this as pure fantasy, there was a problem—this case was real. On 23 January 1974 an explosion on Cader Bronwen (in the Berwyn Mountains near Bala) had sent people from the village of Llandrillo scurrying into the streets. Glowing lights were seen atop the nearby hill, but the matter was quickly written off by the RAF as being produced by a bright meteorite. No UFOlogist seemed to dispute that idea. But many of the details in the full APEN report matched, and they were claiming this was a UFO landing with major overtones.

As time has gone by, the Llandrillo case has risen dramatically in profile until in 1997 it almost ranks alongside the infamous Roswell crash from New Mexico. Thanks to efforts by local UFOlogist Margaret Fry, winning the confidence of numerous villagers, and a series of fortuitous leaks of data from sources unaware that they were adding pieces to a giant puzzle we know the following.

Something did crash on the mountain that night. A "military force" cordoned off the area using Land Rovers, theodolites and the like. Farmers were even barred from going onto the hillside to tend to their sheep. The district nurse sent up to join police in what they thought was the grim search for survivors to an aircrash were quickly denied access to a site where a strange craft was sitting on the ground. A local hotel reported a sudden influx of "men in suits" with English accents who filled the rooms (normally half empty in winter) and went onto the mountain at first light, returned at night, and stayed for a week. They refused to discuss what they were up to. A scientist measured unusually high levels of radiation on Cader Bronwen during a routine survey a week or two later. And a local doctor (unaware of any of the above information) had contacted the science editor of a national newspaper in 1992 to say that he had noted a big rise in the levels of childhood cancers in this area for reasons he could not explain. They had occured since the early to mid 1970s. This was becoming a big case.

Jokers or not, APEN were aware of the significance of this incident immediately after it happened, years before anybody else—except, possibly, the British government.

The Go-between

The threatening mood of APEN continued, even after they stopped contacting me—perhaps because I refused to take them seriously. Most worrying was an extract from what was purported to be the APEN magazine. It proved to be a Nazi party organ. The title translated into English as "Spearhead." UFOlogists received it, complete with further intimidating words.

But a new clue arrived in October 1975 when APEN came into the open for the first time. A stranger called me to say he was Peter Bottomley from Manchester. He had been interested in UFOs for several years but had just joined BUFORA in August. As he later explained in his written statement, "One night I was sitting at home watching TV. The kids were in

AERIAL PHENOMENA ENQUIRY NETWORK

REF :- A-b/b2-03

COPY OF INITIAL REPORT CONCERNING NORTH WALES LANDING. TRANSMITTED 24...AM.

. . . .

U.F.O.
PRIORY.
VIA T/P IINK 03.
PRIORITY ONE.
RELEASE AUTHORIZATION.....
TO REFERENCE CENTRE.
FROM :- AGENTS 71 & 349.
CASE No. 174L.74:71/349ST.

LOCALITY :- LLAN........ NORTH WALES.
INCIDENT :- LANDING AND CONTACT (ALMOST PROVEN).
RECOMMENDED ACTION :- "TIME REGRESSION" HYPNOSIS (A.S.A.P.).
DESCRIPTION OF OBJECT :- DISCOID, DOMED, BALL & TRIPOD UNDERCARRIAGE, 4 PORT
SIZE :- 20'0"X 50'.
COLOUR :- METALIC (POLISHED).

EXTRA EQUIPT. NEEDED :- LAND ROVER, TELESCOPIC STRETOSCOPES, (5).
AT WHAT DATE NEEDED :- TOMORROW (25 MAY 74).
NUMBER OF EXTRA PERSONNEL NEEDED :- .... D AT LEAST ONE TO BE FEMALE).
ANY OTHER COMMENTS :- REQUEST REA.... C INITIAL REPORT FORMS BE DELIVERED
TO MY HOME ADDRESS AS ... AT OF AGENT 349.

Having interviewed Mr. W....... at length (2½ hours) as instructed. he fou
to be very sincere. He was unshakable as far as his story is concerned and
description of the craft (and aliens) was more detailed than that to which
have become accustomed, perhaps this is because he is an ex-soldier/engineer
He described a typical "Adamski" Scout Ship with a few "extra" details. His
description of the Aliens was also reminiscent of Adamskis' Aliens. The des
cription was similar to the Lake District report and also the Rossendale Va.
area report (summer 1972). The Aliens are said to have spoken to him, give
ing instructions to contact us only and also furnished him with one of our X-D .

bed and my wife was visiting a friend. There was a knock at the door and on answering I saw two gentlemen whom I did not recognize. They announced themselves as 'APEN operatives' but preferred not to give names."

These two men were like typical MIB. They wore smart suits, claimed to be from some secret investigative body and looked quite human. Their talk was a mixture of logic and nonsense, Peter Bottomley did not see how they arrived, as he had assumed APEN were a well-known UFO group and this visit was quite mundane. He knew nothing of the previous 18 months of letters, tapes and threats.

According to these strangers, APEN was "a very widespread organisation with a headquarters in America." Their aim was simple—"to initiate and sustain a fully coordinated research/investigative network." The reason they had to stay undercover was because "they can operate more efficiently in this manner" and their "constitution" required it of them.

As Bottomley told me, "to me this all sounded reasonable." So he did not flinch when they explained that they had decided to pick a "neutral" to serve as their mediator. He was their choice, but they refused to tell him how he had been selected.

What APEN wanted Peter Bottomley to do was take an address to contact them and use their unlisted phone number. He would also be given a code that personally identified him to the organisation. He must swear to secrecy, but in exchange for acting as their go-between he would be paid "expenses" and be given "help" in his research.

These APEN "operatives" left, saying that they would contact Bottomley shortly for an answer. When he mentioned this

Opposite *One of the many mysterious letters sent to me from APEN in early 1975. It has all the usual James Bond style imagery found in their other letters and heard on their tapes and was typical in that it was untraceable to any source. It discusses the January 1974 UFO landing at Llandrillo in North Wales—an event then considered trivial by all except APEN but now seen as far more important by the UFO community. It appears to have had covert government agency associations—something quite unknown at the time.*

meeting to his immediate mentor in BUFORA (a man called Gordon Clegg, who was investigations' coordinator for the region) the newcomer was surprised by his relative lack of enthusiasm for the plan. When, as advised by Gordon, he phoned me and found my complete distrust of APEN, Peter was truly puzzled. The two men had seemed quite persuasive to him.

After discussing the issue with his wife, she summed it up by saying APEN seemed like children, and if Peter intended to be taken seriously for his UFO work then he would be advised to stay clear of them. Which is what he decided to do. When telephoned for his reply, he politely declined. APEN did not try to press him and seem never to have attempted this tactic again.

A few weeks later I moved house. Waiting to greet me was a "Welcome to Your New Home" card. It was from APEN and bore a sticker saying, "Never call anyone bigger than yourself stupid."

Sinister Overtones

After this strange affair APEN tactics became far more subtle and yet dangerous. A group in the East Midlands had stored UFO case files in a terraced house. One night there was a break-in. Nothing was stolen but the files were messed about to make it clear that someone had looked through them. A few days later an APEN letter arrived apologizing "for the actions of our local agents."

Another group in Leicester had even more trouble. They were visited by the police, demanding to know why they were reporting bogus UFO sightings. The group were not doing so, but the police insisted that their name and address was cited and they could be prosecuted for wasting police time. Soon afterward a letter arrived at the group. It was from APEN, again issuing an apology for the behavior of its local agents and saying that "photo identity cards" were going to be issued in future. Passport sized photographs of supposed local APEN operatives were sent out to several UFO associations after that.

Nobody has ever recognized any of these people.

I was dragged into the fray after a couple of years of such tactics, when I discovered by accident that several people had stopped communicating with me because of the "letters" I had sent to them. Only after much effort did I get to see one of these letters. It possessed a signature with a passing resemblance to my own. The letter was offering these people a job in a top secret government sponsored UFO group. All they had to do in return was withdraw from normal UFO research and tell nobody what they were doing. Naturally the recipients assumed that I had sent this and if I was offering them the chance to join the élite I must be some secret agent too and was not to be trusted.

APEN have never completely disappeared from the scene. From time to time stories of new activities come to light. In 1980 I received phone calls from people wanting to join APEN. They had been given my phone number to apply for this in a local newspaper ad!

Then they contacted one group in the mid to late 1980s regarding the famous UFO sightings connected with a US Air Force base in Rendlesham Forest, Suffolk. They wanted this group to get me to meet APEN in the dead of night at a railway station miles from home to discuss "the truth." That, apparently, had something to do with a secret government plan to create fake UFOs. I was not foolish enough to agree to this bizarre nocturnal invitation.

THE UFO MADHOUSE

It would be easy to read all sorts of sinister things into some of these activities—to think that some government agency was using sophisticated tactics to try to blacken the name of serious witnesses or objective UFO groups. Perhaps the whole point is to prevent them from working together and to sow seeds of doubt about their true allegiance to maximise disruption.

Of course, that is all possible. However, the UFO world contains some very strange characters, and the simplest explanation for many of these things is that they are responsible. The activities of APEN—just like the member of SCUFORI who acted as an MIB—probably result from twisted ideas of what is fun by someone attracted to the UFO community.

That we need to be careful of making prejudgments regarding exotic explanations is shown by one case from Heywood in Lancashire that occurred in May 1989. Strange lights had appeared over a housing estate and were witnessed by many people, including the staff at an ambulance station and a police patrol brought from the adjacent station house. The lights were not especially spectacular. Because of the objective stance that NARO has taken in attempting to explain UFO sightings, the police called us in immediately after the sighting (at 4 A.M. in fact!). Within 24 hours we had solved the case, thanks to the support of Manchester Airport air traffic control, radar operators based there, weather centers and great assistance from Jodrell Bank, who ran a special computer programme to assist our investigation.

Although we took this case step by step and eventually demonstrated (to a reasonable level of confidence) that the UFOs were a mirage of stars low over the hills disorted by a weather phenomenon known as a temperature inversion layer, the media were not so easily dissuaded. They featured the story before the investigation was complete and could not wait even one day for the outcome as UFO news is news to them only when it happens. So, whilst NARO members (Peter Hough and two other men) were interviewing police and ambulance workers on site about the way in which the ambulance station phone had "stopped working" during the encounter, and I was chasing the scientific data to verify our theoretical solution, the press were talking spaceships. This inevitably attracted other UFOlogists to Heywood.

One such group was later to publish the startling news that the police and witnesses from the emergency services had apparently been silenced by MIB within hours of the sighting. This conclusion arose because they had visited the site on the evening after the events and these witnesses had decided not to proceed with the investigation. Men in Black were known to be to blame as this UFO group had seen three of them—complete with the usual attire of smart dark suits—leaving the building just as they had arrived to try to talk to the witnesses.

Unfortunately, the truth is considerably more mundane. These three MIB certainly did exist. They had also visited the witnesses and were possibly even responsible for their subsequent silence. But this was not as a result of any dark threats. It was because the three men had explained about the possible solution to this case and identified the reason why the phone had stopped working. A radio station had called the ambulance crew to do a ''live'' report whilst the UFOs flickered in the sky for more than an hour. It appeared that the radio office had failed to replace the receiver in their studio for a short time, making the ambulance phone temporarily unusable through perfectly explicable factors.

I know all of this to be correct because we can positively identify these particular MIB. They were the smartly dressed—and far from intimidating—men from NARO, who were engaged in a very sensible investigation of this case. It is all too easy to see conspiracies where none exist.

13

EVIDENCE
OF ALIENS

Although MIB cases are undoubtedly very strange and feature some degree of complexity in their occurrence, very little has been reported in this book so far which could not be put down to terrestrial forces. By that I mean either some government agency that is investigating UFOs (in an admittedly bizarre manner) or cranks and crackpots who might be clinging to the perceived glory of the UFO community and engaging in some sort of fantastic party trick.

However, there are some incidents where it is difficult to imagine any human being as responsible. If these are being reliably reported, then they may offer that elusive evidence that points toward something more alien being involved.

DOCTOR IN THE HOUSE

In September 1976 Dr. Herbert Hopkins, physician of Orchard Beach, Maine, USA, had minimal awareness of MIB and UFOs. What little he did know about UFOs had come about because a friend had asked him to investigate an incident that befell local man David Stephens the year before. Along with another witness, Stephens had encountered strange lights in a wood at the nearby town of Oxford.

This October 1975 case is well respected in UFO circles. Stephens and his friend (who became so distressed after the events that he packed up and shipped out of town) lost time after encountering floating lights on a late night drive. They then suffered what can only be described as hallucinogenic after-effects, spending some hours drifting in and out of a peculiar state of consciousness and seeing things which were definitely not present (such as indoor snowflakes).

There is no evidence that these witnesses were under the influence of any substance and they knew as well as anybody that they were "seeing things," which is not suggestive of someone rather the worse for wear. Some force had seemingly altered their perception of reality in an astonishing manner and not unlike the "Oz Factor" (see p. 107) which precedes many close encounters.

Hopkins' task in the aftermath of these events was to check out the witness, attest to his mental welfare and then use regression hypnosis to see if memories of the missing time could be coaxed out from his subconscious. It will be little surprise that such memories were brought forth—and Stephens recounted a classic abduction story of being in the presence of small alien beings with heads shaped like lightbulbs that were carrying out tests on the two men.

Dr. Hopkins had no real idea how to interpret all of this. But he was happy to cooperate when on 11 September (the only evening he chanced to be home on his own in quite some time) he received a phone call from an outside phone booth and the man announced that he was with the New Jersey UFO Research Organisation. He wanted to come and chat with the doctor about the Stephens case—after assuring himself that Hopkins was alone.

No sooner had Hopkins agreed to this and switched on the living room light to set things up than the "UFOlogist" was seen to be approaching the front door. In retrospect Hopkins realized this was amazingly fast. He could not even have got there from the main road, let alone the nearest phone booth, in the few seconds involved.

However, this minor puzzle was put aside and the doctor let the stranger in, despite his odd appearance. It was only later (as so many MIB witnesses have reported) that Hopkins realized just how out of character was his own behavior on that evening.

To say the visiting UFO enthusiast was odd is perhaps an understatement. He was dressed entirely in black and looked like an undertaker. When he took off his hat he revealed a bald head but he also had no eyebrows or lashes. He also wore lipstick on a very pale face, as proven later when it smeared on the back of his glove as he wiped his mouth.

In fact, as Dr. Hopkins noted with astonishment, the lipstick was "drawn on" to the man's chalk white face as if to imitate lips. There were no real lips at all. He looked just like a china doll wearing clothes so clean and fresh that they might have come from a store window dummy.

Batteries Not Supplied

The stranger spoke with a flat monotone in perfect English, allowing the doctor to relate the sighting back to him and detail his investigation of it. Once the story was told, this encounter quickly went into real X File territory.

Now the MIB announced that the doctor had only two coins in his left pocket. Indeed he had. He was asked to take one out, and brought out a one cent piece. Holding this between his fingers, the stranger asked Hopkins to watch the coin as if he were about to perform a magic trick.

Then, as Hopkins reports, "It suddenly began to develop a silvery color—and the silver became blue, and then I had trouble focusing. I could focus on my hand perfectly well—that was my reference point—but the coin was simply gone. Not abruptly. It simply slowly dematerialised—it just wasn't there any more, I didn't smell anything. I didn't feel anything. I didn't hear anything."

Hopkins reports that he noticed the weight of the coin gradually vanishing. He is sure it was not sleight of hand. He saw it literally vanish on the spot. The MIB made some curious remark that "nobody in this plane" would ever see the coin again. Then he asked the doctor if he had heard of a famous

UFO witness who had recently died but had lived nearby. Dr. Hopkins agreed he had heard the name but had never met the man and knew nothing of his death. The man in black said, "Just as you do not have a coin, so he no longer has a heart."

The threat was implicit but obvious. Whilst the facts of the death of this witness do not support this frightening allegation, Herbert Hopkins did not know the details at the time and was understandably spooked. Immediately he agreed to the request politely made of him by the man who now was very obviously *not* a UFOlogist. This was that he should destroy all of the tapes made during the interviews with David Stephens. Not only did Hopkins demagnetise them but he physically got rid of all records on the case. Days later—when rationality returned—the MD began to see the folly of what he had done. The Stephens' case was already public knowledge. No purpose was served by his act.

At the conclusion of the session the man began to talk in a curious way. His voice slowed down like a battery tape recorder needing a recharge. "My—energy—is—running—low—must—go—now—goodbye," he said and left.

Hopkins watched him walk out, negotiating the steps as if they were the slopes of Everest, and clinging to the wall at the side of the house for a long time before turning the corner. Moments later a very brilliant bluish/white light—too bright to be a car headlight—sped laterally across the front of the house.

Needless to say, there was no New Jersey UFO Research Organisation and the identity of this man remains a mystery. In so far as Herbert Hopkins is concerned this MIB was not a visitor from the secret services or some government investigation unit. Although we might imagine that all of these oddities could be reproduced (perhaps even the disappearing coin was just a trick), the doctor is adamant that what he witnessed was not humanly possible. "There are other dimensions," he concludes. "I think this man was undoubtedly from such a place."

A MUNDANE CASE

We may have to take Hopkins' idea about other dimensions
seriously when we consider the following case. Unfortunately,
I must protect the individuals involved for reasons that will be
explained. But I had sufficient association with this case to
confirm that the story is genuine.

It began in late August 1971 in a major town in the East
Midlands of England. The witness, Jim Wilson, had observed
a white light moving slowly across the sky. It appeared to be
a completely mundane sighting and on its own would not generate much interest amongst even the most enthusiastic UFOlogist.

Yet, rather curiously, two men arrived at Wilson's house.
They drove in a dark car and wore smart business suits. Flashing identification cards, the men announced that they were
with the Ministry of Defence and asked Jim to recount his
sighting. Then they politely instructed him that he might as
well forget all about the event because they had identified the
light as a Russian satellite called Cosmos 408, which was passing over his town at that time.

Superficially, this explanation made much sense and I would
have been inclined to accept it. The white light seen by the
witness resembled an earth-orbiting satellite. But what did not
jell was the extraordinary decision of the MoD to send two
men to interrogate a witness and give him this news first hand.
If the sighting was easily explained, why investigate at all?
More importantly, why not simply write to Jim Wilson and
tell him this fact, as is customary practice even with UFO
groups, let alone the MoD.

Some time later I was able to talk with Ralph Noyes (see
Chapter 15), who was in charge of the MoD UFO investigation team at this particular time. He is adamant that he sent
nobody to the East Midlands and has no knowledge of these
alleged visitors in this case. Moreover, as my alert colleague
Derek James could soon calculate, by checking with the satellite information center then based in Farnborough, Cosmos
408 was over Canada at the time of the sighting and had not

passed over England at all. The MIB's seemingly plausible explanation would have convinced most witnesses. Yet it was a sham.

But who would want to invent such an explanation—and why? Jim Wilson's sighting by any UFO criteria ought to be of no interest to MIB if they are government investigators. Cases like it happen every day and 99.9 percent of them have simple explanations. Even those that do not are hardly going to change the world.

The MoD responded to Derek James' request for information with their usual sidestep, saying "we investigate reports to see if there are any defense implications." They declined to answer the more direct question as to who had visited Jim Wilson with MoD identification cards?

Casing the Joint

However, once again this case was about to head for the Twilight Zone without a passport. The terrified witness called to report that his house was being stalked by a black Jaguar car (just as Cadillac seem to supply American MIBs, Jaguars are the vehicle of choice for their UK equivalent!). Inside the Jaguar were two men. They parked outside Wilson's home at night and he was sure they must be watching him.

After discussion as to what to do next, a plan was hatched. Derek James had by chance a relative who was a high ranking police officer in the East Midlands town in question. It was not thought prudent to ask the police to investigate an MIB case. Nor was it considered likely they would take the prospect very seriously. However, by good fortune Jim Wilson lived quite near a major toy manufacturing company, and it seemed not unreasonable to suggest to the police that the two men in the car (who by now had been parked outside for several successive nights) might be "casing the joint" with a view to planning a robbery at the factory.

A police patrol car was duly asked to keep a look out on 19 October. The Jaguar was there, waited half an hour or so and then drove off. On 20 October the same thing happened, and the car registration and other details were recorded. A subsequent check found that the vehicle did not exist, and by now the police were really interested. So, at 9:05 P.M. on 21 October, the police patrol was instructed to bring in the occupants of the Jaguar for questionning by the CID.

The patrol car parked on the main road out of sight of the Jaguar so as not to alert its occupants. Following standard procedure the two bobbies walked toward it—one either side—and got to within a few inches. They were just about to knock on the window and question the driver and his passenger. Although they could see little in the dark, the two men inside were smartly dressed.

Suddenly, the car disappeared. It literally just melted away into nothingness in front of the two terrified police officers. When they regained their senses a search was made of the area, but they were in no doubt that the vehicle and the two men had simply vanished on the spot.

After discussions between the officers and their senior, a "cover story" was decided upon. It was not thought wise—or indeed possible—to enter into the logs that a suspect vehicle and its occupants was last seen heading for another dimension. As one put it, "This isn't the Starship Enterprise. What we write has to be possible in the real world."

I can hardly blame them for that. Unfortunately, of course, it makes this case hard for anyone to verify. But, given the obvious similarity with the disappearing coin trick engineered by the MIB who called on Herbert Hopkins, it might suggest that we should think again about the prospect that these visitors are from Whitehall or the Pentagon.

FROM OTHER WORLDS

The idea that these MIB might be paraphysical or interdimensional visitors is so fantastic that we cannot just accept it, in the way that we might be prepared to accept some government department nosing into UFOs. We can prove that government departments exist. But other dimensions are at best a scientific theory. Unfortunately, we cannot just ignore the uncomfortable bits of evidence because we do not like them.

The image on the Jim Templeton photograph still has to be explained. That it was some momentary penetration from an alternative dimension is as feasible as any theory the rationalists have come up with. And many have tried. Certainly that being was not a man from the ministry.

Equally, there are cases where too much knowledge of an individual appears to be in the possession of the MIB. They know not only about their sighting but intimate details of the witness's life—the sort of thing that even widescale phone tapping, bugs in every living room and spies in all the UFO groups in the kingdom could not explain.

Then again, the story told by people like Cynthia Appleton in Birmingham is very hard to entertain as any kind of role-play by some ministerial employee. Once again we have a figure materialising and dematerialising as if that were just as easy as switching on a light, although later modes of arrival through this inter-dimensional portal were by way of the more earthly big black car.

John Keel reports that there are a number of recorded instances throughout history where important discoveries seem to have been handed to individuals by mysterious strangers who simply disappeared. He cites the example of Thomas Jefferson, who reputedly received the "Great Seal," part of the United States regalia, when a man dressed in black turned up in his garden and gave it to him.

Crazy as this sounds, I have come across just such a situation. A man (whom I always considered to be an ordinary man interested in UFOs but who professed to be an alien) persuaded my colleague Peter Warrington and I to arrange a meeting with one of the country's leading experimental physicists. We felt complete idiots making the request and expected to be told that we were crackpots. Instead, the scientist invited us to his laboratory at a London University college.

The three of us went down there and spent a fascinating day. The scientist demonstrated a form of free gravity device that he was attempting to perfect and which appeared to rely upon a novel understanding of energy. After telling us to keep his identity secret until he was ready to face the world (a request we have always complied with), he then announced that he was given research that set him on this path by a man who professed to be an alien. He had no idea if this person really was from Mars or from Millwall, but he was evidently able to offer useful scientific ideas.

The "alien" that we brought with us added a new batch of inter-dimensional physics to this scientist's notebook. Although we could not decipher if it was gibberish or brilliance, the scientist seemed intrigued by the data. We went home not much the wiser, but mindful of the motto that there are indeed more things in heaven and earth than we can dream of in our philosophy.

All of this could no doubt be explained in mundane ways. But "strangers in our midst" who "direct the flow" of human knowledge are far more common than you might think. Several UFOlogists have mentioned similar incidents to me.

Of course, the scientists involved in these secret confrontations prefer not to talk about these things, because they have to live in the mundane reality of research grants and university tenures where one whiff that your work is based on help from another dimension and you might as well fill out your P 45.

Who can say what the truth is, but perhaps we should not be quite so scornful of this fantastic possibility.

14

A HISTORY
IN BLACK

We face a challenge if we are to accept that reports of MIB encounters are real and thus require some sort of explanation. The stark choice seems to be between meetings with sinister government agents or some sort of "alien" with the ability to appear in human form. But in order to determine which option works best the antiquity of the MIB legend becomes important.

It is often assumed that MIB stories are a product of the space age, post-dating the Second World War and only contemporary with modern versions of UFO and alien sightings. This would certainly favor the idea of some kind of secret investigative unit of earthly origin that is following through on close encounters for their own reasons. However, there are some grounds for suspecting that this might *not* be the case. There are stories not greatly removed from today's meetings with MIB that exist far into the past.

Indeed there are countless legends about sinister figures whose origin is uncertain—people who seem to act in an intimidating manner or issue threats of silence against those whom they choose to contact. Such episodes have been reported throughout history and may possibly be relevant to the debate in hand. But it is wise to be cautious, because the context of these old stories can be very difficult to define. It is often couched in the mythology and superstition of the day, and little more than a century ago bizarre beliefs were still remarkably dominant amongst large sections of the community.

Telling which—if any—of these centuries-old incidents reflect a reality (as opposed to a fantasy or some collective mythology) is far less straightforward than with more recent evidence.

A FAIRY STORY

Almost every culture on earth has a belief in other-worldly entities that sit between man and the angels in terms of physical and spiritual evolution. So widespread are these beliefs that folklorists struggle to understand the origins—if not, as the legends themselves usually allege, based upon a reality defined by actual eye-witness accounts. Astonishingly, claimed meetings with these strange denizens of some other dimension do still occasionally surface today.

In 1976 veteran folklorist Katherine Briggs published a 500-page compendium with potted descriptions of some of the more significant of this hierarchy of beings. Her title, *A Dictionary of Fairies*, uses the modern word that conjures up rather misleading impressions about these entities. However, as she notes, these beings are of widely differing appearance and character and are more correctly known as "elementals," because they seem to live between the elements of the natural world—the solidity of earth and the refinement of air—and are therefore largely invisible to ordinary mortals.

It seems that only those gifted with "second sight" can see these entities for much of the time—which is fascinating, given the way in which we are discovering that the same clue demarks potential witnesses to today's so-called alien contacts. We might even speculate that these beings are one and the same.

Moreover, fairies were not what you might imagine them to be. The word does not even derive from a particular type of elemental. Instead, it relates to the practice of *fae-erie*—or enchantment—imposed by these mystical creatures. The elementals could make their victims enter what we now recognize as both an altered state of consciousness and a form of hypnotic trance. In this state time slowed down and strange things happened, such as sounds of the environment suddenly disappearing—at least according to documented reports down through the ages.

This is remarkably like the condition UFOlogists call the "Oz Factor," to describe those claims of witnesses meeting UFOs or aliens and entering an altered state during close encounters. It is also intriguingly akin to the various hints about hypnotic conditioning during MIB visits where the intimidators are allowed to enter a home against the will of the victims. Indeed these people often seem to have no control over their own mental state, as if they are indeed under "enchantment."

ELEMENTALLY SPEAKING

In folklore and gathered stories of supposed real-life meetings across hundreds of years, these elementals were reported to perform a wide range of tasks that are most interesting in the light of MIB cases in this book. They abducted young women for the purposes of enhancing the "fairy race" through childbirth. They had the ability to disguise themselves as anything from hairy monsters to ordinary looking humans who could walk the streets without fear of being recognized. These entities could also bestow gifts, in terms of knowledge of the future and powerful visions—although these were not always to prove true visions, of course, because the fairies were intent on deception. This all sounds rather familiar from our study of aliens and MIB.

If a person did not do as they were told by elementals, then they would meet with ill fortune and various attacks remarkably like the poltergeist phenomena reported by some victims of UFO encounters. Objects would move about rooms, numerous small fires would be ignited indoors or pools of water would appear in the middle of the house. You crossed these ethereal beings at your peril.

There are also fascinating reports of horses and carts being stopped in the presence of these beings—rather like today's stories of cars being stalled and suddenly transported to a different location thanks to aliens. Indeed at the very spot where Peter Taylor suffered three days of vehicle interference in 1973 (in Daresbury, Cheshire), there are older stories in which fairies were said to interfere with the passage of travelers. It is almost as if we have simply substituted an extraterrestrial species of elemental for the fairies, goblins and demons of the past.

As can be surmised from the fact that elementals and humans supposedly interacted in a very physical way in these stories, they were certainly more like us than popular children's tales lead you to expect. In fact, those "fairy story" images of tiny little beings floating on wings or hiding under toadstools date from the Victorian era when the church tried to outlaw belief in non-Godly forces and started the process with the young. It was propaganda (hence the now derogatory meaning of the phrase "fairy story" as an untrue account), not a representation of reality (even a mythical reality).

In truth, there were two major types of elemental creature, albeit given a host of names in cultures all over the world. One group of elfin beings were about three feet tall but otherwise fairly human-like and playful rather than wicked. They often kidnapped humans and took them to "a strange world." They also stole items from the possession of those who saw them. Other elementals were tall and dark and rather more sinister in nature. Their purpose was more difficult to define.

The imagery of today's UFO world seems curiously apt, with the little "grays" that abduct folk and the men-in-black who join in to stifle any research immediately afterwards. One could look at the comparisons and wonder if we are indeed playthings of the gods.

MEN IN BLACK MAGIC

Researcher Peter Hough has investigated early accounts of supernatural events that were attributed to the power of evil spirits whilst writing his book entitled *Witchcraft: A Strange Conflict*. Events that were on the one hand interpreted as the act of a "possessed" soul could on other occasions be seen as the intervention of elemental beings.

One of the cases Hough researched came from medieval times and is cited from French court records of 1603. A young boy in a wooded rural area was tried for murder. He had kidnapped a child and then killed him in a wanton act of violence hard for the people of that age to accept from someone expected to be quite "innocent." The youth defended his actions by saying that evil forces commanded him to kill.

Of course, this is a comment that has been repeated many times down through the centuries. Serial killers even today often suggest that voices or dark apparitions have appeared and told them they must commit their heinous crimes. A form of hypnotic control—such as that exhibited by the MIB—is also commonly alleged, as if that made it impossible to resist these evil urgings.

This French youth maintained he had seen a stranger who was specific in insisting what must be done. From religious teachings he "knew" this was Satan, who appeared in the form of a tall man with dark complexion and dressed in black. Of course in today's culture we might impose a different perspective on this same experience, adopting the now stereotypical idea that this figure was an MIB.

Researcher Janet Bord has drawn our attention to other similarities through many reports of the supernatural at large in the centuries before "enlightenment" dawned on the world. For example, Lancashire witch Margaret Johnson told of how she was visited by a "devil in the similitude and proportion of a man, apparelled in a suit of black." This was during the seventeenth century. The Man in Black in this case issued threats and warnings that she must obey his orders or suffer

the consequences. Other such episodes like this are not difficult to trace in the annals of medieval history.

THE HIDDEN RACE

Much of our knowledge of these elementals in the western
world comes from Scottish church minister Robert Kirk, who
wrote *The Secret Commonwealth* in 1691. This epic work told
of what he had uncovered from eyewitness accounts reported
by local people. He learned, for example, that the beings often
appeared in disguise because they love to deceive those who
meet them. He also reported that they had the ability to become insubstantial and pass through solid objects or disappear
suddenly. Again, these attributes are often found in connection
with today's UFO entities.

Researchers like Kirk, who over the next two hundred years
attempted to document reports of elementals, faced an unexpected problem. Witnesses were often scared to talk. Those
who did reveal their contacts sometimes explained that these
beings visited their homes and warned them to stay silent. If
they disobeyed they would suffer. This certainly has a familiar
ring to it. As poet and writer W.B. Yeats warned of these
elementals in a manuscript on fairy lore that he wrote in 1888,
"[they] are very secretive, and much resent being talked of."

Indeed, the Reverend Kirk paid a heavy price for his research. It appears that just as modern day UFOlogists sometimes report MIB threats that they must cease investigations,
so too did he offend the elementals with his furious attempts
to expose their reality. Although the beings warned the minister to be silent, he refused to be coerced by their threats. His
body was found soon afterwards, dumped beside a fairy knoll
at Aberfoyle. In legend it has certainly been attributed to the
wrath of the beings he had become so obsessed with proving
to the world.

THE DEVIL AND HIS DISGUISES

As time has progressed there is evidence that the elementals have continued to manifest in ways that were contemporary and relevant to the era in question.

In the Victorian period, for example, there were many tales about the deeds of "Spring Heeled Jack"—a sinister apparition that had the ability to leap great distances,—even from rooftop to rooftop. Jack was always dressed in black (but his clothing was Victorian). Those who suffered his attacks claimed he had eyes of fire and spat blue flames just like the devil himself.

Of course, in these reports it was a devil steeped in the melodrama popular for the day and which presaged the horrors of the Whitechapel murders where, for a time, the idea that "Jack the Ripper" *was* "Spring Heeled Jack" turned vicious killer was even mooted. Nobody was ever apprehended for the "Spring Heeled Jack" attacks and the sightings—which spanned several decades—gradually faded. The last known appearance was in Liverpool in 1904.

Researcher John Keel, an American investigator of modern day "Men in Black" stories, spent much time in the study of ancient magical texts. He has argued that the devil has *always* appeared in a variety of deceitful shapes (like Jack), according to the differing traditions all over the world. Indeed, just as "God" is widely believed but takes on many different perspectives from culture to culture, so the devil is an equaly powerful symbol regarded as capable of visiting earth in a humanoid form.

"The devil and his demons can, according to the literature, manifest themselves in almost any form and can physically imitate anything from angels to horrifying monsters with glowing eyes," Keel says. To Keel, there is some force co-existing with us on earth that is to blame. Indeed, he believes, these elementals have always shared our planet but constantly manipulate the way in which people have perceived them. They enjoy impressing us with the wrong idea. He named his opus on the theme "Operation Trojan Horse," sensing some kind of large scale infiltration plan at work.

Be it the devil, fairy folk, alien day trippers or interfering Men in Black, according to Keel's view of the universe this was all part of some diabolical scheme with the intent to mislead. It is a ploy that has gone on throughout the ages and our view today that "aliens" have landed is every bit as much a deception as Spring Heeled Jack in 1897 or men from the ministry suppressing UFO data in 1997.

THE NAME GAME

Nigel Kneale's fictional story based on fact, "*Quatermass and the Pit*," was first seen as a TV serial on the BBC in 1958 and remade ten years later as a chilling Hammer horror movie. Kneale developed the story from the concept of this demonic interference in the affairs of mankind as witnessed through the idea of "Devil Names."

He talks of goblin-like creatures being seen in the vicinity of a London underground station when improvements were being made to the line. The station is presumed to be named after a famous cricketer called Hobbs but (as research soon shows) was formerly spelled with just one "b" as Hobs. This name was coined hundreds of years ago because of dark spirits in the form of small, ugly creatures (hobgoblins) that had plagued the area. They were frequently being seen by the locals, notably whenever some disturbance of the ground was underway—such as digging a well or building the underground railway during Victorian times.

Real evidence has demonstrated that outbursts of demonic forces such as these do erupt in certain locations (especially, as Kneale indicates, when some force or pressure is applied to the ground). They have done so throughout history and still do today. Of course we have sublimated the hobgoblins and demons of the past into the aliens of the present.

Historical research into centers of paranormal activity has found it useful to pay attention to the names ascribed to such locations by those who have lived there across the centuries. A name associated with the devil, demons, goblins or the like usually implies that this place has long been recognized as the focal point of supernatural happenings.

Such "devil names"—as they are called by American researcher Loren Coleman—certainly exist in real life and not merely within Kneale's perceptive story.

We have already come upon the area on the banks of the Mersey in north Cheshire which has generated very strange stories for as far back as people can recall. A fiery dragon was reported during the Middle Ages to have landed in woods around what is now Runcorn and Frodsham. Then people were abducted from local roads by evil spirits and lost all track of time. The village of Daresbury, centered on the Ring O' Bells inn, is one of the most favored spooky spots that—like its many counterparts around the world—is more formally known to researchers as a "window area."

Today the weird occurrences continue in about one hundred "windows" recognized by researchers across the planet, with tales of missing time, abduction by aliens and fiery lights in the sky. Yet this interpretation of events is—as Keel suggested—probably no more than today's illusion.

THE DEVIL LIVES HERE

Loren Coleman has identified many window areas where far more strange things have occurred than chance (or statistics) should dictate. Often he has done so by way of seeking out the "devil names" attached to the area by frightened residents hundreds of years ago. At that time, of course, the paranormal was not a passport onto TV or radio talk shows but a source of true supernatural dread.

These locations with "devil names" do seem to be liberally scattered around the world. Coleman notes, for example, that ominous black creatures have been reported frequently in parkland east of San Francisco, California. Sightings congregate in the so-called Devil's Hole and on the slopes of Mount Diablo (Spanish for devil).

Another area he has researched is the Devil's Lake area of Wisconsin. Here there have been reports ranging from lake monsters to dark prowling terrors that scare campers at night. Indian legends also tell of a maiden who was driven by some sinister force to throw herself from a cliff.

We also have seen UFOs, aliens and MIB recorded in locations such as Draguinan (Dragon Town) in France, focusing on the slopes of what has come to be called "The Evil Mountain." Visitations by Men in Black are recorded in almost all of these areas which seem to have attracted "devil names." Can this merely be coincidence?

An example of this in action concerns a window area on the mid-Wales coast, where at the turn of the century strange lights were seen moving about the skies. They were popularly attributed to the work of a local woman, Mary Jones, who was leading a religious revival amongst the small village communities when they were still in many ways decades behind the rest of the world.

The media were fascinated by the crusade of this lay preacher and the "miracles" seemingly associated with her, although in his marvelous study of the events (*Stars and Rumours of Stars*) researcher Kevin McClure has noted how the balls of light that rolled along hillsides were remarkably like the "earthlights" said to inhabit "window areas" all over the planet and believed by many UFO experts to be a natural atmospheric process generated by the local rocks when under strain.

The mid-Wales lights have continued to be seen long after Mary Jones and her revival were forgotten. Other strange events have also been recorded, ranging from alien abductions to a local sea monster that has appeared from time to time at Barmouth.

Then, in 1995 and 1996, a local land conservation officer began to investigate stories from walkers that the hills were literally humming. Using monitoring equipment, he did indeed establish that some kind of local frequency emission was being generated by the earth itself and was being heard—as a humming noise—if you stood at the focal point of its strongest emissions.

Nor have MIB been absent. For instance, during the height of the religious revival in 1905 a woman reported how "a man dressed in black" had appeared inside her house as if he were suddenly transported there. He told her "secrets" that she was instructed not to reveal.

VICTORIAN ALIENS

Around the time of this revival, through the autumn of 1896 and the spring of 1897, the first real UFO encounters in any modern sense occurred in waves, first across the far western USA and then in the mid-western states. People saw gigantic floating airships of fantastic design well ahead of the then current technology but akin to the science-fiction of the day as popularised in stories by Jules Verne.

Again we see an example of John Keel's thesis that the elementals are shape-shifters who change their appearance to suit the expectations of the day. If we were *inventing* a presence that was visiting us from beyond—perhaps as a part of our collective unconscious—then inevitably its form would adapt to the rapid progress that we have made in understanding and in technology.

Reports of "airship pilots" (the Victorian equivalent of aliens) were also made, and these usually entailed conversations in which bearded men admitted that the sightings were a result of their own fabulous invention. It would all be revealed to the world very soon, but of course never was.

There were also stories of strangers who turned up in the wake of airship sightings and then just as mysteriously disappeared. Often this was after an episode where physical evidence of some form had been left behind. For example in one case some pieces of metal or fabric reputedly rained down on farmland after an overflight by one of the airships. These were collected by the townsfolk, but a stranger then appeared, claimed the metal as his own and fled the scene, taking with him any proof that the event had ever happened. As you have seen, this behavior occurs today in connection with many MIB events. The procurement of physical evidence often seems to be the primary reason for the visits.

Airship reports spread from the USA to Britain during 1909 and 1913. The fear was mounting that real airship technology, by then in its infancy, might be exploited by the Imperial Germans for spying missions on Britain. This fuelled the paranoia. Research by Granville Oldroyd and Nigel Watson into some of the British airship encounters was published in *Magonia* magazine.

The peak of the 1909 wave centered on East Anglia in mid-May and generated a fascinating MIB episode. On 7 May at 10:30 pm a man called Egerton Free was locking his beach-front house at Clacton-on-Sea, Essex, when a cigar-shaped object hovered above nearby cliffs. After some minutes it drifted away to the north-east. In daylight the next morning Mrs. Free discovered fragments of steel and rubber with words on the side that appeared to be German. Naturally they assumed that this was from the overflying airship which had been spying on a land it planned to invade. In fact, later events suggested that this debris might have been part of a Royal Navy air target.

News of the sighting appeared in the local paper on 15 May and the very next day two strangers turned up at the Frees' isolated home. They did not make themselves known but inspected the surroundings for a considerable time, paying attention to the stables where the material was stored. After several hours the Frees' servant was forced to disturb these men on her way to church. She heard them jabbering to one another in a peculiar accent, using words she did not recognize. Then they approached her, walked on either side of her and began to talk in a bizarre manner. At this point she became quite terrified and fled back to the sanctuary of the house. The men then disappeared.

History was to prove that the Germans were *not* using airships to spy over Britain as was feared. So what was going on here? Did the elementals mold themselves to fit the pattern of the day so that the visiting strangers appeared contemporary and not wildly out of place? If so, they still displayed the typical eccentricity so often reported today within tales of the Men in Black.

OUT OF TIME

During the Second World War a truly strange case occurred which today we would have no difficulty slotting into a more modern framework. Back then, of course, it was simply weird. It was reported to me by a man called Bernard from a small town amidst the south Pennine Hills. Although the incident occurred in 1942 it was etched on his mind so firmly that he has spent decades visiting doctors, psychiatrists, in fact anybody who might be able to help, before being led almost in desperation to a UFO researcher, hoping that I might provide the key to a mystery that he has never resolved.

That summer he had befriended a girl of his own age (11) with the delightfully symbolic name of Angela Shine. She had been evacuated from Surrey. They climbed a local hill to look for spent bullets one hot day and were suddenly overcome by a sense of peace that caused them to enter a trance-like state. Bernard's account is almost exactly like many tales of trips into fairyland or the tale of Rip van Winkle falling asleep for many years.

Suddenly they found themselves on the grass surrounded by two men who talked of the two children in a curious manner. "Here they are . . . They are beautiful children, aren't they?" they said. Then they began to chat to one another in a strange way, discussing what appeared to be the nature of time.

When it was clear that Bernard and Angela were aware of their presence the men began to tell them about the future and promised that they would meet again, without specifying how or when. These are all things we are well used to hearing from today's alien abductees.

Bernard asked these men who they were and they looked

at one another, smiling, as if perhaps thinking of an explanation that might be acceptable to these children. ''I come from a long way away,'' one of the men said, staring at the sky almost wistfully as he did so.

But these two strangers also issued the classic MIB warning. ''Do not tell anyone that you have seen us. Whatever the pressure you are put under to tell, you *must* not do so.'' A bright light then enveloped the two children and they evidently fell asleep.

Awaking soon after, or so they thought, Bernard and Angela set off to walk down the hill, as they had promised only to be away from home for a couple of hours. As they walked Bernard noticed a bluish/purple mark on his elbow. Angela had one in exactly the same position. Bernard later worked in the medical profession and now knows that the mark was on the brachial artery.

Coming to a farmhouse, the children were met by an anxious stranger who asked their names. It turned out that they were being sought by worried parents as a whole day and night had passed since they had gone onto the hill and disappeared.

Soon afterwards Angela returned to London and Bernard has never heard from her again. He complied with the strangers' request for silence for over 40 years, but needs to resolve the matter for his peace of mind. His quest to find a childhood friend is understandable. He told me that he *knew* this event had occurred but needed the assurance that his companion could give that it was more than just the hallucination, daydream or fantasy that he has always been offered in explanation by those he told.

COSMIC BATTLEGROUND

Just as there is God and the Devil, so, some researchers believe, there are angels and there are Men in Black. The two interfere in life on earth—angels for our good and MIB to serve the ministrations of dark forces. This is because, they suggest, these ''good and evil'' beings are engaged in a cosmic war.

Intriguingly, this concept runs right through modern-day alien abduction stories just as readily as it did several hundred years ago when witches were hunted down or when elemental beings threatened strangers with evil consequences if they revealed their presence on earth. Remember Shirley Greenfield's images of a terrible battle and the coming ''sequence of events'' (see p. 15).

In 1965 a Venezuelan gynaecologist who met the familiar tall aliens was advised that there were also small beings coming to earth and they had less friendly intentions toward us. There was no love lost between the two species and a kind of war in heaven was underway whilst we on earth were simply ''in the way.''

A whole family abducted near Aveley in Essex in October 1974 met both of these types of entity—ugly, demonic beings with (devil-like) pointed ears and horrible faces that served the will of taller ones. The small beings performed medical experiments. The tall ones, through both magical technology and advanced psychic powers, tried to reason with the witnesses, explaining why they were attempting to help life on earth and why they must do so covertly.

They added that they had done this for centuries, boosting our moral, ethical and physical powers through indirect means rather than any obvious form of contact like landing on the White House lawn or parading in front of interested scientists armed with cameras.

In her series of epic novels begining with *Shikasta* celebrated feminist writer Doris Lessing builds a fascinating picture that extrapolates from these ideas. She debates a long-term contact with earth that began millions of years ago from some supernatural race. We are descendants of this alien race of paranormally advanced beings who have ''fallen from grace.'' As such we have forgotten our origin out there in space. Perhaps now we subconsciously strive to return, hence our wanderlust desire to reach the stars and today's cultural obsession with all things alien.

During this long-term strategy the aliens have constantly located operatives on earth, disguised as humans and aiming to help us grow as a culture. We must be guided upwards through a spiral of evolution and, as such, all the major religions of the world were ''set up'' by alien emissaries as ways to get us moving on the right track.

Equally our meetings with fairies in the past or aliens today may be seen as examples of subtle mental prodding. By acting out roles and spelling out messages with much deception to blur the truth, the hope is that we will find our way home, both physically and spiritually.

But there is a problem—a cosmic war between good and evil. To learn that we are in the middle of a battle between vastly superior intelligences who create our whole structure of beliefs on a whim, and to whom ESP, levitation or altered states of reality are routine, would prove a devastating blow to our society. The effects on the church alone are easy to imagine.

If there is any truth in this dramatic concept does it provide a built in incentive for someone to stop the news of this ethereal domination from leaking out via the credible witnesses with the kind of solid evidence which might prove influential to a widespread acceptance?

BEHIND THE SECRECY

We hear much about a purported cover-up by the military and government authorities that masks this phenomenon. But *why* hide the truth about UFOs in the first place?

Of course, what if someone is hiding an answer that they feel might destroy our entire culture? Did aliens plant us here and build our civilisation, and are they the template from which all our dreams of heaven and God emerge? Such a shock may well prove terminal and could need suppression.

Lessing may well see her *Canopus in Argos* stories as just a fictional adventure, but more has been hinted by some commentators. Indeed I had the great privilege of appearing with her on a BBC radio programme (''Woman's Hour'') some years ago, and whilst she was not in a mood to give too much away I did get a sense that she suspected that something had inspired her to write these books.

Others (such as Michael Craft in his book *Alien Impact*) have even written that Lessing may actually believe she ''channelled'' this remarkable literary saga—that it was fed directly to her from some outside source. Whether this is true or not her stories stir the emotions and strike a chord with so many of us that it might infer a deeper meaning which at some inner level we somehow understand.

Lessing's vision of contact across millions of years is important to our interpretation of MIB cases. It is not just that— if true—all of our legends and myths (from demons to devils and angels to MIB) could result from hypothetical intervention by a wise race of beings possessed of supernatural powers. It is not even just because we could then see abductions to fairy-land and today's spacenappings by little green men as being part of the same phenomenon. More significantly it is the pointer that indicates why anyone should wish to prevent the truth about UFO reality from coming out.

Taking Shirley Greenfield's story (p. 8) as it stands, for example, we might be able to accept her UFO sighting, and, if we are liberal-minded enough, to accommodate the possibility of her alien abduction. What is more difficult to imagine is that there are people who would need to threaten a teenage girl into silence about such things. Why on earth would anyone want to do that?

Of course, if there is a ''cosmic battleground'' in which we are tin soldiers, then just as role-playing ''goody'' aliens might seek to guide us toward enlightenment, so might character-acting ''baddy'' entities want to step in and do their bit to disrupt the universal plan.

On the other hand, perhaps there are forces at work within the bureaucracy of government who know—or merely suspect—the truth behind the real nature of alien contact. Such a shocking truth strikes at the core of our ego-driven belief that the universe revolves around human life. Indeed they may fear the repercussions should sufficient proof emerge that not only are we not alone, as Steven Spielberg put it in his movie *Close Encounters* but we are not even in control of our own destiny.

A mundane UFO sighting is hardly going to change the universe and set Whitehall and the Pentagon in a frenzy. But what about cases where there is physical evidence—fillings falling out and baffling dentists, marks on people's bodies that show clear signs of irradiation? That could make people sit up and take notice. You may need to try to stop important evidence from becoming too well known and to stop it may require the use of covert government intimidators scaring the pants off vulnerable witnesses.

You may even need to try to find ways to discredit these people by visiting in the guise of "Men in Black," for should they choose to defy your demands for silence they will appear credulous. In other words, be these Men in Black terrestrial agents or some kind of elemental being who exists far beyond the confines of our knowledge, then there are reasons why their seemingly bizarre activities may be thought necessary.

Needless to say, all of the stories about dark forces and mysterious visitors through the ages may have other explanations. They could be simply imagination, as indeed may all of the modern MIB reports (although personally I doubt it). But if the MIB are really out there, then they may have been out there for a very long time and that would certainly suggest that they do not come from a locked room in a dark corridor on Whitehall or some covert planning agency buried within the Pentagon. If you believe that MIB have always been around to threaten and cudgel the human race, then they simply must be an integral part of whatever forces create the UFO mystery.

Incredible as it seems, and misleading as it may prove to be, we should keep this possibility in mind as we assess the more terrestrial prospect that the MIB are very human and very determined to get their way.

15

ENFORCERS OF
THE COVER-UP

It is likely that many people will struggle to accept the idea that MIB are supernatural visitors from another dimension engaged in a million-year-old cosmic war. I do not blame them. Whilst there are cases that might support such a staggering concept, it is quite impossible to prove.

Whilst we cannot just ignore the idea, it is clear that the overwhelming weight of evidence seems to point rather more close to home when seeking the origin of the MIB. Indeed, we may have to look toward the Pentagon or the MoD for the *real* suspects.

Of course, even if we were to regard this down to earth interpretation as the most reasonable explanation for MIB reports, there are major questions outstanding—notably *how* and *why* such extraordinary activities are undertaken.

FRIENDLY ADVICE

We have seen many MIB cases where government forces profess a quite open involvement. Sometimes UFO investigators find themselves sought out just as much as a witness may be and then given friendly advice by these sinister visitors. That advice, of course, is to keep your mouth shut!

Yvonne Smith is a hypnotherapist from Verdugo City, California. In 1992 she told me about one of her most puzzling

cases. The witness was a 25-year-old police officer called Hiroshi who had undergone a close encounter during which he
believed that he was abducted by aliens. The sighting itself
had some chilling attributes, the strangest of which was the
sensation that the little gray-skinned creatures were performing
some sort of surgical procedure on his brain. But after coming
through this trauma he chose to assist others and become a
UFO investigator himself. In this way he hoped to bring his
expertise from the police force to bear on the subject. It was
to prove a fateful decision.

One of Hiroshi's first cases involved a large property in
southern California in which the occupants had seen a UFO
flying overhead. The officer visited the site and began what
seemed to be a straightforward investigation of a routine case.
But on the Sunday morning after his trip two men arrived at
his home. They announced that they worked for the top secret
intelligence unit the NSA (National Security Agency) and appear to have persuaded the UFOlogist that they were sincere.

These NSA agents told Hiroshi that it was not in his best
interests to continue with UFO investigation and that he should
cease all study of this case specifically. He was informed that
if he wanted his career in the police force to progress this was
the only option.

It is interesting to note that these MIB were not concerned
about the police officer's own spacenapping. Nobody tried to
stop him working with Yvonne Smith when that had first happened. Nor had the NSA agents even *asked* him about these
personal events during their visit.

It was Hiroshi—the UFOlogist—that somehow perturbed
these government people—or rather the man who was investigating this one (seemingly ordinary) case. That case is what
they wanted to stifle. But *why* would such an innocuous event
prove so important to the NSA?

Answer a question like this and we may understand the real
nature of the Men-in-Black.

OVERNIGHT DEPARTURES

Over the years many UFOlogists have quit in sudden, dramatic fashion, seemingly after receiving threats like the one made to Hiroshi. The group NARO had a very active member—Malcolm Fenwick (pseudonym). He lived on Merseyside and was interested in UFOs as a result of his aviation expertise—working, in fact, for British Aerospace designing military weapons systems.

One night Fenwick announced very unexpectedly that he was leaving the group and abandoning his UFO research, which had included high-tech investigation into UFO photographic cases. Fenwick refused to discuss his reasons and it was almost two years before the group's chairman, Peter Hough, secured a proper explanation other than his vague comment upon departure that "something terrible has happened to me."

Malcolm Fenwick now alleged that a phone call was made to his home late at night. It exhibited deep knowledge of his work and his association with the UFO group. The man on the line told him that the two things did not go together and if he cared for the safety of his family he must leave UFO research immediately. Unhesitatingly he did so and has never returned.

The implication behind this technician's story is that a government agency was somehow very worried about his UFOlogical research, apparently for fear of what he might discover. Was the link with UFO photographs the key, as this so often seems to attract the notice of the MIB?

Of course it is part of the conspiracy mindset so beloved of UFO buffs that "they" are out to get you. TV series like *Dark Skies* build their plot around the fact. So it is almost inevitable that the field should generate speculation about UFOlogists being silenced even when there is scant evidence.

In cases such as that of Malcolm Fenwick the prospect seems strong that they were indeed intimidated out of the subject, but there are other instances where I suspect the truth was much less dramatic than the UFO community believes. Investigators can get fed up for a whole host of reasons.

Indeed it might even be predictable that if MIB did not exist then the paranoia of UFOlogy would force them to be invented. Perhaps that is precisely what happened—although not necessarily by the UFO buffs themselves, as we will see later.

SECRET SERVICES

Even so, complex bureaucratic bodies like the American state generate secrecy almost for the sake of it, and such an unwieldy structure is interlaced with agencies, surveillance operations and black budgets never reported to the taxpayer. Some departments survive the periodic changing of the guard in the White House and run to their own (often unspoken) agenda.

Whilst the USA is the prime example, simply through sheer global power, the same is true of most major nations. Britain's own "official secrecy" is notoriously endemic. You can be charged for trying to reveal the make of tea bags used in the MoD canteen. If PG Tips makes them paranoid, one can only guess what the possibility of alien contact must do.

It is also worth bearing in mind that these secret services engage in all sorts of nefarious operations—from building stealth aircraft to testing weapons in locations where ordinary people may accidentally be exposed. At times UFOlogists may simply stumble into areas beyond their conception which, in fact, have nothing to do with aliens.

There are sufficient examples that have been revealed in the past. For example, in the 1950s low level radiation exposure was inflicted on uninformed American citizens and the outcome was judged a useful test of medical knowledge. For fear of revealing the truth about this unfortunate exposure elaborate cover stories were fed out.

There was also a cover-up concerning an air crash and resultant fire at a British air base. Nuclear weapons were affected and radiation leaked out. News of this was hidden for 40 years—even though there are suggestions that the health of children living nearby might have been adversely affected.

So we *know* that governments can—and do—get up to some pretty horrible things that have no connection with UFOs or aliens. They stop at nothing to protect what they consider to be a "necessary" secret. If, for some reason, a major UFO case falls into that category it is understandable that any UFO-logist who gets in the way by striving to investigate might be targeted as a threat.

We cannot know what Hiroshi chanced upon during that innocuous case in southern California. But if his MIB really were from the NSA, then it was evidently something rather disturbing and about which the US government did not want people to know.

This is where UFOs can be such a godsend. Radiation levels rise over a Welsh mountain irradiating a few sheep. No problem. Seal off the area. Clear up the evidence. Place a tent in a judicious spot that "happens" to glow like a UFO, then come up with a cover-story. Say nothing happened. It was just a meteorite. If that shuts everybody up then fine. If it doesn't, the UFO buffs will find the "evidence," proving that it was really an "alien contact," and shout that from the nearest roof-top.

Exactly this may well have happened in January 1974 during that strange affair at Llandrillo (see p. 162). Certainly, the end result of such an intelligence disinformation exercise is that nobody ever finds out the real truth. At least nobody that matters very much. The UFO enthusiasts will preach to one another, and the audience who watch episodes of *The X Files* will whinge about an alien cover-up. But that will not convince anyone in the House of Commons, the US Congress or the United Nations. And that's what counts.

Does this mean that a secret organisation might send MIB to spread confusion in the wake of an incident that threatens national security? Might it even sometimes follow that UFO-logists who are promoting "tall tales" about aliens are used to *spread* this disinformation when what really happened was not a part of the UFO mystery at all?

I strongly suspect that the MIB (if they are earthly intelli-

```
RUEAHCC/CMC CC WASHINGTON DC
RUEALGX/SAFE
R 301246Z MAR 90
FM ████████
TO RUEKJCS/DIA WASHDC
INFO RUEKJCS/DIA WASHDC//DAT-7//
RUSNNOA/USCINCEUR VAIHINGEN GE//ECJ2-OC/ECJ2-JIC//
RUFGAID/USEUCOM AIDES VAIHINGEN GE
RHFQAAA/HQUSAFE RAMSTEIN AB GE//INOW/INO//
RHFPAAA/UTAIS RAMSTEIN AB GE//INRMH/INA//
RHDLCNE/CINCUSNAVEUR LONDON UK
RUFHNA/USDELMC BRUSSELS BE
RUFHNA/USMISSION USNATO
RUDOGHA/USNMR SHAPE BE
RUEAIIA/CIA WASHDC
RUFGAID/JICEUR VAIHINGEN GE
RUCBSAA/FICEURLANT NORFOLK VA
RUEKJCS/SECDEF WASHDC
RUEHC/SECSTATE WASHDC
RUEADWW/WHITEHOUSE WASHDC
RUFHBG/AMEMBASSY LUXEMBOURG
RUEATAC/CDRUSAITAC WASHDC
BT
CONTROLS
████████            SECTION 02 OF 02 ████████    05049
```

SERIAL: (U) IIR 6 807 0136 90.

BODY
COUNTRY: (U) BELGIUM (BE).

SUBJ: IIR 6 807 0136 90/BELGIUM AND THE UFO ISSUE (U)

MAR TV SHOW.

████████

PAGE:0015

6. (U) DEBROUWER NOTED THE LARGE NUMBER OF REPORTED
SIGHTINGS, PARTICULARLY IN NOV 89 IN THE LIEGE AREA AND
THAT THE BAF AND MOD ARE TAKING THE ISSUE SERIOUSLY. BAF
EXPERTS HAVE NOT BEEN ABLE TO EXPLAIN THE PHENOMENA EITHER.

7. (U) DEBROUWER SPECIFICALLY ADDRESSED THE POSSIBILITY
OF THE OBJECTS BEING USAF B-2 OR F-117 STEALTH AIRCRAFT
WHICH WOULD NOT APPEAR ON BELGIAN RADAR, BUT MIGHT BE
SIGHTED VISUALLY IF THEY WERE OPERATING AT LOW ALTITUDE IN
THE ARDENNES AREA. HE MADE IT QUITE CLEAR THAT NO USAF
OVERFLIGHT REQUESTS HAD EVER BEEN RECEIVED FOR THIS TYPE
MISSION AND THAT THE ALLEDGED OBSERVATIONS DID NOT
CORRESPOND IN ANY WAY TO THE OBSERVABLE CHARACTERISTICS OF
EITHER U.S. AIRCRAFT.

gence agents) may exist to protect secrets other than UFOs. Nuclear contamination, experiments with new weapons and crashes of top secret aircraft may all be part of their remit. If their antics are mistaken for something more supernatural that could even prove an advantage by working to discredit otherwise reliable sources.

HUNTING THE MIB

One man who is certain that governments practice disinformation and seek to use the UFO community as puppets in this process is William Moore. There are many reasons why Moore, if anyone, should know. This Burbank, California UFOlogist caused shockwaves throughout the UFO world when he admitted that in the early 1980s he had been sounded out by intelligence operatives who offered him an exchange of information.

His part of the deal was to assess the outcome of bogus documents fed out to a UFO witness in New Mexico. An intelligence agency "leaked" these via Moore, and their data concerned a mythical top secret government UFO project called "Aquarius."

Moore eventually understood that the intelligence agency was spreading fake information, and that no such project really existed. But they wanted Moore to report on the reactions displayed by the witness to whom the data was sent and which

Opposite *Do MIB serve to clear up "UFO sightings" generated by secret earthly technology? Strange triangular UFOs were seen over Belgium in late 1989/early 1990. Colonel Debrouwer of the Belgium Air Force asked the US government if they were flying any stealth aircraft over his country. They denied this, but former French Minister of Defence Robert Galley tells how he found himself in a similar situation. The USA told him that they would not "spy on an ally." However, he persisted, sent French Air Force jets in pursuit and a US spy plane was covertly filmed near a nuclear plant. Something new and top secret but very terrestrial might well have been hiding behind the UFO smokescreen during the Belgium wave . . .*

he evidently *believed* to be "explosive" and real.

In return for this, Moore anticipated that his contacts would provide him with genuine material about government UFO studies. Given that he came to realize how he was acting as a channel for disinformation such faith that "they" would treat him differently seems rather naive. But in Moore's circumstances, can we really judge him too harshly?

The witness who was here targeted was Paul Bennewitz, who ran a science development company in Albuquerque. In 1980 he had allegedly filmed some strange objects flying over the nearby Manzano weapons site of Kirtland Air Force Base. His company had also recorded unusual electromagnetic effects. Freedom of Information documents later released news of several UFO sightings during August and September 1980 also above Kirtland in which the nuclear weapons stores were overflown and the radar was somehow jammed by electromagnetic interference. These events appear connected and suggest something was definitely going on. The famed Sandia scientific labs used the site for secret weapons testing. Their guard patrols also saw some odd things at the time.

However, the story became even more confused when Arizona UFO group APRO received a letter which purported to tell the remarkable story of an airman called Craig Weitzel. Weitzel said he was temporarily stationed at Kirtland and on 16 July 1980 at nearby Pecos had witnessed not only a "dull metal" craft but a figure dressed in a silvery spacesuit. He successfully photographed the UFO but was unprepared for the consequence of doing so.

On the evening of 17 July, Weitzel reported that a tall man dressed in a dark suit and sporting sunglasses arrived at his room on the Kirtland base. The man claimed to be a "Dr. Huck" who worked at Sandia on a secret contract with the government. The helpful Dr. Huck told Weitzel that he had "seen something you should not have seen." It was a secret test aircraft built at Los Alamos and the photographs Weitzel took (which Huck knew all about) would have to be confiscated. Weitzel reported he no longer had these photographs but had given them to another airman on the base.

Huck administered the traditional MIB warning that Weitzel must not tell anybody of his experience and then left. However, not having heard of this scientific facility operated by Sandia, Weitzel called the Air Force Office of Special Investigations to ask them what to do. AFOSI took statements and then *they* confiscated the photographs from Weitzel for themselves. Evidently he had filmed something that he ought not to have seen and government forces were intent on cleaning up this trail of solid evidence. How often this seems the cause of MIB visits.

Given this fascinating trail of evidence we might wonder if this is why Bennewitz was "destabilised" by the intelligence community. He was not a military man like Weitzel, so they could not march in and just take his photographs and order silence by reminding him of his oath to serve the USA. Maybe to prevent this scientist from being taken seriously whilst in possession of impressive evidence about the incidents at Kirtland, an intelligence unit was forced to try different tactics—using a fellow UFO enthusiast (Bill Moore) to filter out misleading information and so discredit Bennewitz.

SELECTIVE JUDGEMENT

Once again with this case we see typical MIB selective judgment at work—picking out reports with key UFO photographs, especially in an area of military research. The comparison with MIB interest shown in Jim Templeton's photographs near the plant building Blue Streak rockets is clearly intriguing. The involvement of the NSA in Hiroshi's case further reminds us of how the Taylors had a close encounter (see p. 105) near the NSA's most significant base in Europe—Menwith Hill.

This slots together into a rather disturbing picture where UFO witnesses and researchers are at times more of a threat to the intelligence community for reasons far removed from those which they would expect. Aliens may not enter into the equation—but national security usually does.

If these people have accidentally come across something top secret that was reported as a UFO—such as the testing of a new weapons system—one can envisage a situation in which the inflated opinions of the UFO community might be manipulated by intelligence operatives to their own advantage. UFOlogists would be certain that visitations by MIB, confiscation of evidence and the undoubted cover-up of what took place was carried out because the aliens are here and the Pentagon or MoD do not want the world to learn the truth. But that would be just what the government *wanted* them to believe, of course! The plan was that by allowing the UFOlogists to claim things that cannot be proved and which seem, frankly, absurd, nobody asks the key question—what *really* happened?

The UFO buffs then place themselves in the role of hero—acting like James Bond or Fox Mulder, defying the might of bureaucracy to prove to the world that ET has landed. Any witnesses involved will be taken along for the ride—either because they look up to the UFOlogists for guidance or because they themselves are half minded to believe that they have had a close encounter.

In fact, in such circumstances, both UFOlogist and witnesses are being played for suckers by the powers-that-be, who will publicly deny (and quite honestly) that they are hiding knowledge of an alien intrusion. The witnesses and the UFOlogists become discredited in the eyes of many objective thinkers even though they are in fact *right* that something serious has indeed taken place. They are simply very *wrong* in terms of judging what that something was.

Perhaps more often than we realize (and certainly more often than most UFOlogists will care to admit), their passion for the subject is their biggest enemy. It is turned against them with remarkable ease, and the MIB could well be just a means to that end.

However, in order to see if this is really practical, we need to look more closely at what the government of a major nation does (both officially and covertly) when tackling the UFO problem. Could this really involve the use of agents to interrogate and terrify witnesses?

BEYOND WHITEHALL

British government records reveal that there has been official investigation of UFOs at the Air Ministry and Ministry of Defence since at least 1952 when Prime Minister Winston Churchill ordered a study. There are plenty of cases available on the files of the Public Record Office (PRO) at Kew. But what you see are poor attempts to document sightings made to the authorities by members of the public. What is missing are extensive records of cases involving the Army, RAF or Navy.

Yet such cases certainly exist. Well documented investigations involving RAF planes vectored onto radar tracked UFOs, chasing them and watching as the objects streak away at vast speed, or of UFOs overflying naval vessels, or of military bases at which strange things defy all top level security are all an ongoing reality. These have occurred across Britain and I have investigated many of them. There has to be a reason why almost *none* of these cases are on the records at the PRO.

As each new year comes along we can search for the official files on cases which are freshly released from the chains of the Official Secrets Act after 30 years have elapsed. Not to our very great surprise those top cases referred to above are never there. By now it is obvious that the best evidence is simply not being released into the public domain regardless of what the British government claims.

What *is* being released comes from a department at the MoD now known by the acronym "Air Staff 2A" (formerly named "Defence Secretariat 8"). This is operated by a civil servant of rank equivalent to a captain and who (perhaps a little unfairly) I would liken to a clerical officer shuffling papers. Certainly he or she never leaves their desk in Whitehall to chase up sightings.

In the past 40 years there have been at least 15 people in this position, and I know the names of most of them. I have had dealings with quite a few—mostly by letter, occasionally by phone and once or twice by actual meetings at the MoD main building.

REPORT OF AN UNIDENTIFIED FLYING OBJECT

A. <u>Date, time and duration of sighting.</u> (Local times to be quoted.)

B. <u>Description of object.</u> (Number of objects, size, shape, colours, brightness, sound, smell, etc.)

C. <u>Exact position observer.</u> (Geographical location. Indoors or outdoors. Stationary or moving.)

D. <u>How observed.</u> (Naked eye, binoculars, other optical device, still or movie camera.)

E. <u>Direction in which object was first seen.</u> (A landmark may be more useful than a badly estimated bearing.)

F. <u>Angle of sight.</u> (Estimated heights are unreliable.)

G. <u>Distance.</u> (By reference to a known landmark wherever possible.)

H. <u>Movements.</u> (Changes in E, F and G may be of more use than estimates of course and speed.

J. <u>Meteorological conditions during operations.</u> (Moving clouds, haze, mist, etc.)

K. <u>Nearby objects.</u> (Telephone lines; high voltage lines; reservoir, lake or dam, swamp or marsh; river; high buildings, tall chimneys, steeples, spires, TV or radio masts; airfields; generating plant; factories, pits or other sites with floodlights or other night lighting.)

L. <u>To whom reported.</u> (Police, military organisations, the press etc.)

M. <u>Name and address of informant.</u>

N. <u>Any background on the informant that may be volunteered.</u>

O. <u>Other witnesses.</u>

P. <u>Date and time of receipt of report.</u>

Up until the late 1980s these people claimed that they spent very little of their working day on UFO matters. "Two percent" was a figure quoted to me directly by Pam Titchmarsh, who held the job in 1983. The rest of the time they looked into other RAF-related matters of public relations, such as low flying aircraft complaints. I believe the percentage has increased somewhat in recent years, but there is no doubt from the attitudes of those civil servants—and the data that you can read on file at the PRO—that most of these people have always seen their job as a chore.

UFO enthusiasts wrote endlessly to them convinced of a massive cover up of alien spaceships. But these civil servants *knew* that their department had just a few scraps of paper discussing lights in the sky, and these were mostly shown to be mundane things. At no time did they even speak to witnesses by phone, let alone drive around in big black cars and warn them to remain silent. The cover-up was probably regarded as a joke to the workers at Air Staff 2A, and it is small wonder the MoD personnel thought UFOlogists were potty for claiming otherwise. Unfortunately, these MoD staff were being duped, just like everybody else.

The problem is that Air Staff 2A is a bit like a shop window. It exists to field questions from the public and reassure them that the MoD has everything under control. It never has been in even the remotest sense a UFO investigation department such as groups like BUFORA or NARO—something they freely admit. If any dynamic work into UFOs goes on, then it is out of sight at the back of the store and the chances are that

Opposite *Air Staff 2A receive UFO sightings via the MoD command unit at West Drayton in Middlesex. These come via civil and military airports, coastguard stations and main police HQ. They principally report sightings made to these sources by the public. Up to five hundred cases per year arrive this way and each location uses a standardised MoD UFO reporting form asking the questions listed opposite. When released on the public record after the lapse of thirty years, answers to several of these questions—eg those identifying witnesses—are usually censored.*

it happens at a security level well beyond the need to know of Air Staff 2A. In fact, the staff working at this Whitehall department will quite legitimately be unaware of the real locations from whence any governmental MIB visitations may occur.

A NEW BROOM

One man who disputes my opinion on this is Nick Pope. Between 1991 and 1994 he took the tour of duty at 2A and has since decided to come into the open to tell the world what he learned. Whilst his 1996 book *Open Skies, Closed Minds* is a good read and became a best-seller, it was a disappointment to many UFOlogists and contained little that we did not already know.

This is not, I suspect, because Nick Pope is "covering it up." It is because Nick Pope, or indeed anybody working in the position that he held in Whitehall, simply is not at the real center of British government UFO research as they themselves honestly believe that they are.

There is no doubt that Nick brought to the job far more enthusiasm than those who came before him. He tackled the cases that came in during his three year tenure with a commendable professionalism, working closely with UFO groups and spending far more time, I suspect, than anybody had done before in following up sightings that he considered important. But even he never had chance to visit witnesses or do any study beyond the confines of his office.

Although Nick Pope came across a few interesting cases during his three years, most of the sightings were—as any glance at the PRO files shows that they *always* have been— just lights in the sky and simple misidentifications. There is little sign of the sort of evidence that would be persuasive of an alien contact or cause the MoD to need to cover anything up.

Pope told me, "They would have banned my book if they could. The idea was discussed. But I have done nothing wrong and they knew that if they had tried to ban it they would have created an even bigger story.'' So the MoD merely stress that these are Pope's personal views—not MoD policy.

I find Nick a very easygoing person and, whilst he has clearly recognized the lucrative potential of his job at Air Staff 2A (making substantial money as a result of his writings and lecturing), few will begrudge him that. I am sure that he is genuinely interested in UFOs and learning some of the confusing realities of the field as he gains in experience. He could be a useful ally.

MIB: THE OFFICIAL VIEW

Naturally, I have asked Nick Pope from his position of authority whether he accepts the reports of MIB as expressed in this book. If so, might they refer to government agents being sent to interview witnesses, as many of those witnesses themselves certainly think they are? Pope's answer is specific. He is convinced that the MIB are *not* government related.

Pope tells me that during his time at 2A he never sent anybody to investigate a sighting first hand. From case files that he has seen at the MoD covering earlier years, nobody else has ever done so either to his knowledge.

I believe this is a sincere reply. Certainly this view concurs with most of the data on the PRO for the period so far released (up to 1967), where there is little sign that anybody from the MoD ever went first hand to interview a UFO witness.

The one instance where that *did* occur comes in the files released to the PRO in early 1997 and concerns a sighting at Wilmslow, Cheshire in March 1966. A young police officer (Colin Perks) spotted a fluorescent green object over a town center cinema and reported it officially via Jodrell Bank and Manchester Airport. The case was picked up by the media and investigated by BUFORA. I have read their report and—intriguingly—BUFORA concluded that it was a bright meteor, although I note that I re-evaluated this for the organisation in 1975, changing the status to ''unknown'' largely on the strength of an independent witness who had seen the same thing as Perks.

In fact what PC Perks and this other witness saw was a green fireball exactly like those that had plagued the secret research facilities around Los Alamos in the USA in the late 1940s and the NSA research site at Orford Ness in Suffolk during the 1980s, causing concern about intrusions into airspace where top secret research was underway. This could be very important.

Whilst Perks makes no mention of this in his detailed account to BUFORA (signed in May 1966), the government files at the PRO indicate that this case *was* considered serious enough to warrant the dispatch of two agents from the military intelligence unit attached to the Air Ministry. This was not Air Staff 2A but associated scientific and technical support staff. Unfortunately, for that reason there is little indication as to why the Ministry chose the sighting of PC Perks to follow through in this way when it has ignored hundreds of other encounters. However, it even mounted a creditable survey of the site looking for physical evidence. One must ask why?

But is this case unique? I doubt it. If you chase up some of the cases on the PRO the witnesses sometimes tell you that they *too* were visited. The "intelligence files" are usually missing from the PRO. Only this comment by the witness years later lets us know that an intelligence officer from the MoD paid a visit and advised them not to discuss in public what they saw.

I took a batch of 15 old cases from the PRO (dated 1964 and 1965) and tried to trace the witnesses 30 years later. Many were unreachable, but I found two who had been advised not to talk—either by phone or personal visit. Nick Redfern, who has scoured the PRO files for his forthcoming book *A Covert Agenda*, also tracked down a witness who had been coerced into silence by the MoD.

Just how does that jell with the non-interventionist policy Air Staff 2A employ?

I put to Nick Pope that, as he and his predecessors were not responsible for such visits (and I am sure they were not), then this must infer that some other more secret department exists from which these "government agents" are coming? Again he insists no and, to be fair, he was unaware of the discovery of the PC Perks file *proving* such a visit in 1966, as this was released after our interview.

Pope is confident there cannot be another government department working on the UFO problem, arguing quite logically that this is "because they could not do this job without contacting me. I get the case reports."

Certainly he got the cases from the public, or calls from air base public relations officers, but I am not convinced he was getting *all* of the cases that were subject to high level government response. I have interviewed numerous military witnesses where a major case *has* definitely happened. But where *are* the official records on these case files? They are not on the PRO and appear to reside in locations outside the reach of both the public and civil servants like Nick Pope.

IN SEARCH OF WALTER MITTY

Nick Pope told me that he was sure that if there was a secret department serving to siphon off the best cases then he would have got some inkling about this at Air Staff 2A—but he did not. So who then *are* these visitors who go to see witnesses or demand photographic and other hard evidence?

"There are a lot of Walter Mitty types out there," was Pope's fascinating answer.

"Do you mean the witnesses are making these stories up?" I countered, as we walked along the darkened banks of the Thames with Big Ben glowing in the background.

No, he corrected, but such "Walter Mitty" types might be the ones *doing* the visiting.

I tried to point out that these cases seem very consistent and have been occuring for many years over a big area. That suggested some sort of organisation behind them all, not a few maverick eccentrics. But perhaps the same people keep pretending to be MIB, he suggested.

Nick Pope was undoubtedly sincere in his opinion that the MIB were play-acting individuals peripherally linked with the UFO community. If so, then the phenomenon discussed in this book would have no substance outside that scenario. Perhaps he is right, but I seriously doubt it.

"What if the Walter Mitty types work for the British government?" I offered probingly—to which Nick Pope gave a polite smile. He was genuinely convinced that this *was* not the case.

Unfortunately, having studied the evidence and met the witnesses—as Nick Pope has not had the chance to do, of course—I cannot dismiss the probability that there is more going on here than that.

On only two occasions did Nick Pope have a problem answering my questions. He would not discuss the level of his security clearance—which was perfectly reasonable, of course—but it leaves me wondering if he would *really* be told should some secret department be despatching agents to visit witnesses in possession of evidence contravening national security. Maybe the awareness of this went higher than the civil service rank of Captain. After all, Ed Ruppelt was a Captain at Project Blue Book and he was clearly cut out of the loop—as I suspect Nick Pope may have been when it was necessary.

More significantly, Pope reacted ashen-faced when I asked him to discuss what DSTI and DI55 do within the British government. He would not even tell me what these acronyms stood for as he was, again quite honorably, bound by the Official Secrets Act. I have no quibble at all with that, but it is a matter that we must address, for it is the predecessor of one of *the* intelligence units (DI 64) that paid a call on PC Perks.

THE REAL UFO COVER UP

Thankfully, I already knew who these two departments were. These are the other units associated with the MoD who *do* study UFOs—or, at least, the ones thay we can *prove* to exist.

That there are other places where UFO data is examined

was already known by me thanks to Ralph Noyes. This man waited until retirement before he chose to tell what he knew about UFOs following thirty years at the MoD and a most distinguished career. He has, like Pope, not hidden his support for UFO reality, speaking in public several times. But he has not had the same level of exposure, preferring to work behind the scenes. In 1985 Noyes and I jointly submitted a briefing document to Lord Peter Hill-Norton, former chief-of-staff of the entire MoD and an ex-Admiral of the Fleet. This is another man publicly accepting of UFO reality. We did so in connection with a major case near a military base in Suffolk and also sent letters to the Defence Minister with the active support of Liberal Democrat MP David Alton (who perceptively saw this as a freedom of information issue). We made little real headway, but I think this shows the committment of Ralph Noyes.

I have talked with Noyes many times since he first came forward in 1984 and his views are well documented in several letters to me and in an interview that I filmed at his home in 1996.

Noyes was at a higher level than Pope has yet attained (reaching, in fact, the equivalent of an air commodore on the civil service rankings). Between the 1950s and the 1970s he had not only *supervised* the MoD department containing what is now Air Staff 2A, but Noyes had also worked directly for the Air Minister's department with high level access at a time when UFOs were first being debated in cabinet. This came during the mid to late 1950s as a result of a series of military close encounters involving radar trackings and pursuits by RAF jets. Almost *none* of the data on these cases is to be found on the PRO files, as you might expect. When the case was public knowledge from the day it happened (as in a radar encounter at RAF West Freugh in Scotland in 1957), the data *is* on file—probably because it would be noticed if it was omitted from release. But in the many other instances kept secret at the time (but confirmed later by RAF pilots or radar staff), the reports have disappeared.

Ralph Noyes is adamant that he knows of no proof at the MoD of aliens or spaceships, but that the Ministry is very well aware that there is a real UFO phenomenon and is completely baffled by its paradoxical behavior—appearing more like an apparition in many respects than a solid aircraft, and yet occasionally capable of leaving hard evidence in its wake. This baffles "nuts and bolts" MoD staff.

Noyes has further told me of gun camera film taken from RAF planes sent up to chase UFOs—again, *not* in the PRO files at Kew or seeming to be evidence coming to Nick Pope and his associates at Air Staff 2A. Pope told me be has seen no such film. Noyes insists he has. That suggests to me that Noyes had a high enough security clearance to do so and Pope did not. This film, incidentally, showed merely unexplained fuzzy lights and *not* invading alien starships, Noyes is quick to assure me.

One MoD location where UFO data is secured is in a part of the building requiring a high security clearance even to get onto the same corridor. A map showed sightings logged and flagged. This is not Air Staff 2A but is, I suspect, the sort of place from whence MIB visitors might be sent out.

SECRET DEPARTMENTS

For a long time we had no real clues as to what part of the MoD might outrank Air Staff 2A for UFO data. There were references on the PRO archives to intriguing cases sometimes being discussed with RAF intelligence staff (even occasional mentions of the mysterious DSTI as beings recipients of UFO data). But we were not clear precisely what was taking place during such an exchange, as the records of these other units were not entering the public domain alongside the Air Staff 2A files.

In the mid 1980s, however, the MoD made a curious decision and started to release a few modern files to interested UFOlogists (myself included). This was well in advance of the thirty year rule. It was done sporadically and in a limited way. Possibly they were pre-empting a Freedom of Information act then being threatened, just as the Australians had prematurely eleased UFO data to UFOlogist Bill Chalker. Whatever the reason, in the process of this early release programme the MoD seemingly made a crucial mistake. At least, I *assume* it was a mistake, as they quickly stopped doing it!

All identifying details of the witness were eliminated from these files and it was difficult to follow the crumbs of data left in the reports toward any real conclusion. They exhibited no evidence of any MoD follow-up and were merely raw sightings data received through the central military radar and communications site at West Drayton. From here they were being passed onto Air Staff 2A.

But in 1987 a handful of these then very recent files were released, complete with a series of letters at the bottom of the page under the word "Distribution." This *was* the distribution list used by the MoD for all of their incoming UFO data. Of course it showed that a copy of each case was going to Air Staff 2A. But, in fact, three other places received copies of all the incoming UFO files *as well*. Between them they got four times more copies than 2A, suggesting they had more of a need for the data.

The origin of one location (coded DD GE/AEW) remains unclear, although I suspect this is a defense department dealing with "Airborne Early Warning" systems (hence AEW). That is, however, little more than an educated guess on my part. But the other two departments receiving UFO cases reported to the MoD were already known to me because of their occasional mention in the the PRO files. They proved easier to identify and were code named DSTI and DI 55.

DI 55 (my contacts in the MoD and RAF have advised) is a defense intelligence unit whose operations include data collection from surveillance and interview, concerning matters potentially affecting national security. I can discover little else as the operation is covered by the Official Secrets Act. But if the MoD are *not* sending out people to interview witnesses, then why would DI 55 be receiving copies of all incoming UFO files?

As for DSTI, I guessed that this stood for Directorate of Scientific and Technical Intelligence, since Australia has a similar acronym (*and* a Freedom of Information rather than an Official Secrets act!), and this is what their DSTI means "down under." I am advised that this is correct.

In any case, this is the place where security cleared scientists and top rank intelligence staff from the RAF come together to evaluate novel technology that is recovered in some way (such as film taken by gun cameras on RAF jets that might give an idea about the capabilities of the latest enemy aircraft on spying missions over the North Sea). It assesses information about the technological progress of foreign powers garnered by the secret services as well, and is not unlike the role of Wright Patterson's Foreign Technology Division in the USA in this respect. It is worth noting that DSTI get *twice* the copies of the UFO files as do Air Staff 2A—almost by itself enough to suggest that there is more going on beneath the surface than we are being told.

These records may be the key to British UFOlogy—for, whilst there are references to DSTI staff being consulted in PRO files as far back as cases from the 1960s, there is no sign, to my knowledge, of any intelligence analyzes on the many thousands of UFO reports that they must have received over the past 30 years. The DSTI records are not being released— officially on the grounds that they would affect national security to do so. As indeed I am quite sure they would!

I would not be surprised if this secret evidence were far more interesting than the fluff fed out to the PRO each year care of Air Staff 2A. In my view, this batch of rather feeble data is a sop to keep us from asking about the really important stuff.

WHO ARE DSTI?

In April 1996 I showed on British television the MoD document that proved what I have just reported. This was in a half-hour documentary which I wrote and presented for the BBC called *Britain's Secret UFO Files*. It caused a national furor with highbrow newspapers waging a bitter campaign to brand ne as some kind of fanatical conspiracy monger. None of these commentators bothered to check the facts for themselves, as they could so easily have done. The distribution list was (quite literally) in black and white and available for anyone to dig into. Instead, they preferred to laugh, as is unfortunately so often the case when UFOs are debated.

Three weeks later the *Daily Mail* reported a story carried in the official RAF newspaper. The MoD had been forced into making a new public statement about UFOs as a consequence of my documentary. In fact it was a statement which they had already faxed to me a few weeks earlier at the BBC in London and which we filmed on its arrival. The scene was used to conclude my documentary (although, yet again, the media missed the relevance of what the MoD had told me in this document).

This statement was the usual waffle, indicating that the MoD investigate sightings for the purpose of discovering if they have any "defense implications," but that they do not have the facilities to proceed to the point where they can fully identify a specific report. Nor is it their job to do so. Standard fare indeed. But the significant *new* feature was the remark that, whilst they had no evidence that UFOs are alien in origin, the MoD did not rule this possibility out. *They* raised this issue. I had very carefully *avoided* any implication that UFOs were extraterrestrial during my BBC documentary.

Although the *Daily Mail* for some reason directed their story to suggest that the MoD had now *rejected* UFOs (which in fact this statement clearly does not do), they missed once again the fact that the government had left the door open for the possibility of alien contact

The *Mail* also quoted an anomymous MoD "official" (a man who was evidently talking to the paper in confidence about events behind the scenes). He noted that in the weeks since my programme had been transmitted Whitehall had been swamped with inquiries on UFOs and the RAF were thus *ordered* to publish this statement in a sort of retaliatory strike. The MoD official even suggested that this act was unprecedented and hinted that the MoD were shaken.

UNCLASSIFIED

LTO225 17/1956 22902391

FOR CAB

ROUTINE 17 4007 AUG 87

FROM   RAF WEST DRAYTON
TO   MODUK AIR

UNCLASSIFIED
SIC Z6F
SUBJECT: AERIAL PHENOMENA A. 161900Z AUG 87, 30 SECS I. ONE, DARK
ROUND OBJECT, NO LIGHTS, NO SOUND C. AT HOME ADDRESS-OUTDOORS-
STATIONARY D. NAKED EYE E. TO THE SOUTH OF PINNER F. 45 DEGREES
WHEN SIGHTED PASSING TO OVERHEAD G. N/K H. STEADY SOUTH-NORTH J.
CLEAR/CAVOK K. RESIDENTIAL AREA L. WATCH MANAGERS DESK LATCC M.

O. NIL P. 171230Z AUG 87
BT

DISTRIBUTION   Z6F
F
CAB   1   Sec (AS) ACTION (CXJ   1 AERO)
CYD   1   DD GE/AEW
CAV   1   DI 55
CAV   2   DSTI

But shaken by what? Was it my demonstration that DSTI and DI 55 existed?

Five months later—in September 1996—the same highbrow press that had ridiculed my programme noted in a "defense correspondence" item that there was to be a change to the rules announced by the MoD. They had now decided to *allow* the distribution list to be released on UFO files that were going to be released each year to the PRO (albeit still thirty years late, of course).

Nobody in the press saw the connection here, but it was surely more than a coincidence that I had just exposed the truth—that Air Staff 2A was *not* the only source of MoD UFO study—and I had done it by screening their "top secret" distribution list to five million viewers. So there was hardly much point in the MoD continuing their pretence, was there?

As such, they simply waited a few months and discreetly announced this decision as if it were a free choice made to ward off cries of "cover up." The highbrow media were hooked like a codfish without seeing the subterfuge it entails.

The truth is, of course, that the existence of DSTI and DI 55 had been *hidden* for 30 years (just as even now their files are *still* being hidden). I think it possible that the mistake in 1987 in revealing proof of their existence might not have been spotted. If some office clerk quickly corrected the error might they have chosen to say nothing, hoping that nobody in the UFO world would figure out the significance? Why risk the wrath of your superiors if nothing may come of your slip?

Opposite *One of the dramatic 1987 MoD UFO files that was released with the distribution list intact. It was the first solid proof that three other locations beyond the publicly admitted SEC (AS)—ie Air Staff 2A—retain data on the subject. These more covert intelligence agencies may be the key to the MIB phenomenon—as suggested by PC Perks' visit by agents from DI 64 back in March 1966. Just how often has this occurred, but the files never been released? The MoD could not hide the PC Perks case as the story was put onto the public record at the time although no details of his MIB encounter were given. He followed orders and remained silent.*

But then, when, during the course of the interview, Nick Pope realized that I knew about these locations (but not, at that point, that I had *proof* in the form of the distribution list on the released files), he may well have been genuinely taken off guard.

Of course he would presumably have seen the distribution list on files that he was getting whilst at Air Staff 2A. He clearly knew of the involvement of DSTI and DI 55 and had actually stated in letters to the UFO community during his tenure at 2A that there were other staff working with his department (presumably as far as he was allowed to go in talking about these other units).

I emphasize that I do not suggest Nick Pope was lying to me. I believe that he was bound by the Official Secrets Act not to discuss DSTI and DI 55 and may well himself never have had access to their findings. In other words, he may genuinely not know what UFO work they do.

Is the DSTI or DI 55 the home of the MIB in Britain? Perhaps. Certainly someone in the British secret service is taking far more notice of UFO phenomena than you have been led to believe. Air Staff 2A is in essence a PR exercise—a carrot leading us donkeys away from the truth.

PLAYTIME AT THE PENTAGON

Whilst we may not be able to pinpoint the home of any hypothetical governmental agents acting as MIB in Britain, beyond these few tantalising glimpses, we can discover more from the USA thanks to their Freedom of Information Act. Researcher Bill Moore (who, as we saw earlier, has had quite a few adventures in the realms of US government secrecy) has probed the Pentagon power base and in the *Irish UFO Journal* in 1995 offered his thoughts on MIB. He says, ''Men in Black really do exist and they really do make occasional appearances to UFO witnesses in order to obtain critical evidence.'' Remember, this stems from his first hand experience of the US intelligence community, but it is well borne out by the data in his book.

Many of the cases where an MIB visit is "risked" by a government department that officially does not exist are those in which solid evidence (notably photographs) were captured by witnesses. It appears as if these are deemed too important to allow into the open and a stop is put upon them wherever possible.

I have noticed a curious fact here that I think is relevant. Camera ownership has rocketed during the past 40 years. Film stock is now vastly superior. Yet 80 percent of all the high quality and well-attested UFO photographs pre-date 1970. Indeed, over 50 percent predate 1960. By all logic we should be getting countless impressive pieces of visual evidence every year, far more than we did a few decades ago. But the reverse is true. Good UFO photographs are now a rarity. Where has all this evidence gone?

Of course we might anticipate some possible reasons for a decrease. Modern investigation techniques make it less easy to carry off a crude hoax that may have fooled millions in the past, and we are more familiar with camera faults and processing errors which can make someone wrongly conclude that they have photographed a UFO.

However, once again this is counter-balanced by new technology allowing truly incredible "fake UFOs" to be created by the determined amateur. There is also the media appetite to purchase and promote visual evidence with numerous TV series competing for ratings and coming up with programmes about the phenomenon. This provides such an opportunity to promote photographic evidence that the cumulative outcome of these factors should be more evidence, not less.

What of those cases where no visual evidence is involved—Shirley Greenfield, for example, or Sandra and Peter Taylor? In the Taylors' case a seemingly unique clue was offered (the unusual door in the side of the UFO). The proximity to the NSA base at Menwith Hill also no doubt alerted the authorities.

It strikes me that we can see see how certain cases are being selected for visitation—primarily those which offer impressive hard evidence (medical effects and photographs, for example or something new that might provide insight about the nature of UFOs that these intelligence operatives have not come across before. Assuming that the MIB *do* come from a government department, this finding confirms what I suspect from all of my research into UFOs and what both Nick Pope and Ralph Noyes insist.

The cover-up is not one of great knowledge being withheld from the public. It is a cover-up of ignorance. The powers that-be know there are UFOs but may well not know precisely what UFOs are. If my theory is true, then most routine sightings will offer nothing toward a conclusion. But the occasional incident stands out as being something different. It may then be tempting to go out into the field and gather first hand intelligence from those novel situations.

Of course to do so in the open would destroy the well crafted illusion that the government is not interested in UFOs. You cannot confiscate film, scare witnesses into silence or do face-to-face interrogations whilst successfully maintaining the pretence that you simply have an office with a civil servant shuffling papers. But you *can* do it if nobody is ever going to believe that the people who pay the visit come from a government department—because they act so peculiarly, dress so oddly and fit the legend (and all too *cranky* image) of the MIB.

This touch of absurdity is like wearing a cloak of invisibility. It ensures that people think as Nick Pope does, as a matter of course—that Walter Mitty types are the only ones who would act so absurdly. No government would be as childish in its intelligence gathering.

But Moore points out, "[The MIB] did not create the legend at all, but rather have taken opportunistic advantage of it in order to provide cover for their shady operations." We can see what he means. The birth of MIB legends in UFO circles—as told in the early chapters of this book through cases like Tacoma, Washington and Albert Bender's mysterious three men—provided the idea that intelligence agents could use to wonderful advantage.

Think about it. We have seen situations where secret aircraft are being flown in locations that would not ordinarily be possible because there would be civilian witnesses. Of course if you use the UFO mystery as camouflage you can fly with impunity. Simply ensure that your aircraft looks enough like a UFO to be reported as such and nobody will take the sightings seriously enough to bother your continued operations.

The same principle may well operate at the level of the MIB. This gift from the imagination of the early UFO mythology provides a smokescreen for those masters of disinformation. It allows them to go out into the world and mingle with the UFO witnesses and investigators, to procure evidence and evade detection safe in the knowledge that they are simply living up to the crackpot expectations of the UFO community. Extremist UFOlogists believe in MIB visits but argue about them being "alien in origin." Outsiders regard them as such a dubious feature of the UFO literature that just to report one in the context of an otherwise impressive close encounter will destroy objective credibility.

Considered in this fashion, it is a brilliant scheme.

AMERICA'S MIB

Bill Moore has scoured the available evidence released by Freedom of Information in the USA and delved into the information on offer about covert intelligence operations. As a result he believes that he has located America's "government people in disguise"—as he insists these MIB to be. He says they are part of a unit known as "Air Force Social Activities Center" (AFSAC). This is devoted "primarily to the collection of . . . intelligence obtained by covert means directly from human sources as opposed to that which has been intercepted from electronic sources or gleaned from printed material."

His research into the official records has revealed the history of AFSAC—which began circa 1950 as the 1006th Air Intelligence Squadron. It went through changes to the 1127th Field Activities Group in 1959, the 7602nd Air Intelligence Group

in the late 1970s and became AFSAC in 1983. As of 199
Moore claims that it was still operative and based at Fort Bel
voir, Virginia, but under the command of the Air Force intel
ligence unit at Kelly Air Force Base in Texas.

Various documents released under the US Freedom of In
formation Act offer support for his belief that AFSAC are the
source of modern MIB visitations. There are references to the
use of "three man teams" in AFSAC data gathering. The con
nection with UFOs is also well indicated. Although there is a
sea of black ink censoring much of the history of this cover
unit, what you *can* read links them with "Project Moon
Dust"—a retrieval operation for hard evidence connected with
"objects from space." From a number of released document
about "Moon Dust" operations we know that this can mean
the recovery of a fallen meteorite getting intelligence from a
foreign military satellite should it crash to earth and, of course
any hypothetical traces or visual evidence relating to a UFO
encounter. This may be circumstantial, but it suggests that
Moore could well be correct.

Bill Moore also notes a curious file from the Air Force
Office of Special Investigations made available years after i
was written. This concerns an investigation into "Donald Key
hoe"—the ex-Marine and pioneer UFOlogist who first pub
licly introduced the concept of a government cover-up. I
seems that in 1965 Keyhoe was subject to an intelligence stud
and the report on this stated in part that "files relating to the
UFO are maintained in principally two places." The documen
then goes onto specify these locations as being Wright Patter
son (which is, as we might expect, the Air Force intelligenc
unit—Project Blue Book—and the only publicly admitted lo
cation). More dramatically, the file locates UFO records quite
unexpectedly as also being "at the 1127th Field Activity
Group at Fort Belvoir, Va." This, of course, means AFSAC

When Blue Book was closed in 1969 all official interest in
the subject was supposedly ended. In April 1997 a Pentagon
press release stressing this very point made world headlines
Yet the terminating memo for Blue Book insists that "UFO
data affecting national security" will still be collected by othe

hannels set up to do so! What other channels? There were
ot supposed to be any. But very evidently there were.

The similarity with the position found in the UK should be
oted. Both nations seem to have a twin track system with
3lue Book (and Air Staff 2A) officially the only UFO data
athering source that is interacting with the public to collate
JFO information. At the same time (and covertly) the high
:vel files are stored away at some peculiar air intelligence
nit where all the best data is presumably retained well out of
1e way of the prying eyes of the likes of you and me. In the
JSA this covert location is called AFSAC. In the UK it ap-
ears to be DI 55 or DSTI.

MASTERS OF DISGUISE

n a study of the US intelligence community published in 1985
y J.R. Richelson, AFSAC (and its earlier incarnations) is dis-
ussed. Although not intended to be read in a UFO context, it
s very tempting to do just that. Richelson tells us, "The Air
'orce Special Activities Center at Fort Belvoir ... [has activ-
:ies that] include clandestine collection as well as the debrief-
1g of defectors." Its predecessor, the 1127th, was described
s "an oddball unit, a composite of special intelligence groups.
'he men of the 1127th were con artists. Their job was to get
eople to talk."

Bill Moore contends that what this means is that they were
motley crew of burglars, impersonators, disguise artists plus
'eccentric geniuses and useful flakes ... recruited from all
ver the country, even from prisons when necessary." Whilst
1e AFSAC tasks that are publicly admitted involved trickery
o get would be traitors to talk about their deeds, it does not
eem much of a stretch to imagine such interrogation special-
sts from revelling in the MIB scenario.

As Bill Moore says, "The sensationalist paranoia of the
JFO community and the accompanying incredulity of more
esponsible individuals would provide all the cover they
eeded. No-one but the lunatic fringe would ever believe such

stories were true . . . It was the perfect deception.''

Indeed, if this speculation is correct, it suddenly makes sense of the quirkiness of many of the MIB stories: ''the Commander'' with one arm; the man who sits with a box on his knee all night; the two visitors who always talk to one another using numbers, not names. These features might be deliberately introduced to add to the general air of crankiness.

The patterns will be important as well. Black Cadillacs and sunglasses in the USA. Big Jaguar cars and MoD identity cards in the UK. These ensure that the story fits the legend and so is recognized as part of the MIB myth by the UFO Community who, as a result, promote it as such and indirectly assist the intelligence agencies in their destabilising tactics. I would no doubt keep government intelligence prop and make up artists chuckling for a few years as well.

Most of the things we find within the MIB reports are easy to duplicate by human means. They are not ''supernatural'' or ''extraterrestrial,'' and they come across as just plain daft so far as most people are concerned. What they do is provide memorable hooks that the witness is hardly likely to forget should they choose to defy the MIB warnings and report their story.

What they also do is add that touch of eccentricity that virtually guarantees that the witness is demeaned in the eyes of most rational observers. These victimised witnesses do not realize that by telling the truth they are destroying their own credibility. Witnesses and UFOlogists alike shoot themselves in the foot without even being aware that they are doing so. This may well be the whole point of such an intelligence exercise. What a spectacular ruse, if so.

As Moore says, it would be the perfect deception, because it uses the hysteria of the subject's own researchers to make its best witnesses look like idiots in the eyes of the majority of the world, but at the same time it allows a covert data gathering operation to proceed.

No doubt plenty of people are scared into not discussing the strongest UFO encounters, when these just might—in sufficient numbers—turn the tide of public opinion toward taking

is subject seriously. If not and they still do speak out, simply
lling the truth about their ''weird'' visitors devalues their
vidence and permanently tarnishes the validity of their close
ncounter. It is a double-edged sword of beautiful simplicity.

THE QUESTION OF WHY

ut why would any government agency not want the truth to
merge? Is it, as UFO buffs insist, because knowledge of an
lien invasion would undermine our ecomony or religious
aith? I doubt it. More likely, I suspect, it is to preserve a
overnment or militaristic edge over its foreign rivals.

Tell the world the truth—that incredible things are flying
round and outstripping all of your defenses, that you don't
ave much of an idea what they are, whether they are natural
henomena or intelligently controlled devices. You cannot
ven be sure if they are friendly or hostile. Nor can you do
uch about them. All this does is undermine public confidence
a your ability. What President or Prime Minister needs that
xtra headache? So silence is surely a preferred option. Al-
ough silence necessarily coupled with investigation, because
ou cannot afford to ignore any possibility.

More importantly, there is another reason, as one very sen-
or figure in the MoD has put it to me (indeed I doubt there
ere many more senior than he at the time!). This conversa-
on occurred on the day in December 1980 that I was invited
o the Houses of Parliament to talk about UFOs with a gath-
ring of members of both the Commons and the Lords. This
oluntary group wanted me to brief them on the UFO situation
a Britain, but I took the chance of asking searching questions.

I was reminded that the job of the MoD was not to explain
hat UFOs are but to defend Britain from them if necessary,
lthough as far as anyone knew it was not. Failing that ne-
essity, any defense ministry *must* find out how to harness the
otential science behind UFOs so that we could use it to our
dvantage. Inherent in this is the need to comprehend the truth
efore anybody else does, and, as a result, the fostering of the

illusion that you don't give two hoots about UFOs is in the national interest. Doing this persuades "enemy" foreign powers that you are inactive. This is exactly what you want them to believe, in the hope that they will not start to research the data for themselves.

No doubt there is some cooperation between friendly governments. The way in which the NSA are allowed to operate freely in Britain and certain cases where, for example, USAF intelligence staff and Project Moon Dust agents have collected data about incidents on British soil all imply that this must sometimes be true. We also saw earlier how the Australian government appear to have sent film of a UFO over New Guinea to the CIA for study. It may well sometimes be a combination of sharing bits of knowledge and keeping secret from one another—all at the same time and in the name of international cooperation!

However, what any government needs is for its own security-cleared scientists to study UFO data and try to figure out the theory behind the phenomenon—then put that theory to some practical use. The last thing you need is meddling, non government controlled scientists taking sufficient interest in UFOs to start investigating the cases for themselves, compiling the evidence and maybe even announcing breakthroughs at some open international conference. That destroys the political rat race by which all government and military forces live or die.

So you do what you can to ridicule the field—just as the CIA recognized as long ago as 1953 when the Robertson panel met. MIB are a superbly crafted weapon in that quest to belittle the subject.

COVER-UP OF IGNORANCE

These MIB stories come from *somewhere*. I am personally satisfied that some of the witnesses in this book are telling the truth. This means that we have to find an origin for these range intimidators. Nick Pope could be right. They might be "Walter Mitty" types wandering around the country playing games. John Keel might be correct. These beings could be visitors from another dimension.

We know with assurance, however, that all of the major governments of the world investigate UFO reports, have done so for nearly half a century and continue to invest money in this operation despite recessions and limited finance. They are not doing this for no good reason. And if they are willing to spend money to chase weird phenomena, we cannot rule out that they might be behind the MIB.

The UFO cover-up exists for reasons probably irrelevant to whether UFOs are extraterrestrial visitors or unusual natural phenomena. Either way they are fascinating things that puzzle the scientific and military minds within a government. They offer a possible golden key toward the best Christmas present any defense ministry can want—a weapon that your enemy does not have.

In the face of such logic I think it would be a positive necessity to find ways to ensure that UFOlogy continues to be seen as a fool's paradise and that the daftest possible ideas and cases get the maximum attention. And any government's number one ally in this task is the typical hapless UFO enthusiast who is easily led into believing just about anything so long as it is extraordinary.

As for witnesses, any mechanism by which they can be made to look foolhardy seems an asset. MIB are a wonderful invention—probably a product of the UFO community itself in the first place, but enthusiastically adopted. Any intelligence community that was on the ball would relish the opportunity of putting on the make up, revving up the dark car and shouting lights, camera, action.

The sad part is that it has a built-in denial factor. Unless we can *prove* that this is happening—and with tight security and official secrets acts that is highly unlikely—just to suggest the possibility falls into the very trap that the MIB provide. Any-

one who moots the possibility is made less credible by the
very act of taking it seriously. Unless we can find a way
around this problem, it seems heads they win and tails you
lose.

16

CONCLUSION: DARK THOUGHTS

The MIB phenomenon is no thing of the past. It still occurs. Unfortunately, because witnesses tend to be deterred from speaking by its very nature, it can take several years before a researcher is likely to find out about an incident. As a result, the number of cases for the 1990s remains small, although there are some on record and all past evidence suggests that this number is virtually certain to grow with time.

A TOUCH OF IRISH

Dianne Tesseman cites a case from County Tipperary in Ireland in the summer of 1990. Farmer James McCleary had found a number of those gently flattened "crop circles" in his fields. To McCleary they were just a nuisance as they were destroying his personal economy, crushing flat his oats and potato crops. One Sunday after the last of half a dozen circles had formed during June and July, he went for a brisk walk on his land, as was his usual custom. Suddenly a strange man almost leapt out at him from behind a shed. He was tall and thin, almost too thin in fact, and had a face so pale that he looked as if he had died and been dug up!

The man wore a dark suit but one that appeared some 50 years out of fashion. He also spoke in a curious way. Although he had an educated manner without an accent he could not quite fit the proper words into place. The sensation this provided was just vague, not anything the farmer could really pin down. But it did not seem quite right. As you will appreciate, this is pure MIB.

"Tell us about those designs in your crops," he was asked. Throughout the conversation the word "us" was emphasized but never explained.

McCleary tried to politely get the man to move out of his way and return to the main road but he did not seem to want to budge. He used peculiar expressions such as "bunches" to define each circle and treated the farmer as if he would have all the answers, getting irate when he was unable to provide them. Finally, he issued the customary threat that McCleary should remain silent and talk to him alone as it was "in your best interest" to do so. Then he added after a pause—"or else!'

Unfazed by this, the farmer headed off and left the strange man to his own devices. Thankfully he was not in the least terrified by this meeting—never having heard of the MIB legend and not realizing with whom he may have just come into contact.

THE LIGHTS OF LINCOLNSHIRE

Then there is the strange case of Peter Gregory from Mablethorpe in Lincolnshire. He first contacted me in 1993 to advise that odd things were happening around him. At 2:30 A.M. on 16 April he had got out of bed to go to the bathroom and had watched a ball of light float toward the seafront and then vanish. It was so bright that the image remained "burned" onto his retina for some minutes.

The following night Peter had a vivid experience and saw himself "inside a room" surrounded by strange equipment and with a blue haze and humming noise filling the air. Several beings were standing nearby. These were human-like but quite tall, with shoulder-length hair and piercing blue eyes. Although he wanted to talk to these entities Peter felt "like an unseen phantom in their world.'' His hand passed through the beings as if they were projections.

These encounters were visionary but Peter told me they seemed so realistic that ''the memory of it would remain with me for the rest of my life.'' Then, on 31 May, he managed to take some camcorder images of a white ball of light moving through the evening sky over Mablethorpe. It is hard to pick out the light against the pale blue background of the sky, but he sent a copy to BUFORA so that we could assess its content. There is no doubt that a real object was photographed. Many other lights were seen during that summer, mostly in the vicinity of a microwave repeater tower at the nearby small coastal town of Sutton on Sea.

On 21 June a far more spectacular event took place right outside his bedroom window. This was a huge flattened triangle with red and yellow lights at the edges. It was very low down and nearly filled the window with its bulk. Grabbing his camera, Gregory took several seconds of video footage before it shot across the sky so fast that it left a trail of light. This film was highly impressive.

Peter extracted a color still print from his video to enable him to show other people what the triangle looked like, so he was not unduly surprised when two men arrived at his house on about 24 June. At that time his new photographic success had received no publicity, but he had mentioned it to UFOlogists. When these visitors announced that they were members of a certain Grimsby UFO group, he was happy to let them in. Grimsby was his home town and this immediately put him at ease.

The men seemed ordinary enough but were smartly dressed. They asked many enthusiastic questions and Gregory was pleased that someone was taking so much interest in his investigations. Consequently, when they explained that they could perform a full analysis of the video, including computer enhancement, he did not hestitate. He handed the film over and waited for their report.

The report never came. When Gregory chased up the men he found that their address was non-existent and nobody had ever heard of the Grimsby group. His video was never returned and these mysterious UFOlogists vanished off the face of the earth. As so often in the past, it seems that MIB may have come out into the open to seek prime visual evidence. Once they ensured that it was out of the loop, they disappeared into the night.

MY CONTACT WITH MIB

It would be unfair not to answer the one question that has no doubt occurred to you. Have I ever come across MIB during my time as a UFO researcher? Happily, no strangers have called at my door and warned me into silence. Perhaps they realize that if they did I would ask them to pose for a photograph before getting back into their black Jaguar. However, there was one intriguing episode

The case that brought about this encounter was the remarkable series of events inside Rendlesham Forest, Suffolk during late December 1980. Numerous witnesses observed an object that was also tracked on radar as it crashed through pine trees into the woods just outside the twin NATO air bases of Bentwaters and Woodbridge. It was a major encounter.

US Air Force personnel had a close up view of a cone-shaped object that seemed to "warp space and time" in its immediate vicinity before it took off from the ground and sent the local wildlife into a frenzy. Physical traces were discovered in the forest the next day. Radiation levels up to ten times the normal background count were sprinkled through this area eight miles from Ipswich and senior base personnel tape recorded some of these events live on an office-type dictaphone they had taken into the woods. This recording provides astonishing evidence of what to many is the best documented UFO encounter to have occured in Britain.

I received one of the first generation copies of that tape from an unknown military source in the USA during July 1984. Many copies were made from that original, of course, and these were not difficult for any UFOlogist to obtain. Researcher Harry Harris had also received a copy from a US base commander in Texas and he no doubt created copies for others. UFO group Quest were even selling them via their magazine to all who wished to hear this amazing recording.

This was the background by the autumn of 1989 when I was contacted by a man called Tom Adams who called to say that he was making a BBC radio documentary about UFOs. I deal with journalists almost every day—reporters writing stories, TV researchers trying to find the next show that will cash in on *The X Files*, freelancers writing magazine articles and wanting advice. In those days I usually obliged whoever called.

Adams explained the full basis of his programme and said he wanted to build it around the Rendlesham Forest case. He wanted to come to see me. I do not recall anything odd and had not given the meeting more than a casual thought or two as it was so much a matter of routine. But what was not routine was the interview itself, which in retrospect proved him to be unusually perceptive about the case—asking me many questions about my view that the incident might involve a military accident not a UFO. Then Tom Adams surprised me and insisted that he must have the original audio tape.

Mystery Man

Immediately I said no. I explained that evidence such as this was never allowed out of my possession because it was so easy to lose and irreplaceable. He could have a copy. But a copy was not good enough, he argued. So I pointed out that my "original" was not *the* original. It was obviously copied by the military source that sent it to me, so adding one more generation to the list was not going to make much difference. I played him such a copy to prove my point.

Adams refused to budge and became, I felt, rather annoying. He *must* have the original, he said. Whilst I saw nothing sinister in this—having worked in radio and knowing the importance of good quality audio—I merely assumed he was being overly fastidious. But I was not about to let the tape out of my possession. So I handed him a second generation copy and told him that this was the original. Adams seemed pleased and took it without complaint.

A few weeks later I checked the *Radio Times* on the date I had been given for the programme. It was not listed. Adams had also promised to return my tape (which he thought was precious, if you recall) but had not yet done so.

I called the BBC number (Adams had given me the name of the studio he was working with after I had insisted on this before releasing the tape). They had never heard of the man. I spoke to the head of programming there. They had not commissioned any documentary on UFOs. Needless to say I never heard from Tom Adams or saw my audio tape again, and no UFO documentary has appeared from him anywhere to my knowledge.

Perhaps there is nothing sinister behind all of this. Maybe Adams was inflating his own achievements when he was merely intending to submit a documentary on speculation to the BBC. But I do find it odd that he should be particularly insistent about needing the original tape. This rather infers some ulterior motive. And he did give a definite transmission date which was only possible if he had really been commissioned or was not telling me the truth.

The case of Tom Adams puts the problem of MIB into focus. Should we see in this something mysterious? Was he really a government agent out to steal my tape? Did he come from another dimension? I rather doubt that!

Many would no doubt leap to such unproven conclusions. Is that how MIB cases come to fruition? Play around with the story in your mind, let the legend simmer and a few years down the track the episode may seem much odder than it ever really was. Of course Tom Adams may read this book, offer his apologies and return my tape, and then another MIB story will be put firmly into its place. Or we may never resolve this matter and another teasing MIB scenario will remain.

I saw this in dramatic style in January 1997, with my mind full of the stories in this just completed book. Whilst visiting the bank in Buxton I emerged to confront every UFOlogist's nightmare—a large, dark, old-fashioned Jaguar car with a London registration dating from 1962! It was a classic MIB moment, especially when the eyes of a man in a smart suit standing beside the car fixed on me—no doubt as a result of my stunned expression.

Was I about to be warned against publishing this book? Were all of these stories I had heard from others about to come true? Had I run off then without further inquiry this would be another mystery to leave us pondering questions such as that.

Except that I did not run away. I talked to the man. He was a perfectly legitimate vintage car owner and this chance encounter was pure coincidence.

You see how easy it is to make something out of nothing?

THE SEARCH FOR ANSWERS

Evaluating the cases in this book requires a moderation of mind. Perhaps there are answers to them all—be that answer confusion, misperception, distortion, wishful thinking or who knows what sort of mundane solution that is not immediately obvious.

For me, however, there do seem to be too many cases where that interpretation would be difficult. As I have said before, I am personally satisfied that most of the witnesses in this book are telling the truth.

This does not mean that these people cannot be wrong, of course. Nor does it mean that I judge them correctly. But aside from gut feelings there are patterns that link these cases together—themes that recur so often that one must charge conspiracy between dozens of unrelated people or conscious (certainly at least *subconscious*) fraud. Frankly, I am just not willing to do that here.

My book does not aim to solve the MIB mystery. It provides you with a flavor of the evidence and I think points toward a working hypothesis that these visitors *may* be part of some shady intelligence unit who are deliberately hamming it up to the point of absurdity.

Nevertheless, I really want this book to open up the debate. For this is an area of research that even UFO investigators tend to desperately avoid, because it does not fit with conventional theories. It probably tells us nothing of whether aliens have landed or not. It hardly brings us closer to solving the major riddles of the UFO. It also has that air of incredulity which would be so hard for most people to accept. And UFOlogists have a tough enough time being taken seriously as it is.

Unfortunately, we cannot dictate what evidence we must investigate. These Men in Black are real, and the people who report them deserve our attention. We should strive to find out whether these threatening strangers are just a part of some secret department investigating UFOs or are visiting this world from somewhere beyond our ken.

As I have indicated, I suspect the former. At least it is rational and possible to explore through means that do not require a vast leap of faith. I also know that the MoD and the Pentagon can choose to behave in a way that seems frightfully irrational.

I fear what some covert intelligence operation might believe it has the right to do in the name of national security. When our freedoms are limited and we are not deemed to have a need to know, these questions do not just become academic—they are terrifying.

Indeed, we just might be better off if the MIB *do* come from somewhere beyond our ken!

REFERENCES

Books

Arnold, Kenneth and Ray Palmer, *The Coming of the Saucers*. Amherst, 1952.

Barker, Gray, *They Knew Too Much about Flying Saucers*. Werner Laurie, 1956.

Beckley, Tim Green, *The UFO Silencers*. Inner Light, 1990.

Bender, Albert, *Flying Saucers and the Three Men*. Saucerian Books, 1962.

Briggs, Katharine, *A Dictionary of Fairies*. Penguin, 1976.

Chalker, Bill, *The Oz Files*. Duffy & Snellgrove, 1996.

Clark, Jerome, ed., *UFO Encyclopedia Project*. Omnigraphics, 1990-6.

Coleman, Loren, *Mysterious America*. Faber & Faber, 1983.

Collins, Andy, *Alien Energy*. ABC Books, 1994.

Condon, Edward, ed., *The University of Colorado UFO Project*. Bantam, 1970.

Craft, Michael, *Alien Impact*. St. Martin's Press, 1996.

Evans, Hilary, *Dyfed Enigma*. Orbis, 1984.

Good, Tim, *Above Top Secret*. Sidgwick & Jackson, 1987.

Harold, Clive, *The Uninvited*. Star, 1979.

Hopkins, Budd, *Intruders*. Random House, 1987.

Hough, Peter, *Witchcraft: A Strange Conflict*. Lutterworth, 1990.

Hough, Peter and Jenny Randles, *Mysteries of the Mersey Valley*. Sigma Press, 1993.

Keel, John, *The Mothman Prophecies*. E.P. Dutton, 1975.

Keel, John, *Operation Trojan Horse*. Souvenir, 1970.

Keyhoe, Donald, *Flying Saucers Are Real*. Hutchinson, 1950.

Kirk, Robert, *The Secret Commonwealth*. Stirling, 1933.

McClure, Kevin, *Stars and Rumours of Stars*. Self-published, 1986.

Paget, Peter, *The Welsh Triangle*. Grafton, 1979.

Pope, Nick, *Open Skies, Closed Minds*. Simon & Schuster, 1996.

Pritchard, Andrea (ed.), *Alien Discussions*. North Cambridge Press, 1994.

Pugh, Randall Jones and Ted Holliday, *The Dyfed Enigma*. Faber, 1979.

Randles, Jenny, *The Pennine UFO Mystery*. Grafton, 1983.

Randles, Jenny, *Star Children*. Robert Hale, 1994.

Randles, Jenny and Peter Hough, *The Complete Book of UFOs*. Piatkus, 1997.

Randles, Jenny, *UFO Retrievals*. Cassell, 1995.

Redfern, Nick, *A Covert Agenda*. Simon & Schuster, 1997.

Ruppelt, Capt. Edward, *The Report on UFOs*. Ace, 1956.

Wilkins, Harold, *Flying Saucers on the Attack*. Ace, 1954.

Magazines

The Crop Watcher
3 Selbourne Court, Tavistock Close, Romsey, Hampshire SO51 7TY

Flying Saucer Review
FSR Publications, Snodland, Kent ME6 5HJ

International UFO Reporter
2457 W. Peterson Avenue, Chicago, IL 60659

Magonia
5 James Terrace, London SW14 8HB

New UfOlogist
293 Devonshire Road, Blackpool, Lancashire FY2 0TW

Northern UFO News
1 Hallsteads Close, Dove Holes, Buxton, Derbyshire SK17 8BS

Organisations

The following organisations were helpful in research for this book and have my recommendation as objective and rational. This is by no means intended to suggest that organisations I have not mentioned are untrustworthy or unreliable. Many are first class. If you send a stamped addressed envelope to one of the following organisations they will put you in touch with a reputable local group. European readers can request this information via the Buxton address below.

Australian UFO Research, Box W42, West Pennant Hills NSW Australia 2120

BUFORA (British UFO Research Association), BM BUFORA, London WC1X 3XX

CUFORN (Canadian UFO Research Network), Dept. 25, 1665 Robson Street, Vancouver BC V6G 3C2

CUFOS (J. Allen Hynek Center for UFO Studies), 2457 W. Peterson Avenues Chicago IL 60659 USA

IUFOPRA (Irish UFO Research), Box 3070, Whitehall, Dublin 9 Ireland

NARO (Northern Anomalies Research Organisation), 6 Silsden Avenue, Lowton, Lancashire WA3 1EN

UFO Call is a news and information service recorded weekly and available at premium rates. Contact 0891-12 18 86

If you would like to report any incident connected with MIB, UFOs or paranormal phenomena, please contact the address below. Any request for confidentiality will be fully respected. I will do my best to reply and assist, but please allow for any delay. It will probably not be the big black Cadillacs at work. I just get rather a lot of mail!

1 Hallsteads Close, Dove Holes, Buxton, Derbyshire SK17 8BS

INDEX

AFSAC 225–27
aircraft, top secret testing of 23–25, 126–27, 200–203, 225
Air Staff 2A 147, 207–22, 227
aliens 15, 22, 50, 63–64, 116–17, 158
APEN 161–67
Appleton, Cynthia 62–68, 82, 177
Arnold, Kenneth 22–41, 42
ASIO 55, 58, 59
Aston, West Midlands, UK case 62–68

Barker, Gray 45–51, 154
Barmouth, Wales, UK case 188
BBC 4, 88, 219, 237, 238
Beckley, Timothy Green 155
Belgian wave 203
Bender, Albert 42–51, 60, 149, 224
Bennewitz, Dr. Paul 204–5
Bolton, Lancashire, UK case 9–22, 126
Bord, Janet 183
Bottomley, Peter 163–66
Breiland, Grant 131–34
Bridgeport, Connecticut, USA case 42–51
Briggs, Katherine 180
Brown, Lt. Frank 28–29, 34–41, 42
BUFORA 163, 166, 209, 211, 235
Burgh Marshes, Cumbria, UK case 77–91

car stop cases 61, 107–8, 182
Chalker, Bill 48, 53–57, 88, 217

Charlton, Wiltshire, UK case 69–76
CIA 43–47, 55, 59, 153, 230
Clacton-on-Sea, Essex, UK case 190–91
Clark, Jerome 48, 51, 152, 154
Coleman, Loren 187
Collins, Andy 116–20
Coombs, Pauline 122–24
Craft, Michael 195
Crisman, Fred 31–41
crop circles 69, 233–34

Dahl, Harold 29–41
Dale, Dr. John 14, 63, 64, 66, 67–68
Daresbury, Cheshire, UK case 108, 182, 187
Davidson, Capt. William 28–29, 34–42
devil names 185–87
DI 55 214, 217–18, 221, 222, 227
DI 64 221
DIGAP 13, 17
disinformation 43–44, 74, 201–5, 225, 227–28
Draguinan, France, case 151, 188
Drury, Tom 52–56
DSTI 86, 214, 216–18, 221, 222, 227
Dyfed, Wales, UK case 121–24

Eastbourne, Sussex, UK case 111–16
elementals 180–84, 188–89

EM effects 61, 62, 78, 113, 131
Emmet, Idaho, USA case 25, 27
Evans, Hilary 121, 123

Falkville, Alabama, USA case
    157–58
FBI 27, 46
Freedom of Information Act 13, 26,
    27, 43, 44, 45, 47, 53–57, 90,
    91, 200–201, 204, 216, 218,
    222, 226–27
French, Maj. Richard 99
Fry, Margaret 162

Galley, Robert 203
Girvan, Waveney 72–73, 89
Glanville, Rose & Francine
    123–24
Golborne, Lancashire, UK case
    125–30
Greenhaw, Jeff 157–58

Halo project 127
Harris, Harry 14, 237
Heard, Gerald 29
Heflin, Rex 92–97
Heiden, Richard 152, 154
Heywood, Lancashire, UK case
    168–69
Hill-Norton, Lord Peter 215
Hopkins, Dr. Herbert 170–73
Hough, Peter 13, 126–30, 140–47,
    168, 183, 199
Hynek, Dr. J. Allen 153
hypnotic control 20, 48, 50–51, 63,
    112–14, 180–81
hypnotic regression 14–15, 20, 22,
    137–38, 143–44, 171
Hyre, Mary 101, 104

IFSB 42–51
Ilkley Moor, West Yorkshire, UK
    case 139–47

James, Derek 175
Jarrold, Edgar 47–48, 54, 56

Jing-Yang, Li 150
Jodrell Bank 129, 168, 211
journalists, bogus 100, 110, 145–47,
    236–38

Keel, John 39, 99–104, 154, 177,
    185, 187, 189, 231
Kellar, Dr. Albert 14, 20
Keyhoe, Donald 43, 226
King, Barry 116, 121
Kirk, Robert 184
Kirtland Air Force Base 204–5
Kneale, Nigel 186–87

Langton Budville, Somerset, UK
    case 116–20
Lessing, Doris 193–94
Llandrillo, Wales, UK case 162–63,
    201

Mablethorpe, Lincolnshire, UK case
    234–36
Maccabee, Dr. Bruce 144
Marshall, Tony 142, 145
Maury Island, Washington, USA
    case 23, 41, 222
McCarthy, Colin 58
McChord Air Force Base 34–35, 37
McRoberts, Hannah 134–35
Menwith Hill, North Yorkshire, UK
    case 105–11, 205, 223
Mexico City, Mexico case 152–54
MIB: as aliens 5, 50, 60, 101–4,
    152, 170–78, 179–96, 197–231;
    as government agents 6, 40–
    41, 47–49, 57–59, 83–91, 110–
    11, 145–47, 195–96; as hoaxes
    39, 76, 94–95, 130, 143–47,
    157–69, 213, 230–31; as
    misperceptions 123–24, 167–
    69, 196, 238–39; cases in
    Australia 51–59; cases in
    Canada 130–35; cases in China
    149–50; cases in France 151;
    cases in Ireland 233–34; cases
    in Italy 148–49; cases in

Mexico 152–54; cases in
Papua New Guinea 52–57; 230;
cases in UK 8–22, 60–91, 105–
30, 138–47, 158–69, 173–76,
190–92, 199–203, 234–39;
cases in USA 23–51, 92–104,
136–39, 154–56, 157–58, 170–
73, 197–98; defined 2;
descriptions of 15–16, 31, 48,
66, 84, 93, 97, 99, 101, 115,
117, 123, 124, 126–37, 138–
39, 145, 149, 150, 152–53,
173, 205, 233; questions asked
by 17–18, 49–50, 84–85, 97,
102, 110, 115, 119–20, 132–
34, 146, 150, 153, 173, 234;
silence threats by 19–20, 32,
47, 48–49, 57–58, 102, 111,
115, 118–19, 121, 150, 154,
192, 198, 234; taking evidence
away 52–57, 58, 84–86, 93,
94, 134, 205, 235; vehicles
driven by 19, 47, 48, 65, 83,
95–96, 99, 101, 103, 120, 122,
124, 137, 138–39, 152–53, 175–
76

Ministry of Defence 81–82, 110–11,
145–47, 174, 200, 207–27,
229
Moore, Patrick 73
Moore, William 203–4, 222,
224–29
Morello, Ted 33, 36–37
Mortimer, Nigel 144
Moseley, James 154–56
MUFORA 14, 20–21
Munroe, Martha 136–37

NARO 14, 126, 128–29, 145, 199,
209
Norad 93, 97
Noyes, Ralph 174, 215–16, 224
NSA 105, 198, 205, 212, 223, 230
Nullarbor Plain, Australia, case
57–58, 111
Nyman, Joe 136

Official Secrets Act 207, 215, 217,
222
Orchard Beach, Maine, USA case
170–73
Owatonna, Minnesota, USA case
98–99
Oz factor 84, 107, 112, 171, 181

Palmer, Ray 27–41
Perks, Colin 211–12, 214, 221
Point Pleasant, West Virginia, USA
case 99–104
poltergeist effects 50, 100, 122
Pope, Nick 147, 210–16, 222, 224,
231
Port Moresby, Papua New Guinea,
case 52–57
Project Aquarius 203
Project Blue Book 43, 44, 94, 95,
226–27
Project Moon Dust 226, 230
psychic effects 17–19, 107, 111,
180
Public Record Office, Kew 55, 81,
87–88, 207–10, 211–12, 216

Queensland Flying Saucer Bureau
59
Quest 237

Randall, Dr. Robert 71–76
Rankin, Dick 36, 40
Rankow, Ralph 94–95
Redfern, Nick 212
Rendlesham Forest, Suffolk, UK
case 215, 236–38
Richelson, J.R. 227
Robertson, Dr. H.P. 43, 45, 230
Robinson, John 155–56
Rogers, Capt. John 70–71, 75
Rossi, Carlo 148–49
Roswell, New Mexico, USA case
26, 27, 162
Ruppelt, Capt. Edward 44–45

Sandbach, Roy 107
San Pietro a Vico, Italy, case 148–49
Santa Ana, California, USA case 92–97
SCUFORI 159–60
Sedona, Arizona, USA case
Seers, Stan 59
Silver Mine Mountains, Ireland, case 111–12
Singleton, Jim 143
Smith, Capt. E.J. 25–41
Smith, Yvonne 197–98
Southern, John 75–76
spacenapping 14, 51, 61, 113–14, 116–20, 138, 143, 182, 193, 195, 198
Spooner, Dr. Edward 141
Spring-Heeled Jack 185–86
Stone, Fred 56–58

Taylor, Peter and Sandra 105–11, 182, 223
Templeton, Jim 77–91, 177, 205
Tesseman, Dianne 233
thirty-year rule 207, 216
Tilton, Christa 138–39
time distortions 10, 98, 107, 109, 113–14, 180, 190–92
Tipperary, Ireland case 233–34
Tomlinson, Arthur 13, 15, 140, 145

UFO cover up 148–49, 150, 194–96, 200–32

UFO groups, bogus 136–37, 161–67, 171, 235–36
UFO groups, threat of 44, 59, 158–69
UFO photographs 3, 31, 32, 52–56, 72–91, 92–93, 131–35, 139–47, 199, 204, 205, 223, 234–36

Vaillancourt, Jules 136–38
Vancouver Island, Canada case 131–35
Verdugo City, California, USA case 197–98

Wall, Major Sir Patrick 74
weapons, military tests of 199–205
Weitzel, Craig 204–5
West Drayton 209, 217
West Freugh, Scotland case 215
Wheless, Lt. Gen. Hewitt 96, 97
Wilmslow, Cheshire, UK case 211–13
window areas 108, 151, 187, 188
Woomera, Australia, launch site 53, 57, 71, 87–89, 91
Wright Patterson Air Force Base 26, 27, 42, 86, 218, 226

X Files 2, 7, 130–31, 201, 237

Yangquan, China, case 149–50